P9-EAY-190

Acknowledgments

The Princeton Review would also like to thank Clarissa Constantine and Chad Chasteen for their review of the book.

Special thanks to Adam Robinson, who conceived of and perfected the Joe Bloggs approach to standardized tests and many of the other successful techniques used by The Princeton Review.

Cracking the
TOEFL iBT®

2019 Edition

The Staff of The Princeton Review

PrincetonReview.com

Penguin
Random
House

The Princeton Review, Inc.
110 East 42nd Street, 7th Floor
New York, NY 10017
E-mail: editorialsupport@review.com

The Princeton Review is not affiliated with Princeton University.

Terms of Service: The Princeton Review Online Companion Tools ("Student Tools") for retail books are available for only the two most recent editions of that book. Student Tools may be activated only twice per eligible book purchased for two consecutive 12-month periods, for a total of 24 months of access. Activation of Student Tools more than twice per book is in direct violation of these Terms of Service and may result in discontinuation of access to Student Tools Services.

TOEFL and TOEFL iBT are registered trademarks of the Educational Testing Service (ETS). This product is not endorsed or approved by ETS.

ISBN: 978-0-525-56788-2
ISSN: 1941-2029

Editor: Selena Coppock
Production Editors: Liz Dacy and Kathy Carter
Production Artist: Deborah A. Weber

Printed in the United States of America.

10 9 8 7 6 5 4 3 2 1

2019 Edition

Editorial

Rob Franek, Editor-in-Chief
Mary Beth Garrick, Executive Director of Production
Craig Patches, Production Design Manager
Selena Coppock, Managing Editor
Meave Shelton, Senior Editor
Sarah Litt, Editor
Aaron Riccio, Editor
Orion McBean, Associate Editor

Penguin Random House Publishing Team

Tom Russell, VP, Publisher
Alison Stoltzfus, Publishing Director
Amanda Yee, Associate Managing Editor
Ellen Reed, Production Manager
Suzanne Lee, Designer

Contents

Get More (Free) Content

1 Go to **PrincetonReview.com/cracking**

2 Enter the following ISBN for your book: 9780525567882

3 Answer a few simple questions to set up an exclusive Princeton Review account. (If you already have one, you can just log in.)

4 Click the "Student Tools" button, also found under "My Account" from the top toolbar. You're all set to access your bonus content!

Need to report a potential **content** issue?

Contact **EditorialSupport@review.com**.
Include:

- full title of the book
- ISBN number
- page number

Need to report a **technical** issue?

Contact **TPRStudentTech@review.com**
and provide:

- your full name
- email address used to register the book
- full book title and ISBN
- computer OS (Mac/PC) and browser (Firefox, Safari, etc.)

The Princeton Review®

Once you've registered, you can...

- Access 34 audio tracks for important practice for the Listening Section

- Download a Study Guide to help you maximize your TOEFL prep and manage your calendar

- Access useful strategy and learning documents

- Check for any updates to the TOEFL or this book

Look For These Icons Throughout The Book

 MORE GREAT BOOKS

 HEADPHONES ON!

 PROVEN TECHNIQUES

 APPLIED STRATEGIES

 STUDY BREAK

Part I
Orientation

Chapter 2
Core Concept: Reading

The TOEFL is an integrated exam, which means that each task may measure more than one skill. But the TOEFL is also a standardized test, which means that it consists of definite patterns. Your goal when taking the TOEFL is to make sure your responses conform to the patterns present on the test. The reading selections in this chapter will form the foundation for your listening and writing goals. Likewise, the skills needed to perform well in listening, speaking, and writing are closely intertwined. You'll find that mastering the core concepts of one section will also help you on other sections of the test.

READING ON THE TOEFL

There are three to four reading passages on the TOEFL, each around 700 words. Although the TOEFL test writers attempt to simulate the type of reading you will do in a university or graduate school program, the reading skills required on the test are very different from the skills used in an academic environment. Let's take a look at a passage.

Scientists at Michigan State University are asking a most challenging question. Can a computer program be considered alive? The members of the Digital Evolution Laboratory say yes. Computer scientists at the laboratory have created a program called Avida that has intrigued not only scientists and 5 engineers but biologists and philosophers as well.

The Avida project began in the late 1990s, when Chris Adami, a physicist, sought to create computer programs that could evolve to do simple addition problems and reproduce inside a digital environment. Adami called these 10 programs "digital organisms." Whenever a digital organism replicates, it has a chance to alter the program of the newly created offspring. In this way, the programs mutate and evolve. The goal of the Avida program is to create a model that could simulate the evolutionary process.

15 Initially, the digital creations were unable to process numbers in any way. But Adami designed Avida to reward digital organisms that were able to work with the numbers in some way. The digital organisms that could process numbers were allowed to reproduce in higher numbers. In only six short months, the primitive program had evolved a number of mechanisms to perform addition. 20 And, most surprisingly, not all of the digital creatures performed addition in the same way.

The Avida program now resides at Michigan State University, where it has been growing and changing for years. The digital creatures number in 25 the billions and have colonized more than two hundred computers. The organisms compete with one another for resources, and the most successful ones are able to make more copies of themselves. Just like living creatures, the digital entities also undergo mutations. Mutations that are beneficial ensure greater reproduction; harmful mutations have the opposite effect. 30

As a model for studying evolution, the Avida project has been a great success. Adami's digital organisms have suggested solutions to some of evolution's biggest mysteries. For example, Avida has helped disprove the theory of "irreducible complexity." Opponents of evolutionary theory have 35 suggested that some structures, such as the eye, are too complex to have been created in piecemeal stages. The evolution of Avida's digital organisms proves that even extremely complex structures can be developed in stages over time.

40 The Avida program's success has also raised some unintentional philosophical dilemmas. Does Avida just simulate evolution, or are digital organisms a new form of life? According to the director of the Avida project, the processes undergone by the digital creatures are the same as those experienced by biological organisms. The only difference is that biological 45 entities are based on strings of DNA, whereas the digital creations from

Avida are based on strings of ones and zeros. In a living creature, different sequences of DNA instruct cells to create certain proteins. In one of the Avida creations, different sequences of computer code instruct the program to perform certain functions. In both cases, the reproduction of the organisms 50 is subject to forces such as competition and mutation.

Now, some biologists are maintaining that the programs in the Avida project are alive. The programs live, die, reproduce, compete, cooperate, and evolve—activities that many biologists consider the hallmarks of life. One 55 prominent biologist says, "They don't have a metabolism—at least not yet. But otherwise, they're alive."

Of course, not everyone agrees that the program's creations are alive. One difficulty is that biologists do not even agree on the definition of life. The 60 diversity of life on Earth constantly surprises scientists, and there are simply too many characteristics and qualities to provide one simple definition of life.

Despite these misgivings, the directors of the Avida program remain optimistic that their program, even if not considered alive, is leading to a 65 greater understanding of life in all its forms. It may even facilitate future searches for life on other planets. According to one member of the Avida team, "The problem that we have now is that we are focused on looking for DNA-based life. But there may be other kinds of life out there that we have never dreamed of." The Avida program may provide biologists with another 70 avenue to explore.

This passage is typical of the passages on the TOEFL. It's about 700 words long, and it discusses an academic topic. It contains some challenging vocabulary words and requires you to read about a topic in which you may have no interest or knowledge. Although you may end up reading passages such as this at a university or graduate program, your approach for the TOEFL should be very different. For example, in a college course, you would need to read this passage very carefully, paying close attention to the details and facts presented in it. That type of close reading, however, is neither possible nor necessary on the TOEFL. You should employ a tactic called "active reading" rather than close reading.

Working on Active Reading

In this chapter, we focus a lot on active reading. You might ask yourself how that differs from how you ordinarily read. Active reading requires you to read with purpose; analyzing the material and looking for specific things within that material is something you will be asked to do on this section of the TOEFL. We want to make sure you get into the habit now so on test day you'll be prepared. The reading skills necessary for the TOEFL really are different from the skills you need for other types of reading that you do. Therefore, to do well on the TOEFL, you have to work on active reading. You will have to face many challenges in the Reading section. You've already seen an example of the level of content and vocabulary you may encounter. Perhaps the greatest challenge, however, is to attempt to both read the passages and answer the questions in the limited time provided. If you tackle every question, you have only about a minute and a half per question, and that's without allowing any time for actually reading the passage!

Therefore, instead of attempting to retain all of the information in the passage, you should focus on the big picture. Active reading involves completing three major tasks.

1. **Stating the main idea:** Figuring out what the passage is about
2. **Understanding the structure:** Figuring out key information by mapping the passage
3. **Finding the purpose:** Figuring out why the author wrote the piece

By mastering the skill of active reading, you'll be able to not only find the most important information in a passage but also effectively and accurately answer the questions that follow the passage. After all, you gain no points on the TOEFL for simply reading the passages; you get points only for answering the questions correctly.

STEPS TO MASTERING ACTIVE READING

Step 1: State the Main Idea

All passages on the TOEFL have a main idea. The main idea is the central message or point of the passage. Finding the main idea answers this question: What is the author writing about?

Let's take a look at a passage and work on learning how to find the main idea.

Sometimes it appears that the human mark on this planet is indelible. In only a blink of geological time, 200 years or so, human construction and expansion has resulted in the destruction of more than one-fifth of the world's forests, the recession of the polar icecaps, and the creation of a huge hole in the ozone layer. Additionally, industrial activity has damaged rivers and oceans, as well as groundwater supplies. Environmental scientists and activists warn that if Earth's future is not taken into account, humankind could very well destroy the planet.

10 However, Earth is an amazingly resilient place. In its 4.5-billion-year lifespan, Earth has endured bombardment by cosmic rays and meteors, violent earthquakes, volcanism, and frigid ice ages. In light of all these catastrophic events, many geologists and ecologists say that Earth could recover from any damage caused by human actions.

15
The author Alan Weisman has gone so far as to predict exactly what would happen on Earth if all humans were to disappear. Without upkeep, the concrete jungles of the world's largest cities would be slowly reclaimed by the wilderness around them. Harsh temperatures would cause pavement to crack.
20 Plants would return to areas covered by streets and sidewalks.

Different fates would await humankind's other creations. Litter and leaf matter would accumulate, and it would take only one chance lightning strike to start a raging fire. Many structures would burn to the ground. The steel

25 foundations supporting larger buildings and bridges would corrode and
buckle, especially with the rise in groundwater that would accompany the
clogging of sewer systems.

Without human interference, many of the threatened or endangered fauna
30 would reclaim their ecological niches. Unfortunately, household pets would
suffer. In addition, the rat, one of the greatest pests in large cities, would not
have the waste of humankind to feed off of and would be hunted mercilessly
by growing populations of hawks and falcons. And the cockroach, which to
many a city dweller seems to symbolize invincibility, would disappear from all
35 but the warmest climes without artificial heat to sustain it.

Within 500 years, again barely a heartbeat in geological time, most of
humankind's monuments would be gone, covered over by plants and trees.
It's happened before; the Mayan civilization in Northern Guatemala survived
40 for 2,000 years but was swallowed up by the jungle at its end. And after a few
thousand years, if earthquakes and volcanic eruptions have not obliterated
everything made by humans, the glaciers would come, sweeping down from
the mountains, slowly and inexorably destroying everything in their path.
Several times in its history, Earth has been swept clean by these giant sheets
45 of ice. The legacy of humankind would be wiped from Earth.

Of course, not every man-made artifact would be reclaimed by nature. Plastic
is a synthetic material that does not occur in nature. The strong bonds that
hold plastic together are virtually impervious to natural erosion. Long after
50 concrete and glass have turned back into sand and all processed metals
have rusted away, plastics will still be cycling through the Earth's ecosystem,
resilient to even the most destructive of natural forces. Some scientists
believe that plastic molecules may eventually break down entirely, but
there is no reliable data on just how long complete re-assimilation into the
55 environment might take. Furthermore, it is impossible to predict just what
sort of resources Mother Nature might develop in the distant future. There is
always the possibility that, given enough time, some microbe or bacteria may
evolve the capability to digest plastic. If nature somehow evolved a way to
process plastics, then even humanity's most enduring artifacts might vanish
60 in the space of a few hundred years.

The question of plastics aside, there is some evidence that Weisman's view
may be true. Since 1953, a 150-mile-long tract of land separating North and
South Korea has been declared a no-man's-land. After only a little more than
65 50 years, there is almost no trace of the rice paddies that farmers had created
and used for almost 5,000 years. Even more spectacular are the flocks of red-
crowned cranes that now inhabit the zone. These birds are the second rarest
of all birds, but they have flourished in this area, free from human interference
of all kinds.

To find the main idea, read the first sentence or two of the introduction, the first sentence of each body paragraph, and then the first and last sentence of the conclusion.

After reading each sentence again ask yourself, "What is the author writing about?"

Let's gather up the first sentences of each paragraph and the last sentence of the conclusion to see what we have.

Paragraph 1	Sometimes it appears that the human mark on this planet is indelible.
Paragraph 2	However, Earth is an amazingly resilient place.
Paragraph 3	The author Alan Weisman has gone so far as to predict exactly what would happen on Earth if all humans were to disappear.
Paragraph 4	Different fates would await humankind's other creations.
Paragraph 5	Without human interference, many of the threatened or endangered fauna would reclaim their ecological niches.
Paragraph 6	Within 500 years, again barely a heartbeat in geological time, most of humankind's monuments would be gone, covered over by plants and trees.
Paragraph 7	Of course, not every man-made artifact would be reclaimed by nature.
Paragraph 8	The question of plastics aside, there is some evidence that Weisman's view may be true.
Last sentence	These birds are the second rarest of all birds, but they have flourished in this area, free from human interference of all kinds.

When stating the main idea, we must try to tie together all of these topics. Take a look at the sentences above and write down what you think the main idea is.

_____

_____

_____

A good answer to this question might be as follows:

> If humans were to disappear, plants and animals would soon take over Earth again.

Notice how this sentence brings together all of the elements. The sentences from paragraphs 1, 3, and 4 all mention people; the sentence from paragraph 2 talks about Earth; and the sentences from paragraphs 5, 6, 7, and 8 mention both.

Let's try it one more time. Try to find the main idea of the following passage, which we saw at the beginning of this lesson. Write your answer in the space provided after the passage.

Scientists at Michigan State University are asking a most challenging question. Can a computer program be considered alive? The members of the Digital Evolution Laboratory say yes. Computer scientists at the laboratory have created a program called Avida that has intrigued not only scientists and
5 engineers but biologists and philosophers as well.

The Avida project began in the late 1990s, when Chris Adami, a physicist, sought to create computer programs that could evolve to do simple addition problems and reproduce inside a digital environment. Adami called these
10 programs "digital organisms." Whenever a digital organism replicates, it has a chance to alter the program of the newly created offspring. In this way, the programs mutate and evolve. The goal of the Avida program is to create a model that could simulate the evolutionary process.

15 Initially, the digital creations were unable to process numbers in any way. But Adami designed Avida to reward digital organisms that were able to work with the numbers in some way. The digital organisms that could process numbers were allowed to reproduce in higher numbers. In only six short months, the primitive program had evolved a number of mechanisms to perform addition.
20 And, most surprisingly, not all of the digital creatures performed addition in the same way.

The Avida program now resides at Michigan State University, where it has been growing and changing for years. The digital creatures number in
25 the billions and have colonized more than two hundred computers. The organisms compete with one another for resources, and the most successful ones are able to make more copies of themselves. Just like living creatures, the digital entities also undergo mutations. Mutations that are beneficial ensure greater reproduction; harmful mutations have the opposite effect.
30
As a model for studying evolution, the Avida project has been a great success. Adami's digital organisms have suggested solutions to some of evolution's biggest mysteries. For example, Avida has helped disprove the theory of "irreducible complexity." Opponents of evolutionary theory have
35 suggested that some structures, such as the eye, are too complex to have been created in piecemeal stages. The evolution of Avida's digital organisms proves that even extremely complex structures can be developed in stages over time.

40 The Avida program's success has also raised some unintentional philosophical dilemmas. Does Avida just simulate evolution, or are digital organisms a new form of life? According to the director of the Avida project, the processes undergone by the digital creatures are the same as those experienced by biological organisms. The only difference is that biological
45 entities are based on strings of DNA, whereas the digital creations from Avida are based on strings of ones and zeros. In a living creature, different sequences of DNA instruct cells to create certain proteins. In one of the Avida creations, different sequences of computer code instruct the program to

perform certain functions. In both cases, the reproduction of the organisms
50 is subject to forces such as competition and mutation.

Now, some biologists are maintaining that the programs in the Avida project are alive. The programs live, die, reproduce, compete, cooperate, and evolve—activities that many biologists consider the hallmarks of life. One
55 prominent biologist says, "They don't have a metabolism—at least not yet. But otherwise, they're alive."

Of course, not everyone agrees that the program's creations are alive. One difficulty is that biologists do not even agree on the definition of life. The
60 diversity of life on Earth constantly surprises scientists, and there are simply too many characteristics and qualities to provide one simple definition of life.

Despite these misgivings, the directors of the Avida program remain optimistic that their program, even if not considered alive, is leading to a greater
65 understanding of life in all its forms. It may even facilitate future searches for life on other planets. According to one member of the Avida team, "The problem that we have now is that we are focused on looking for DNA-based life. But there may be other kinds of life out there that we have never dreamed of." The Avida program may provide biologists with another avenue to explore.

Write down what you think the main idea is:

_____

_____

_____

Here are the first sentences of each paragraph and the last sentence of the conclusion.

Paragraph 1	Scientists at Michigan State University are asking a most challenging question.
Paragraph 2	The Avida project began in the late 1990s, when Chris Adami, a physicist, sought to create a computer program that could evolve to do simple addition problems and reproduce inside a digital environment.
Paragraph 3	Initially, the digital creations were unable to process numbers in any way.
Paragraph 4	The Avida program now resides at Michigan State University, where it has been growing and changing for years.
Paragraph 5	As a model for studying evolution, the Avida project has been a great success.
Paragraph 6	The Avida program's success has raised some unintentional philosophical dilemmas.
Paragraph 7	Now, some biologists are maintaining that the programs in the Avida project are alive.
Paragraph 8	Of course, not everyone agrees that the program's creations are alive.
Paragraph 9	Despite these misgivings, the directors of the Avida program remain optimistic that their program, even if not considered alive, is leading to a greater understanding of life in all its forms.
Last sentence	The Avida program may provide biologists with another avenue to explore.

We could state our main idea as follows:

> The features of the Avida computer program have led some biologists to consider the program alive.

Because the Avida program is mentioned in sentences from paragraphs 2, 4, 5, 6, 7, 8, and 9, we definitely need it in our main idea. The sentences from paragraphs 2 and 4 talk about the program "evolving," "changing," and "growing." Later, the program is described as "alive" and likened to a "biological organism." So we also need to put this concept into our main idea.

Main Idea: Paying Attention to Direction Markers

When finding the main idea, pay close attention to direction markers. Some passages introduce an idea or a topic, but they go on to discuss the opposite of it.

Here's an example.

Art has always occupied a special place in society. Many people consider artists to be the ultimate authorities on aesthetics, the nature and expression of beauty. For much of history, the practice of art was inscrutable, and artists were viewed as being somewhat strange and often mad. Even the word
5 most commonly associated with artists—inspiration—has its own magical overtones. Literally, "inspiration" is the breathing in of a spirit. Artists were thought of as people who were divinely inspired to create.

Of course, artists contributed to this mythology. Many artists ascribed
10 their talents to the presence of some supernatural agent or "muse." Whole movements of art have centered on the supposedly otherworldly nature of art. For example, the Romantic poets believed that art was the search for the sublime, a term for them that meant an ultimate expression of beauty and truth. The search for this ideal led them to explore both natural and
15 supernatural themes in their works.

Another persistent view of art regarded its divorce from rationality. Reason and logic were the province of scientists and philosophers, whereas creativity and intuition were the domain of the artists. The two separate spheres of the
20 mind were supposed to remain distinct.

But in 1704, a major transgression occurred. Sir Isaac Newton, mathematician and physicist extraordinaire, published his study of light, *Opticks*. One of Newton's major discoveries was on the nature of color. Using
25 a prism, Newton found that white light is actually composed of all the colors of the rainbow. He even provided a scientific explanation for the presence of rainbows. The artistic community was shocked. A scientist had taken a beautiful and magical experience and reduced it to the simple refraction of beams of light through the prism of a raindrop. A scientist had intruded into
30 their sacred territory.

More than a hundred years later, John Keats, one of the most famous Romantic poets, accused Newton of diminishing beauty by "unweaving the rainbow." His colleague, Samuel Taylor Coleridge, famously remarked that the
35 souls of five hundred Newtons would be needed to make one Shakespeare. And yet, from another perspective, Newton did not diminish the beauty of the rainbow; he enhanced it. In his quest to uncover the secrets of the rainbow, Newton demonstrated the wonder, creativity, and inspiration of an artist. He also gave the world another opportunity to experience the sublime. Newton's
40 discovery paved the way for the development of the science of spectroscopy, a way of analyzing the chemical makeup of light. Now scientists can look at the stars and discern their composition. The sense of wonder this ability creates is not much different from the wonder the poet or artist feels when gazing at those same stars.

Take a look at the topic sentences from the first three paragraphs. (Note: The first sentence of a paragraph is often known as the topic sentence.)

Paragraph 1   Art has always occupied a special place in society.
Paragraph 2   Of course, artists contributed to this mythology.
Paragraph 3   Another persistent view of art regarded its divorce from rationality.

At this point, you may predict that the main idea of the passage will be about views of art and artists. But look at the remaining topic sentences.

Paragraph 4   But in 1704, a major transgression occurred.
Paragraph 5   More than a hundred years later, John Keats, one of the most famous Romantic poets, accused Newton of diminishing beauty by "unweaving the rainbow."
Last sentence   The sense of wonder this ability creates is not much different from the wonder the poet or artist feels when gazing at those same stars.

The sentence from paragraph 4 is an important one because it contains the direction marker "but." The author is introducing an important new idea contrary to the prior topics. We should figure out this new idea. In paragraph 4, the author discusses science's relationship to art. We need to make sure this idea is part of our main idea. Look through the passage again. Do you see any other direction markers that may clue us in to the main idea?

You may have noticed the following sentence in the last paragraph:

And yet, from another perspective, Newton did not diminish the beauty of the rainbow; he enhanced it.

See if you can come up with a main idea that incorporates these elements. Write down what you think the main idea is.

_____

_____

_____

Your answer should look something like the following:

> Science does not diminish art but instead provides another source of wonder.
> Thus, it is important to incorporate all parts of the passage. The first part of
> this passage establishes the view of art, whereas the second discusses the
> intersection of art and science.

Drill #1: State the Main Idea

For each of the following passages, try to find the main idea. Read the topic sentences of each paragraph and paraphrase them. Then, try to state the main idea. Be on the lookout for direction markers!

Passage A

Plants reproduce by seeding. The seed of the plant contains all the necessary genetic information to create a new plant, and more important, it is designed to start growing only when the surrounding conditions are perfect. For example, the seed of a plant growing in a temperate area will "wait" until the cold winter passes before growing. When spring arrives, the seed responds to environmental
5 triggers such as water intake, rising air temperature, humidity levels, and amount of sunlight. Some seeds are programmed in such a way that they will not grow until they've passed through a period of cold weather.

A germinating seed will first display tiny leaves, called cotyledons. Plants are either monocotyledons,
10 producing just a single leaf, or dicotyledons, producing two leaves. These tiny leaves quickly grow into a mature leaf system, which then begins gathering energy for the young plant. Plants gather the light of the Sun and transform it into energy in a process called photosynthesis. This process allows the plant to produce glucose, which the plant then uses to both further its growth and to produce cellulose and starch, two compounds essential to a plant. Cellulose is a strong, fibrous material that
15 gives shape and structure to the cell walls. Starch is stored in the cells and used for energy.

Beneath the surface, the plant's root system grows and provides not only an anchor for the plant but a constant supply of food as well. Some plants possess what is called a taproot system, in which there is one main root. Others have a more dispersed root system, which lacks a main root.
20 In either case, the roots of the plant are covered with microscopic hairs, which spread into the surrounding soil. These hairs greatly increase the surface area of the root system and allow the plant to absorb water and essential nutrients from the soil.

Water drawn in through the roots undergoes a process called transpiration. During this process,
25 minerals are carried up to the leaves of the plant, while oxygen and water vapor escape through tiny pores, called stomata, on the surface of the leaves. Interestingly, the movement of water through the plant is also responsible for keeping the plant upright; a plant that lacks water will wilt and may die. Too much water may also harm the plant by saturating the soil and preventing the roots from absorbing oxygen.
30
Once a plant reaches full maturity, its energy is devoted to reproduction. The plant forms flowers and fruits, the structures essential to reproduction. The flowers of a plant are typically hermaphrodites, meaning that they contain both male and female reproductive organs. Thus, many plants are able to fertilize themselves. The flowers of some plants are unisexual, being all male
35 or all female. These plants require another plant for fertilization. Some plants are polygamous, meaning they have both hermaphrodite and unisexual flowers. Fruits are created from the ovaries of flowering plants. The main purpose of the fruit is to protect the seed, but many fruits aid in the seed's dispersal as well. For example, a soft, fleshy fruit attracts animals, which eat the fruit and thus spread the seeds. Or a pod or capsule will split open and scatter its seeds. Some of the seeds
40 distributed in this manner will take hold in favorable soil, and the entire process begins anew.

Paragraph 1: _____

Paragraph 2: _____

Paragraph 3: _____

Paragraph 4: _____

Paragraph 5: _____

Last sentence: _____

Did you find any direction markers? List them: _____

_____

_____

Main idea: _____

_____

_____

Passage B

The business practices of the Intel Corporation, a technology company best known for the production of microprocessors for computers, illustrate the importance of brand marketing. Intel was able to achieve a more than 1,500 percent increase in sales, moving from $1.2 billion in sales to more than $33 billion, in a little more than 10 years. Although the explosion of the home-computer
5 market certainly accounted for some of this dramatic increase, the brilliance of its branding strategy also played a significant role.

Intel became a major producer of microprocessor chips in 1978, when its 8086 chip was selected by IBM for use in its line of home computers. The 8086 chip and its successors soon became the
10 industry standard, even as Intel's competitors sought to break into this potentially lucrative market. Intel's main problem in facing its competitors was its lack of trademark protection for its series of microchips. Competitors were able to exploit this lack by introducing clone products with similar sounding names, severely inhibiting Intel's ability to create a brand identity.

15 In an effort to save its market share, Intel embarked on an ambitious branding program in 1991. The corporation's decision to invest more than $100 million in this program was greeted with skepticism and controversy. Many within the company argued that the money could be better spent researching and developing new products, while others argued that a company that operated within such a narrow consumer niche had little need for such an aggressive branding campaign. Despite
20 these misgivings, Intel went ahead with its strategy, which in a short time became a resounding success.

One of the keys to the success of Intel's new branding initiative was its close partnership with computer manufacturers. Intel involved the manufacturers in its plan by first offering them a rebate
25 on the purchase of an Intel microprocessor. The money saved on the purchase of microprocessors was redirected into advertising, with Intel offering to pay fully half of manufacturers' advertising costs, provided their computers prominently featured the Intel brand logo. In an even more effective

strategy, Intel also required computer manufacturers to produce products using competitors'
chips. These products noticeably lacked the prominent Intel logo, which had a negative effect on
30 consumers, who had come to expect to see Intel's brand on the computer.

Intel's successful branding campaign led to two important developments. The first was Intel's
positioning of itself as the leader in microprocessors, recognized for creating products that were
both reliable and ubiquitous, appearing in many different computer brands. This occurred despite
35 the public's general lack of understanding of exactly what a microprocessor was or how Intel's
processor was better than its competitors' chips. Second, Intel's campaign led to a boom in
computer advertising. Prior to Intel's branding initiative, many advertisers avoided the computer
industry, which generally spent far more of its money on research and development. But the
success of Intel's branding program led to a new and eminently profitable relationship between
40 computer manufacturers and advertisers.

Ironically, the success of Intel's branding strategy led to a marketing dilemma for the company. In
1992, Intel was prepared to unveil its new line of microprocessors. However, the company faced a
difficult decision: release the new product under the current brand logo and risk consumer apathy
45 or give the product a new name and brand and risk undoing all the work put into the branding
strategy. In the end, Intel decided to move forward with a new brand identity. It was a testament to
the strength of Intel's earlier branding efforts that the new product line was seamlessly integrated
into the public consciousness.

Paragraph 1: _____

Paragraph 2: _____

Paragraph 3: _____

Paragraph 4: _____

Paragraph 5: _____

Paragraph 6: _____

Last sentence: _____

Did you find any direction markers? List them: _____

_____

_____

Main idea: _____

_____

_____

Passage C

On December 18, 1912, an amateur geologist named Charles Dawson and paleontologist Arthur Smith Woodward presented a stunning finding to the Geological Society of London. One year earlier, Dawson had found a piece of a human cranium in a gravel pit near Piltdown Common, Sussex. Further searching by Dawson uncovered remnants of what appeared to be flint tools and the
5 remains of prehistoric animals. Excited by his discovery, Dawson took the fossils to Woodward at the British Museum, and the two men returned to the gravel pit for a systematic excavation.

In the summer of 1912, Dawson and Woodward made the discoveries that would later shock the assembled scientists at the Geological Society. Among the animal bones and primitive tools, the
10 two men found another skull and an almost entirely intact jawbone. The geologic and biologic evidence dated the site to the Pleistocene era, and the bones were clearly of a creature that resembled no other known at that time. Although the skull resembled those of other finds, including the famous ape-men of Java, the jaw appeared to come from some type of heretofore unknown species of ape. Startlingly, however, the teeth were worn down in a human fashion.
15
Dawson and Woodward's announcement of the so-called Missing Link between man and apes, which they called Piltdown Man, set off an immediate firestorm. Across the Atlantic, *The New York Times* reported the story with the dramatic headline "Paleolithic Skull Is a Missing Link." The ensuing controversy over human origins eventually led the *Times* to publish an editorial that cautioned
20 readers from seeing Piltdown Man as the missing link; instead, the editors advised readers to see Piltdown Man as a link to man's prehistoric past, but not necessarily proof of evolution.

Similar editorials sprang up across the United States, and the American public was divided over the issue of human origins. Although no fossil could conclusively prove evolution, scientists had
25 amassed a huge collection of fossils in the early twentieth century. These fossils seemed to indicate a pattern of evolution and demanded attention. In the United States during the 1920s, a movement sprang up to counter the theory of evolution. This movement culminated in one of the most famous trials in history, the Scopes "Monkey" Trial.

30 John T. Scopes was a biology teacher in a Tennessee school. The textbook he used in his class contained a chapter on evolution and natural selection, a violation of Tennessee law. Scopes was brought to trial for the offense, and the ensuing confrontation riveted the American public. Scopes was defended by Clarence Darrow, a noted lawyer, and William Jennings Bryan, a former secretary of state, worked for the prosecution. After a confrontational trial, which even included Darrow calling
35 Bryan as a witness, Scopes was ultimately found guilty.

Although Scopes's conviction was later overturned, the precedent set by the case endured. It wasn't until 1967 that Tennessee repealed its law forbidding the teaching of evolution. And even today, the reverberations of the trial are still visible. One school district in Georgia recently began
40 placing stickers on its biology textbooks disavowing the validity of evolution. The Supreme Court eventually decided that the stickers were unconstitutional, but a cultural battle over the validity of evolution still rages in the United States.

Paragraph 1: _____

Paragraph 2: _____

Paragraph 3: _____

Paragraph 4: _____

Paragraph 5: _____

Paragraph 6: _____

Last sentence: _____

Did you find any direction markers? List them: _____

_____

_____

Main idea: _____

_____

_____

Passage D

One of the most commonplace instructional strategies in elementary and middle schools is that of oral reading. Virtually all teachers, at some point in the school day, engage in this activity, whether by reading aloud to the class or by having the students read to one another. Although some recent educational theorists have challenged the efficacy of oral reading, its popularity in schools and
5 classrooms is unchallenged.

The history of oral reading in the classroom is inextricably linked with the history of the culture that engendered it. Prior to the development of computers, television, and radio, reading was the predominant form of family entertainment. However, printed books were often scarce, and
10 literacy rates were often low. Thus, families would gather around and listen to a book being read to them. Early classrooms were modeled after this phenomenon, and oral reading was such a part of academic life that schools were sometimes called blab schools. In these schools, students often read their lessons aloud simultaneously, even when the students had different lessons. At other times, all students read the same text aloud.
15
With the increasing availability of books, schools began using textbooks to teach reading in the classroom. By the nineteenth century, the focus had moved to teaching students "eloquent reading." Students were expected to recite stories, poems, and prayers for the class, and the teacher graded them on their articulation and pronunciation, as well as their abilities to recall what they had just
20 read. This method persisted into the twentieth century and became known as the story method of instruction. Oral reading was such a focal point of instruction that philosopher William James stated "…the teacher's success or failure in teaching reading is based…upon the oral reading method."

However, as the twentieth century progressed, the effectiveness of oral reading was called into
25 question. Educational scholars in both Europe and the United States wondered exactly what oral reading was teaching students. With oral reading focusing excessively on pronunciation and dynamics, educators doubted that students were even able to comprehend what they were saying. One scholar quoted a study that claimed that eleven-twelfths of students did not understand what they were reciting when they read orally. Friedrich Froebel, a German education specialist, argued

30 that oral reading inappropriately placed emphasis on expression, when the emphasis should be
placed on process.

Also at this time, science was gaining increasing prominence, and across all fields researchers were
placing a premium on empirical studies. Many long-standing beliefs and views were challenged,
35 and educational theories were no exception. Behavioral scientists studied reading practices and
determined that oral reading was no longer in fashion. In fact, they concluded that the only time
students read orally was in school. Most individuals read silently, and this finding led many schools
to change their methods to reflect this change.

40 The new preponderance of written texts also played a role in the history of oral reading. With the
amount of printed material rapidly expanding, silent reading, which was more efficient, became the
reading model of choice. For a number of years, oral reading was absent from many a classroom.
But in time, new research and studies brought oral reading back to the forefront of education.
Pressley's and Afflerbach's influential book *Verbal Protocols of Reading* emphasizes the importance
45 of oral reading, tracing its history back to the methods of Aristotle and Plato. In many ways,
however, the new research reiterates what most teachers already know. For them, the necessity and
effectiveness of oral reading was never in doubt.

Paragraph 1: _____

Paragraph 2: _____

Paragraph 3: _____

Paragraph 4: _____

Paragraph 5: _____

Paragraph 6: _____

Last sentence: _____

Did you find any direction markers? List them: _____

_____

_____

Main idea: _____

_____

_____

Answers to Drill #1

Passage A

Paragraph 1: "Plants reproduce by seeding." For short sentences like this one, don't worry about paraphrasing. Keep things simple.

Paragraph 2: "Seed first has tiny leaves." When finding the main idea, don't worry about strange or difficult vocabulary words (cotyledons). They are not important to the main idea.

Paragraph 3: "Plants have a root system that helps growth." When paraphrasing, you don't necessarily have to note the exact functions of the root system. Details are not important. All we need to know is that the root system is helpful to the plant.

Paragraph 4: "Water comes through the roots." Again, ignore the fancy term *transpiration*.

Paragraph 5: "After maturity, plants focus on reproduction."

Last sentence: "Process starts all over again."

Pay attention to the last sentence. Look for the author's final word. Is there a definite conclusion? The author wraps up things nicely, but some passages may end with a question or a call for more information or research on the topic.

Direction Markers

(We use boldface for same-direction markers and underline opposite-direction markers.)

For example, the seed of a plant growing in a temperate area will "wait" until the cold winter passes before growing.

During this process, minerals are carried up to the leaves of the plant, <u>while</u> oxygen and water vapor escape through tiny pores, called stomata, on the surface of the leaves.

The main purpose of the fruit is to protect the seed, <u>but</u> many fruits aid in the seed's dispersal as well.

For example, a soft, fleshy fruit attracts animals, which eat the fruit and thus spread the seeds.

You may have spotted some others, but the key thing about this passage is that the information is all going in the same direction. The purpose of this passage is to inform the reader, and all the details provide an explanation of a process.

Main idea: "A plant reproduces with a seed, which grows from a tiny leaf into a mature plant capable of making its own seeds."

Each of our topic sentences discusses reproduction and the steps. Notice we did not mention the root system. That's because the root system is mentioned as a part of the growth process. We don't need to explicitly discuss each detail when stating the main idea, especially if the author is not introducing any contrasting ideas.

Passage B

Paragraph 1: "Intel is an example of good brand marketing." By reading the first sentence, we may be able to predict what's coming in the passage. It looks as if we're going to read a description of this company's business practices.

Paragraph 2: "Intel became a major producer in 1978." In addition to direction markers, time markers are also helpful. We know that we're going to read some of the background story.

Paragraph 3: "To save its market share, Intel started a new program." This sentence supports the introduction paragraph.

Paragraph 4: "One key to Intel's success." When the author presents an example, don't worry too much about what the example is. We don't need to know exactly what the details are for the main idea; it's enough to know that this paragraph will describe it.

Paragraph 5: "Two important developments from the program." Again, don't worry too much about what the developments are. The important thing is that the author is giving the results of the program.

Paragraph 6: "Success led to a problem." The author introduces a problem, but we should note that it is the last paragraph. Therefore, we may think the problem isn't a main focus of the passage.

Last sentence: "New product introduced with no problems." This last sentence indicates that everything ended well. The earlier problem was mentioned only to show how good the company's strategy was. Even the problem fits into the overall direction of the passage.

Direction Markers

(Again, we use **boldface** for same-direction markers and <u>underline</u> opposite-direction markers.)

> <u>Although</u> the explosion of the home-computer market certainly accounted for some of this dramatic increase, the brilliance of its branding strategy also played a significant role.

> <u>Despite</u> these misgivings, Intel went ahead with its strategy, which in a short time became a resounding success.

> In an even more effective strategy, Intel **also** required computer manufacturers to produce products using competitors' chips.

> But the success of Intel's branding program led to a new and eminently profitable relationship between computer manufacturers and advertisers.

<u>However</u>, the company faced a difficult decision: release the new product under the current brand logo and risk consumer apathy or give the product a new name and brand and risk undoing all the work put into the branding strategy.

This passage contains quite a few opposite-direction markers. Notice how each one serves to indicate how successful Intel's branding campaign was.

Main idea: "Intel's branding strategy was important to its success and also led to some important developments in the market."

As we predicted from the first sentence, we were going to read about a successful business strategy. We also brought in the developments mentioned later in the passage. The problem mentioned in the final paragraph doesn't need special mention because it again illustrates how successful Intel's campaign was.

Passage C

Paragraph 1: "Two scientists made a stunning finding." This is a good "teaser" introduction: the author doesn't tell us right away what the topic is. In this case, you may want to read another sentence or two to figure out what the finding is.

Paragraph 2: "The discoveries were made in 1912." This is another reference to the shocking discovery.

Paragraph 3: "The announcement set off controversy." If you are not sure what the word firestorm means, keep reading! You'll find hints in the next two sentences.

Paragraph 4: "The public was divided over human origins." Now the author is adding another dimension to the discussion. Often, a passage will introduce a controversy or problem, as is the case here.

Paragraph 5: "Scopes was a teacher." This sentence appears to be off the topic. We should read another sentence to discover why the author brings up Scopes.

Paragraph 6: "Lasting effects from the case." Don't be thrown off by the vocabulary! If you are not sure of some of the words in the sentence, read another line or two. The passage makes it clear that the situation lasted for many years.

Last sentence: "A battle still rages over the subject." The passage ends without a nice resolution; the author indicates that the situation is ongoing.

Direction Markers

(Again, we use **boldface** for same-direction markers and <u>underline</u> opposite-direction markers.)

<u>Although</u> the skull resembled those of other finds, including the famous ape-men of Java, the jaw appeared to come from some type of heretofore unknown species of ape.

The ensuing controversy over human origins eventually led the *Times* to publish an editorial that cautioned readers from seeing Piltdown Man as the missing link; <u>instead</u>, the editors advised readers to see Piltdown Man as a link to man's prehistoric past, but not necessarily proof of evolution.

<u>Although</u> no fossil could conclusively prove evolution, scientists had amassed a huge collection of fossils in the early twentieth century.

And even today, the reverberations of the trial are still visible.

This passage presents a rather controversial topic. There are two sides to the discussion, and the author indicates them by using the direction markers highlighted above.

Main idea: "The discovery of fossils that supported evolution led to a battle over the theory of evolution, which continues to this day."

This passage is neatly divided into three large areas. The first two paragraphs talk about the discovery, the next two talk about the controversy, and the final two talk about the court case and its effects. Our main idea should touch on each of these topics.

Passage D

Paragraph 1: "Oral reading is used a lot in schools." This sentence prepares us to read about an educational topic. We'll learn shortly to think about the author's purpose—why the author is writing. The author may want to support oral reading, attack it, or just give a history of it. Did you spot any clues that indicate what this passage will do?

Paragraph 2: "The history of oral reading is linked to culture." This paragraph discusses the history of oral reading.

Paragraph 3: "Schools started to use textbooks to teach reading." This continues the history and indicates a change in the way reading was taught.

Paragraph 4: "The usefulness of oral reading is questioned." The author introduces a problem.

Paragraph 5: "Changes in research and science." If you're not sure how this sentence fits into the rest of the passage, read another sentence or two. It appears that new research was against oral reading.

Paragraph 6: "Written books played a role in oral reading." Check the following sentence to see how this fits into the discussion. The author states that silent reading was taking over.

Last sentence: "Good things about oral reading were never in doubt." This final sentence seems to go against what we've been reading. The last three paragraphs all discussed negative aspects of oral reading. But the author ends on a positive note. To understand this ending, let's check our direction markers.

Direction Markers

(Again, we use **boldface** for same-direction markers and <u>underline</u> opposite-direction markers.)

<u>Although</u> some recent educational theorists have challenged the efficacy of oral reading, its popularity in schools and classrooms is unchallenged.

<u>However</u>, printed books were often scarce, and literacy rates were often low. **Thus**, families would gather around and listen to a book being read to them.

In fact, they concluded that the only time students read orally was in school.

For a number of years, oral reading was absent from many a classroom. <u>But in time</u>, new research and studies brought oral reading back to the forefront of education.

By looking at these direction markers, you can see that the main idea (and the author's purpose) becomes much clearer. The author wishes to show how oral reading has persisted despite challenges. This explains why three paragraphs discuss negative aspects, but the final sentence is positive.

Main idea: "Despite challenges to its usefulness, oral reading remains an important educational technique."

If your main idea isn't similar to the one above, you may have missed some of the direction markers. This passage isn't presenting oral reading in a negative manner, but rather supporting it. The last sentence of the first paragraph is a very important one.

Summary: Stating the Main Idea

1. Read the first sentence of each paragraph. State what topic the author is writing about.
2. Skim the rest of the paragraph for direction markers. Pay particular attention to opposite-direction markers.
3. Remember to read both the first sentence of each paragraph in the passage and last sentence of the conclusion. The last sentence will contain the author's final point.
4. The main idea should connect all the ideas found in the first sentences of the paragraphs and the last sentence of the conclusion. (If you're having trouble connecting all of the topics, ask yourself what the purpose of the passage is to help you put all the pieces together.)

Step 2: Understand the Structure

Once we've found the purpose as discussed in Step 1, we'll have a better idea of the structure of the passage. The structure refers to the organization or layout of the passage. On the TOEFL, different types of questions will address different parts of the passage. If you are familiar with the types of structures on the TOEFL, you'll know where to look to find the information you need.

What Is the Structure of a TOEFL Passage?

On the TOEFL, all passages will follow a very similar structure, which will look like the following:

1. An introduction paragraph that contains the basic topic of the passage
2. Four or five body paragraphs that provide more information about the topic
3. A conclusion that brings the passage to a close with a final statement

Let's look at the structure of each of these paragraphs in detail.

What Is the Structure of the Introduction?

Here's the introduction of a passage you've already read.

> (1) Sometimes it appears that the human mark on this planet is indelible. (2) In only a blink of geological time, 200 years or so, human construction and expansion has resulted in the destruction of more than one-fifth of the world's forests, the recession of the polar icecaps, and the creation of a huge hole in the ozone layer. (3) Additionally, industrial activity has damaged rivers and oceans, as well as groundwater supplies. (4) Environmental scientists and activists warn that if Earth's future is not taken into account, humankind could very well destroy the planet.

Now let's look at this very same paragraph in terms of its structure, or what each sentence contributes to the passage.

(1) This sentence introduces the topic about which the author is writing.
(2) This sentence provides information to support the first sentence.
(3) This sentence also provides information to support the first sentence.
(4) This sentence uses the information in sentences 1, 2, and 3 to make a point.

As you can see, stripping down the paragraph in terms of its structure makes it easier to comprehend. Many of the passages on the TOEFL will conform to this basic structure. That means for our purposes, when reading the introduction, you should proceed as follows:

1. Read the first sentence—and the last sentence— of each paragraph very carefully. They will most likely contain key information about the passage.
2. Skim through the sentences in the middle. They typically contain background information that merely supports the author's first or last sentence.

Reading the introduction is helpful for answering questions about the main idea or the primary purpose of the passage. The introduction may also contain background information about the topic, ask a question, or answer a question posed by important details which you'll find in the body paragraphs.

Drill #2: Analyze the Structure

For each of the following introduction paragraphs, write down what role each sentence plays in the paragraph. Check your answers at the end.

Introduction A

(1) Scientists at Michigan State University are asking a most challenging question. (2) Can a computer program be considered alive? (3) The members of the Digital Evolution Laboratory say yes. (4) Computer scientists at the laboratory have created a program called Avida that has intrigued not only scientists and engineers but biologists and philosophers as well.

(1) _____

(2) _____

(3) _____

(4) _____

Introduction B

(1) After a seven-year journey, the *Cassini* spacecraft approached the planet Saturn in June 2004. (2) The spacecraft's successful entry into orbit around the world represented the culmination of a vision that took more than 20 years to realize. (3) Launched amid controversy in October 1997, the *Cassini* spacecraft traveled more than one billion miles in its journey. (4) Despite all the public and technological challenges, the *Cassini* mission has been more successful than even its planners imagined.

(1) _____

(2) _____

(3) _____

(4) _____

Introduction C

(1) What causes hallucinations, vivid perceptions of sights or sounds that appear quite real to the person experiencing them? (2) These mystical experiences have long fascinated psychologists, neuroscientists, and anthropologists alike. (3) In many cultures, shamans, prophets, and seers are marked by their susceptibility to hallucinations. (4) Are hallucinations caused by ghosts or spirits? (5) Are they messages from another world? (6) Although researchers don't have all the answers, there is some intriguing information on the topic.

(1) _____

(2) _____

(3) _____

(4) _____

(5) _____

(6) _____

Introduction D

(1) In the Arctic tundra, temperatures are below freezing for nine months out of the year. (2) Soil in the Arctic, called permafrost, remains permanently frozen, making agriculture impossible. (3) Travel over the land, whether covered in snow and ice in the winter or in boggy marshes during the summer, is extremely difficult. (4) And perhaps most distressing of all, the Sun shines for only six months out of the year. (5) Yet this foreboding landscape has been inhabited for more than 12,000 years, longer than any other part of North America.

(1) _____

(2) _____

(3) _____

(4) _____

(5) _____

Introduction E

(1) Alexis de Tocqueville's *Democracy in America* studies the interplay between political power and society. (2) The treatise was the first of its kind and was revolutionary for its use of empirical methods, which were more common in the "hard" sciences—chemistry, biology, and physics—than in the social sciences. (3) Tocqueville distinguished himself from his colleagues by viewing democracy not as a system based on freedom but as one based on power. (4) In fact, Tocqueville argues that democracy is a form of government with more power than any other governmental system.

(1) _____

(2) _____

(3) _____

(4) _____

Answers to Drill #2

As is always the case with our sample written answers, your answers do not have to look exactly like ours. Just be sure the main ideas are similar.

Introduction A

(1) This sentence introduces the main question of the passage.
(2) This sentence states what the question is.
(3) This sentence gives an answer to the question.
(4) This sentence makes a more specific statement about the topic.

Introduction B

(1) This sentence introduces the topic of the passage.
(2) This sentence provides background about the topic.
(3) This sentence provides more background about the topic.
(4) This sentence makes a statement about the topic.

Introduction C

(1) This sentence asks a question about the topic.
(2) This sentence states who is interested in the topic.
(3) This sentence provides more information about the topic.
(4) This sentence asks another question about the topic.
(5) This sentence asks another question about the topic.
(6) This sentence states that some answers will be provided about the topic.

Introduction D

(1) This sentence introduces the topic.
(2) This sentence gives more support for sentence 1.
(3) This sentence gives more support for sentence 1.
(4) This sentence gives more support for sentence 1.
(5) This sentence indicates a contrast to the previous sentences.

Introduction E

(1) This sentence introduces the topic.
(2) This sentence explains why the topic is important.
(3) This sentence indicates why the topic is different.
(4) This sentence states a viewpoint.

You should notice that all of these paragraphs have similar structures. The important stuff is at the beginning and the end, which is typical: the TOEFL is a standardized test and therefore uses the same types of passages and questions repeatedly. So, you should expect to see a similar structure on your test.

What Is the Structure of a Body Paragraph?

Body paragraphs, just like introduction paragraphs, also share a similar structure. Here's an example of a typical body paragraph.

> (1) The harsh terrain demanded much of its inhabitants. (2) Many residents of the tundra were nomadic, moving about in small bands, following the migrations of caribou, seals, and whales. (3) Cooperation among groups was essential for survival in this land, and the cultures developed elaborate rituals of reciprocity. (4) Groups of hunters often waited patiently at the various breathing holes used by seals. (5) If one hunter caught a seal, all would eat of it. (6) Bravery was also rewarded, as evidenced by the Inupiaq people, who risked death by wandering far across sea ice to hunt seals.

Now we'll look at this paragraph in terms of its structure.

(1) This sentence states the specific topic discussed (that much is demanded of people).
(2) This sentence gives an example of something demanded.
(3) This sentence gives an example of how the people adapted.
(4) This sentence provides a detail related to sentence 3.
(5) This sentence provides an additional detail related to sentence 3.
(6) This sentence gives an example of something else demanded.

Looking at the paragraph this way, you can clearly see that these body paragraphs are all about details. Of course, these details are all closely related to the topic sentence. This means that when dealing with body paragraphs on the TOEFL, you should proceed as follows:

1. Read the topic sentence carefully. Make sure you are looking in the right paragraph for the information you need.
2. Sort through the specific details until you find what you need. It is easy to get distracted by all the information in a body paragraph. Stay focused on the information you need. Reading the body paragraphs will help you answer detail and inference questions.

When answering main idea or primary purpose questions, do not read more than the first sentence of the body paragraphs. The information found in the body paragraphs is too narrow. We'll cover these question types more thoroughly in Chapter 7.

Types of Body Paragraphs

The body paragraph we just read supports the author's views. Most body paragraphs on the TOEFL will be of this type. However, some passages have body paragraphs that present an opposing point of view. Usually, these show up in passages that try to resolve a dilemma or convince the reader of something. By stating contradictory opinions, an author provides a more complete understanding of a topic and makes the main point stronger.

You can usually tell when you are reading a body paragraph that contradicts the author by reading the first sentence. The first sentence may have a transition word that indicates the author is now discussing an opposing point of view. Here's an example of such a paragraph.

(1) Of course, not everyone agrees that the program's creations are alive.
(2) One difficulty is that biologists do not even agree on the definition of life.
(3) The diversity of life on Earth constantly surprises scientists, and there are simply too many characteristics and qualities to provide one simple definition of life.

Again, here's the structure of the paragraph.

(1)   This sentence presents an opposite point of view.
(2)   This sentence explains why some biologists disagree with the author's position.
(3)   This sentence supports sentence 2.

The first sentence states, "Of course, not everyone agrees...." This sentence indicates that this paragraph will contradict the author. It is important to recognize these types of paragraphs, especially when answering main idea or primary purpose questions on the TOEFL.

Drill #3: Analyzing Body Paragraphs

State the role of each sentence in the following paragraphs. Also note whether the paragraph appears to support or contradict the passage.

Body Paragraph A

(1) The harsh terrain demanded much of its inhabitants. (2) Many residents of the tundra were nomadic, moving about in small bands, following the migrations of caribou, seals, and whales. (3) Cooperation among groups was essential for survival in this land, and the cultures developed elaborate rituals of reciprocity. (4) Groups of hunters often waited patiently at the various breathing holes used by seals. (5) If one hunter caught a seal, all would eat of it. (6) Bravery was also rewarded, as evidenced by the Inupiaq people, who risked death by wandering far across sea ice to hunt seals.

(1) _____

(2) _____

(3) _____

(4) _____

(5) _____

(6) _____

Supports or contradicts?

_____

Body Paragraph B

(1) Without human interference, many of the threatened or endangered fauna would reclaim their ecological niches. (2) Unfortunately, household pets would suffer. (3) In addition, the rat, one of the greatest pests in large cities, would not have the waste of humankind to feed off of and would be hunted mercilessly by growing populations of hawks and falcons. (4) And the cockroach, which to many a city dweller seems to symbolize invincibility, would disappear from all but the warmest climes without artificial heat to sustain it.

(1) _____

(2) _____

(3) _____

(4) _____

Supports or contradicts?

_____

Body Paragraph C

(1) According to surveys, anywhere from 10 to 25 percent of the population has experienced at least one hallucination. (2) Most often, the hallucination comes in the form of some visual experience, but some people report hearing a sound or even voices. (3) Even rarer, but not unheard of, is a hallucination of a particular smell or aroma. (4) It is not known exactly what causes hallucinations, although one commonly accepted theory is that hallucinations occur when the external stimulus received by the senses no longer matches the level of activity occurring in the brain. (5) Sensory deprivation is one of the surest ways to elicit hallucinations.

(1) _____

(2) _____

(3) _____

(4) _____

(5) _____

Supports or contradicts?

_____

Body Paragraph D

(1) Another connection between the lower classes and the centralization of power is literacy, or more accurately, illiteracy. (2) In aristocratic societies, widespread illiteracy did not result in the consolidation of power because the social structure was so segmented. (3) But in an egalitarian society, the intermediate agencies vanish. (4) Without these agencies acting on behalf of the less-informed citizenry, the responsibility falls to the government. (5) Centralization is therefore necessary to aid and provide for citizens who may otherwise have nowhere else to turn to for assistance.

(1) _____

(2) _____

(3) _____

(4) _____

(5) _____

Supports or contradicts?

_____

Answers to Drill #3

Body Paragraph A
(1)   This sentence states that much is demanded of people.
(2)   This sentence gives an example of something demanded.
(3)   This sentence gives an example of how the people adapted.
(4)   This sentence provides a detail related to sentence 3.
(5)   This sentence provides an additional detail related to sentence 3.
(6)   This sentence gives an example of something else demanded.

This paragraph supports the passage.

Body Paragraph B
(1)   This sentence gives a consequence of a situation.
(2)   This sentence gives a contrast to sentence 1.
(3)   This sentence gives another contrast to sentence 1.
(4)   This sentence gives another contrast to sentence 1.

This paragraph contradicts the passage.

Body Paragraph C
(1)   This sentence gives a fact about the topic.
(2)   This sentence provides more information related to sentence 1.
(3)   This sentence provides more information related to sentence 1.
(4)   This sentence provides another fact about the topic.
(5)   This sentence provides more information related to sentence 4.

This paragraph supports the passage.

Body Paragraph D
(1)   This sentence introduces another connection.
(2)   This sentence provides a detail related to sentence 1.
(3)   This sentence explains sentences 1 and 2 more fully.
(4)   This sentence also explains sentences 1 and 2 more fully.
(5)   This sentence summarizes the other sentences.

This paragraph supports the passage.

As you can see, body paragraphs start with a narrow topic followed by details that are closely related to that narrow topic. Sometimes, as in paragraph C, there are two topics (the percentage of the population experience hallucinations, potential causes of hallucinations), but most body paragraphs deal with only one topic. Most times, the body paragraphs support the author, but occasionally they are used to present contradictory information.

What Is the Structure of a Conclusion Paragraph?

Many of the passages on the TOEFL are edited versions of longer passages. Thus, the last paragraph will usually provide some additional details and a final wrap-up of the topic. Let's revisit a conclusion paragraph.

(1) Of course, other factors increase the centralization of a democracy.
(2) Tocqueville points out that war is an important agent of centralization.
(3) To succeed in war, contends Tocqueville, a nation must be able to focus its resources around a single point. (4) Countries with a centralization of power are far more able to accomplish this task than are countries with fragmented power structures. (5) But it is interesting how Tocqueville sees democracy as a vehicle not for freedom but for power, driven by the very people the democracy is designed to empower.

Again, here's the structure of the conclusion.

(1) This sentence provides a detail that contrasts with the main point of the passage.
(2) This sentence provides more information on sentence 1.
(3) This sentence provides a detail related to sentence 1.
(4) This sentence provides a detail related to sentence 1.
(5) This sentence states the author's final point.

As you can see, the conclusion paragraph offers some specific details similar to a body paragraph. However, it also contains an important final statement that should apply to the passage as a whole. Therefore, when reading a conclusion paragraph, you should proceed as follows:

1. Read the first sentence. If the topic sentence introduces more details, skim through them.
2. Read the very last sentence. Try to figure out what the author's final message or point is.

Conclusion paragraphs can be very useful for primary purpose questions. In addition to containing extra details, conclusions can also provide contradictory points and ask final questions about the topic.

Drill #4: Analyzing Conclusions

For each of the following conclusion paragraphs, specify the role each sentence plays. Also, write down the author's final point or message.

Conclusion Paragraph A

(1) Despite these misgivings, the directors of the Avida program remain optimistic that their program, even if not considered alive, is leading to a greater understanding of life in all its forms. (2) It may even facilitate future searches for life on other planets. (3) According to one member of the Avida team, "The problem that we have now is that we are focused on looking for DNA-based life. (4) But there may be other kinds of life out there that we have never dreamed of." (5) The Avida program may provide biologists with another avenue to explore.

(1) _____

(2) _____

(3) _____

(4) _____

Final point: _____

Conclusion Paragraph B

(1) Newcomers to the Arctic region required the use of advanced technology to make a living in the region. (2) But the native inhabitants of the tundra existed there for generations without the need for guns, steel knives, vehicles, or modern clothing. (3) Rather than struggling against the harsh environment around them, the original inhabitants found ways to live in harmony with it. (4) The Arctic offers an abundance of riches, and these people, through their resourcefulness, were able to harvest them.

(1) _____

(2) _____

(3) _____

Final point: _____

Conclusion Paragraph C

(1) The question of plastics aside, there is some evidence that Weisman's view may be true. (2) Since 1953, a 150-mile-long tract of land separating North and South Korea has been declared a no-man's-land. (3) After only a little more than 50 years, there is almost no trace of the rice paddies that farmers had created and used for almost 5,000 years. (4) Even more spectacular are the flocks of red-crowned cranes that now inhabit the zone. (5) These birds are the second rarest of all birds, but they have flourished in this area, free from human interference of all kinds.

(1) _____

(2) _____

(3) _____

(4) _____

Final point: _____

Conclusion Paragraph D

(1) Regardless of the causes of hallucinations, the effects they have on their subjects are very real. (2) Hallucinations can cause the aforementioned change in heart rate and body temperature, and they can also lead a person to act on the hallucination. (3) Psychologists have found that the memories created by a hallucination are processed by the same part of the brain that handles normal memories. (4) Thus, for the subject of a hallucination, the experience is as real as any other.

(1) _____

(2) _____

(3) _____

Final point: _____

Answers to Drill #4

Conclusion Paragraph A
(1)   This sentence provides information on the future of the topic.
(2)   This sentence provides more information related to sentence 1.
(3)   This sentence presents a quote to support sentence 2.
(4)   This sentence supports sentence 2.

Final point: The Avida program is providing biologists with new things to explore.

Conclusion Paragraph B
(1)   This sentence introduces new information about the topic.
(2)   This sentence contrasts the two subjects.
(3)   This sentence contrasts the two subjects.

Final point: The inhabitants of the Arctic are able to use its many resources.

Conclusion Paragraph C
(1)   This sentence introduces evidence to support a view.
(2)   This sentence provides details about the evidence.
(3)   This sentence provides more details about the evidence.
(4)   This sentence presents a new piece of evidence.

Final point: Without human interference, the land and animals can flourish.

Conclusion Paragraph D
(1)   This sentence introduces another point about the main topic.
(2)   This sentence provides a detail related to sentence 1.
(3)   This sentence provides a detail related to sentence 1.

Final point: Hallucinations are experienced as real.

Following the Direction of the Passage

We've been practicing all these steps to mastering active reading. Based on our analysis of passages so far, you should begin to see that each passage on the TOEFL is broken down into pieces, each with a main topic and supporting details. The key to active reading is to focus only on the larger topics and not be distracted by details that you can come back for if a question requires more detail.

Our next step when analyzing structure is to pay attention to the direction of the passage. We've already seen paragraphs that either support or contradict an author's position. We say a passage is going in the same direction if the information or paragraph supports the author. If a paragraph contradicts the author, we say that it is going in the opposite direction. Read the passage below, and circle the changes in direction.

Art has always occupied a special place in society. Many people consider artists to be the ultimate authorities on aesthetics, the nature and expression of beauty. For much of history, the practice of art was inscrutable, and artists were viewed as being somewhat strange and often mad. Even the word
5   most commonly associated with artists—inspiration—has its own magical overtones. Literally, "inspiration" is the breathing in of a spirit. Artists were thought of as people who were divinely inspired to create.

Of course, artists contributed to this mythology. Many artists ascribed
10   their talents to the presence of some supernatural agent or "muse." Whole movements of art have centered on the supposedly otherworldly nature of art. For example, the Romantic poets believed that art was the search for the sublime, a term for them that meant an ultimate expression of beauty and truth. The search for this ideal led them to explore both natural and
15   supernatural themes in their works.

Another persistent view of art regarded its divorce from rationality. Reason and logic were the province of scientists and philosophers, whereas creativity and intuition were the domain of the artists. The two separate spheres of the
20   mind were supposed to remain distinct.

But in 1704, a major transgression occurred. Sir Isaac Newton, mathematician and physicist extraordinaire, published his study of light, *Opticks*. One of Newton's major discoveries was on the nature of color. Using
25   a prism, Newton found that white light is actually composed of all the colors of the rainbow. He even provided a scientific explanation for the presence of rainbows. The artistic community was shocked. A scientist had taken a beautiful and magical experience and reduced it to the simple refraction of beams of light through the prism of a raindrop. A scientist had intruded into
30   their sacred territory.

More than a hundred years later, John Keats, one of the most famous Romantic poets, accused Newton of diminishing beauty by "unweaving the rainbow." His colleague, Samuel Taylor Coleridge, famously remarked that the
35   souls of five hundred Newtons would be needed to make one Shakespeare. And yet, from another perspective, Newton did not diminish the beauty of the rainbow; he enhanced it. In his quest to uncover the secrets of the rainbow,

Newton demonstrated the wonder, creativity, and inspiration of an artist. He also gave the world another opportunity to experience the sublime. Newton's
40 discovery paved the way for the development of the science of spectroscopy, a way of analyzing the chemical makeup of light. Now scientists can look at the stars and discern their composition. The sense of wonder this ability creates is not much different from the wonder the poet or artist feels when gazing at those same stars.

Here's the passage again, with the direction changes indicated. To make it easier to tell them apart, in this passage the same direction words are **bolded**, whereas the opposite direction words are <u>underlined</u>.

Applied Strategies

Art has always occupied a special place in society. Many people consider artists to be the ultimate authorities on aesthetics, the nature and expression of beauty. For much of history, the practice of art was inscrutable, and artists were viewed as being somewhat strange and often mad. **Even**
5 the word most commonly associated with artists—inspiration—has its own magical overtones. Literally, "inspiration" is the breathing in of a spirit. Artists were thought of as people who were divinely inspired to create.

Of course, artists contributed to this mythology. Many artists ascribed
10 their talents to the presence of some supernatural agent or "muse." Whole movements of art have centered on the supposedly otherworldly nature of art. **For example**, the Romantic poets believed that art was the search for the sublime, a term for them that meant an ultimate expression of beauty and truth. The search for this ideal led them to explore both natural and
15 supernatural themes in their works.

Another persistent view of art regarded its divorce from rationality. Reason and logic were the province of scientists and philosophers, <u>whereas</u> creativity and intuition were the domain of the artists. The two separate spheres of the
20 mind were supposed to remain distinct.

<u>But</u> in 1704, a major transgression occurred. Sir Isaac Newton, mathematician and physicist extraordinaire, published his study of light, *Opticks*. One of Newton's major discoveries was on the nature of color. Using
25 a prism, Newton found that white light is actually composed of all the colors of the rainbow. He **even** provided a scientific explanation for the presence of rainbows. The artistic community was shocked. A scientist had taken a beautiful and magical experience and reduced it to the simple refraction of beams of light through the prism of a raindrop. A scientist had intruded into
30 their sacred territory.

More than a hundred years later, John Keats, one of the most famous Romantic poets, accused Newton of diminishing beauty by "unweaving the rainbow." His colleague, Samuel Taylor Coleridge, famously remarked that the
35 souls of five hundred Newtons would be needed to make one Shakespeare. **And** <u>yet</u>, from another perspective, Newton did not diminish the beauty of the rainbow; he enhanced it. In his quest to uncover the secrets of the rainbow, Newton demonstrated the wonder, creativity, and inspiration of an artist. He

also gave the world another opportunity to experience the sublime. Newton's
40   discovery paved the way for the development of the science of spectroscopy,
a way of analyzing the chemical makeup of light. Now scientists can look
at the stars and discern their composition. The sense of wonder this ability
creates is not much different from the wonder the poet or artist feels when
gazing at those same stars.

When reading actively, use direction words to help you understand the organization of the
information in the passage. Same direction markers mean that the information you are about
to read supports the topic. Once you notice this, you can often skim through this information. However, pay particular attention to changes of direction in a passage. These indicate an
important shift.

Look for the following common direction words:

Same Direction	Opposite Direction
And	Although
Because	However
Even	Yet
Therefore	Despite
Another	But
For example	In contrast to
One reason	On the other hand
Due to	Rather
Also	Even though

Drill #5: Finding Directions

Read each paragraph, circle the direction markers, and identify whether they are same direction or opposite direction words.

Direction Paragraph A

Hallucinations can also be elicited in a number of other ways. Some of the most common experiences of hallucinations happen when a person is in the throes of an epileptic fit or suffering from a high fever. Other methods of bringing about a hallucination include fasting or sleeplessness. Admiral Richard Byrd reported having hallucinations after spending several months alone in the Antarctic. Hallucinations can be so powerful that members of many cultures seek them out, undertaking "vision quests" in the hopes of having a hallucinatory experience. Usually, the participants who go on these quests journey out into the elements without food or shelter.

Direction Paragraph B

Another connection between the lower classes and the centralization of power is literacy, or more accurately, illiteracy. In aristocratic societies, widespread illiteracy did not result in the consolidation of power because the social structure was so segmented. But in an egalitarian society, the intermediate agencies vanish. Without these agencies acting on behalf of the less-informed citizenry, the responsibility falls to the government. Centralization is therefore necessary to aid and provide for citizens who may otherwise have nowhere else to turn to for assistance.

Direction Paragraph C

It is also suspected that the brain has its own chemicals designed to produce hallucinations. For example, some patients suffer from delirium tremens, a violent period of hallucinations accompanied by sweating, an increase in heart rate, and a rise in body temperature. Through experience treating episodes such as this, it is also known that certain chemicals can stop hallucinations. The drug Thorazine is often used to treat patients suffering from psychotic disorders that involve hallucinations.

Direction Paragraph D

The career of Phillip Johnson, one of America's foremost architects, was a study in contrasts. Initially, Johnson was a staunch proponent of the Modernist school of architecture, and he achieved his early fame by working in this style. After a time, however, Johnson apparently became bored with Modernism, even though he claimed that he loved the experience of the new above all things. Johnson decided to move from Modernism to Classicism, a style that he explored thoroughly. He soon tired of the Classical school as well and moved back toward Modernism, although his later works still incorporate Classical elements.

Answers to Drill #5

Direction Paragraph A

Hallucinations can (also) (same direction) be elicited in a number of other ways. Some of the most common experiences of hallucinations happen when a person is in the throes of an epileptic fit or suffering from a high fever. (Other) (same direction) methods of bringing about a hallucination include fasting or sleeplessness. Admiral Richard Byrd reported having hallucinations after spending several months alone in the Antarctic. Hallucinations can be so powerful that members of many cultures seek them out, undertaking "vision quests" in the hopes of having a hallucinatory experience. Usually, the participants who go on these quests journey out into the elements without food or shelter.

Direction Paragraph B

(Another) (same direction) connection between the lower classes and the centralization of power is literacy, or more accurately, illiteracy. In aristocratic societies, widespread illiteracy did not result in the consolidation of power (because) (same direction) the social structure was so segmented. (But) (opposite direction) in an egalitarian society, the intermediate agencies vanish. Without these agencies acting on behalf of the less-informed citizenry, the responsibility falls to the government. Centralization is (therefore) (same direction) necessary to aid and provide for citizens who may otherwise have nowhere else to turn to for assistance.

Direction Paragraph C

It is (also) (same direction) suspected that the brain has its own chemicals designed to produce hallucinations. (For example) (same direction), some patients suffer from delirium tremens, a violent period of hallucinations accompanied by sweating, an increase in heart rate, and a rise in body temperature. Through experience treating episodes such as this, it is (also) (same direction) known that certain chemicals can stop hallucinations. The drug Thorazine is often used to treat patients suffering from psychotic disorders that involve hallucinations.

Direction Paragraph D

The career of Phillip Johnson, one of America's foremost architects, was a study in contrasts. (Initially) (same direction), Johnson was a staunch proponent of the Modernist school of architecture, and he achieved his early fame by working in this style. After a time (however) (opposite direction), Johnson apparently became bored with Modernism, (even though) (opposite direction) he claimed that he loved the experience of the new above all things. Johnson decided to move from Modernism to Classicism, a style that he explored thoroughly. He soon tired of the Classical school as well and moved back toward Modernism, (although) (opposite direction) his later works still incorporate Classical elements.

Summary: Understanding Structure

1. Identify the structure of the passage because this knowledge will help you to find information quickly.
2. Remember, TOEFL passages are made up of the following paragraph types: introduction, body, and conclusion. Know what type of information is usually found in each type of paragraph.
3. Use the first sentence of the paragraph as a guide to the information contained in the rest of the paragraph.
4. Keep in mind that the remaining sentences provide details about the topic.
5. Pay attention to direction markers. Same-direction markers indicate the author is continuing the discussion. Opposite-direction markers highlight contrasting ideas.

Step 3: Find the Purpose

People write for many reasons. Some write to entertain, whereas others write to inform. If you know the purpose of a passage, then you know what the writer is trying to accomplish, and you can determine what is important and unimportant about the piece.

The majority of passages on the TOEFL will do one of the following:

-   **Explain:** The purpose of these passages is to present you with information on specific topics, and they contain mostly facts.
-   **Resolve:** The purpose of these passages is to find solutions for some sort of dilemma. There is usually a debate or question that needs an answer.
-   **Convince:** The purpose of these passages is to try to argue the validity of a certain viewpoint or idea. They give opinions and support them with evidence.

A written passage can be broken down into three basic parts: the introduction, the body, and the conclusion. The introduction seeks to give the reader background about the topic. The body of a passage provides details and explanations of what was covered in the introduction. The conclusion summarizes everything in the passage and usually leaves the reader with a few new thoughts on the topic. In the next section, we will practice active reading by looking at each part of a passage. To find the purpose of the passage, we'll start with the introduction (the first paragraph).

The Introduction Paragraph

Let's return to the sample passage at the beginning of this chapter. Here's the first paragraph again.

> Scientists at Michigan State University are asking a most challenging question. Can a computer program be considered alive? The members of the Digital Evolution Laboratory say yes. Computer scientists at the laboratory have created a program called Avida that has intrigued not only scientists and engineers but biologists and philosophers as well.

The introduction paragraph is one of the most important paragraphs in the passage—it should give you a pretty good idea of what the author wants to accomplish. Look at it sentence by sentence and identify clues that will help you find the purpose.

First, examine the opening sentence.

> Scientists at Michigan State University are asking a most challenging question.

Now, focus on the important stuff. You do this by asking yourself what and why. The first question to ask yourself is this: What are you reading about? This is the subject of the sentence. Write down the subject.

_____

Now ask yourself this question: Why is the author writing about this? Write down what you think the author wants you to know about. _____

_____

So far, you are reading about the scientists. And why are you reading about them? Because they are asking a question. If you are still unsure about this information after reading the first sentence, then continue to the second sentence.

> Can a computer program be considered alive?

This clarifies the first sentence. Now you know that the passage is about scientists and a computer program that may be considered alive. Do you think the author wrote this passage to inform, to resolve, or to argue? Write it down.

_____

Now move on to the body paragraphs.

The Body Paragraphs

When looking for the purpose, don't get bogged down in the details. For most passages, you can get everything you need by reading just the first sentence or two of each paragraph. Try that on the passage below. Here are the first four body paragraphs.

The Avida project began in the late 1990s, when Chris Adami, a physicist, sought to create computer programs that could evolve to do simple addition problems and reproduce inside a digital environment. Adami called these programs "digital organisms." Whenever a digital organism replicates, it has
5 a chance to alter the program of the newly created offspring. In this way, the programs mutate and evolve. The goal of the Avida program is to create a model that could simulate the evolutionary process.

Initially, the digital creations were unable to process numbers in any way. But
10 Adami designed Avida to reward digital organisms that were able to work with the numbers in some way. The digital organisms that could process numbers were allowed to reproduce in higher numbers. In only six short months, the primitive program had evolved a number of mechanisms to perform addition. And, most surprisingly, not all of the digital creatures performed addition in
15 the same way.

The Avida program now resides at Michigan State University, where it has been growing and changing for years. The digital creatures number in the billions and have colonized more than two hundred computers. The
20 organisms compete with one another for resources, and the most successful ones are able to make more copies of themselves. Just like living creatures, the digital entities also undergo mutations. Mutations that are beneficial ensure greater reproduction; harmful mutations have the opposite effect.

25 As a model for studying evolution, the Avida project has been a great success. Adami's digital organisms have suggested solutions to some of evolution's biggest mysteries. For example, Avida has helped disprove the theory of "irreducible complexity." Opponents of evolutionary theory have suggested that some structures, such as the eye, are too complex to have
30 been created in piecemeal stages. The evolution of Avida's digital organisms proves that even extremely complex structures can be developed in stages over time.

Now, read only the first sentence of each paragraph and ask what and why. Look only at the first sentence of the first body paragraph. Write down what the author's subject is and what you think the author is telling you about it.

What? _____

What about it? _____

Do the same for the other three paragraphs.

What? _____

What about it? _____

What? _____

What about it? _____

What? _____

What about it? _____

Please note that your answers may be worded differently from ours and still be correct. Just check to be sure they share the same general idea. Your answers should look something like this.

What? Avida project
What about it? To tell us how it began

What? Digital creatures
What about it? They are able to work with numbers.

What? Avida program
What about it? It's been changing.

What? Studying evolution
What about it? Digital creatures can help scientists learn more about evolution.

Check back on the prediction you made earlier. Does this new information change it? Let's look at the remaining body paragraphs.

The Avida program's success has also raised some unintentional philosophical dilemmas. Does Avida just simulate evolution, or are digital organisms a new form of life? According to the director of the Avida project, the processes undergone by the digital creatures are the same as those
5 experienced by biological organisms. The only difference is that biological entities are based on strings of DNA, whereas the digital creations from Avida are based on strings of ones and zeros. In a living creature, different sequences of DNA instruct cells to create certain proteins. In one of the Avida creations, different sequences of computer code instruct the program to
10 perform certain functions. In both cases, the reproduction of the organisms is subject to forces such as competition and mutation.

Now, some biologists are maintaining that the programs in the Avida project are alive. The programs live, die, reproduce, compete, cooperate, and
15 evolve—activities that many biologists consider the hallmarks of life. One prominent biologist says, "They don't have a metabolism—at least not yet. But otherwise, they're alive."

Of course, not everyone agrees that the program's creations are alive. One
20 difficulty is that biologists do not even agree on the definition of life. The
diversity of life on Earth constantly surprises scientists, and there are simply
too many characteristics and qualities to provide one simple definition of life.

Again, read only the first sentence of each paragraph and answer the questions.

What? _____

What about it? _____

What? _____

What about it? _____

What? _____

What about it? _____

Take a look at your responses. Do they match the following?

What? Are digital organisms a form of life?
What about it? The digital creatures meet many of the criteria for life.

What? Biologists
What about it? They think the program is alive.

What? Other people
What about it? They don't agree with the biologists.

By now, we should have a pretty good idea of why the author has written this passage.

Write down your reason here. _____

_____

You'll check your final prediction in a moment, but before you do so, you have one more paragraph to review.

The Conclusion

Here's the final paragraph, but for this paragraph, read both the first and the last sentence.

> Despite these misgivings, the directors of the Avida program remain optimistic that their program, even if not considered alive, is leading to a greater understanding of life in all its forms. It may even facilitate future searches for life on other planets. According to one member of the Avida
> 5 team, "The problem that we have now is that we are focused on looking for DNA-based life. But there may be other kinds of life out there that we have never dreamed of." The Avida program may provide biologists with another avenue to explore.

Now answer the questions regarding the first and last sentences in this conclusion.

What? _____

What about it? _____

What? _____

What about it? _____

Here are our answers.

What? Directors of the program
What about it? The program is helping people understand life.

What? The Avida program
What about it? The program gives biologists something to explore.

Putting It All Together

Look back at what you've written. Based on only the six or seven sentences you've read, does it seem as if the author is trying to argue a point, resolve a dilemma, or simply provide you with information? The purpose of this passage is to provide us with information—to explain something. It introduces the scientists and their Avida program. Next, it describes the beginning of the project and the current state of the Avida program. After that, the author talks about how the director of the project and other people view the project. Finally, the author indicates that scientists hope Avida will lead to new avenues of exploration. Thus, we could write down the following for the purpose:

Purpose: To give us a brief overview of the Avida computer program and its implications

Remember, you won't have time to read and comprehend every single word and sentence on the TOEFL. Therefore, with active reading, you'll read fewer sentences, but your comprehension will increase because you'll read only the important parts.

Drill #6: Find the Purpose

Apply the techniques you've just learned to each of the passages that follow. Check your answers at the end of the drill.

Passage A

Alexis de Tocqueville's *Democracy in America* studies the interplay between political power and society. The treatise was the first of its kind and was revolutionary for its use of empirical methods, which were more common in the "hard" sciences—chemistry, biology, and physics—than in the social sciences. Tocqueville distinguished himself from his colleagues
5 by viewing democracy not as a system based on freedom but as one based on power. In fact, Tocqueville argues that democracy is a form of government with more power than any other governmental system.

Born in France in 1805, Tocqueville had a conflicted relationship with his reformist ideals.
10 His grandfather, a liberal aristocrat, lawyer, and politician, was a powerful force for social reforms prior to and during the French Revolution. Despite this, he was condemned as a counterrevolutionary and executed along with several members of his family. Tocqueville adopted his grandfather's liberal ideals, but never lost a profound distrust for the potentially violent extremes to which the drive for democracy can push a nation. Tocqueville's famous
15 study of the United States was the product of a nine-month trip to the young republic, beginning in 1831. Tocqueville had traveled to the United States to produce a study of America's prisons. That initial study was published in 1833, a year after he returned to France. He then labored another nine years over *Democracy in America*. The book itself was written in two distinct volumes. The first volume focused specifically on Tocqueville's
20 observations of American culture. He stressed the growth of social equality promoted by a stable social order, an issue that was close to his heart given France's repeated violent efforts to establish a lasting democracy. The second volume, written four years after the first had been completed, was more abstract. Tocqueville turned his attention to the conflict of individuality and centrality in democratic cultures.
25
Tocqueville ascribes the power of a democracy to its tendency to centralize power. In a democracy, there are no guilds, estates, or sharply defined social classes. These institutions, in earlier times, represented a check on the powers of kings and tyrants. But in their absence, the government holds the ultimate authority. According to Tocqueville, it is the
30 lower classes that primarily drive the centralization of power in a democracy.

One reason the lower classes prefer a centralization of power relates to the historical role of the aristocratic class. In many class-based societies, the lower classes were subject to the rule of classes above them. Local affairs were overseen by aristocrats, who often acted like
35 petty tyrants. Only by surrendering authority to a central government could the lower classes achieve equality.

Another connection between the lower classes and the centralization of power is literacy, or more accurately, illiteracy. In aristocratic societies, widespread illiteracy did not result in the
40 consolidation of power because the social structure was so segmented. But in an egalitarian society, the intermediate agencies vanish. Without these agencies acting on behalf of the less-informed citizenry, the responsibility falls to the government. Centralization is therefore

necessary to aid and provide for citizens who may otherwise have nowhere else to turn to for assistance.

45

But perhaps the most profound effect the lower classes can have on the centralization of power in a democracy concerns the nature of the democratic leader. In an aristocracy or a monarchy, the ruler was always viewed as a person apart from the lower classes, a person whose birth made him (or her) superior to his subjects. In a democracy, the lower classes
50 can identify more closely with a leader whom they can view as one of them and thus are willing to rally around him (or her) more readily.

Of course, other factors increase the centralization of a democracy. Tocqueville points out that war is an important agent of centralization. To succeed in war, contends Tocqueville,
55 a nation must be able to focus its resources around a single point. Countries with a centralization of power are far more able to accomplish this task than are countries with fragmented power structures. But it is interesting how Tocqueville sees democracy as a vehicle not for freedom but for power, driven by the very people the democracy is designed to empower.

Paragraph 1

What? _____

What about it? _____

Paragraph 2

What? _____

What about it? _____

Paragraph 3

What? _____

What about it? _____

Paragraph 4

What? _____

What about it? _____

Paragraph 5

What? _____

What about it? _____

Paragraph 6

What? _____

What about it? _____

Paragraph 7

What? _____

What about it? _____

Overall Purpose? _____

Passage B

Sometimes it appears that the human mark on this planet is indelible. In only a blink of geological time, 200 years or so, human construction and expansion has resulted in the destruction of more than one-fifth of the world's forests, the recession of the polar icecaps, and the creation of a huge hole in the ozone layer. Additionally, industrial activity has
5   damaged rivers and oceans, as well as groundwater supplies. Environmental scientists and activists warn that if Earth's future is not taken into account, humankind could very well destroy the planet.

However, Earth is an amazingly resilient place. In its 4.5-billion-year lifespan, Earth has
10 endured bombardment by cosmic rays and meteors, violent earthquakes, volcanism, and frigid ice ages. In light of all these catastrophic events, many geologists and ecologists say that Earth could recover from any damage caused by human actions.

The author Alan Weisman has gone so far as to predict exactly what would happen on Earth
15 if all humans were to disappear. Without upkeep, the concrete jungles of the world's greatest cities would be slowly reclaimed by the wilderness around them. Harsh temperatures would cause pavement to crack. Plants would return to areas covered by streets and sidewalks.

Different fates would await humankind's other creations. Litter and leaf matter would
20 accumulate, and it would take only one chance lightning strike to start a raging fire. Many structures would burn to the ground. The steel foundations supporting larger buildings and bridges would corrode and buckle, especially with the rise in groundwater that would accompany the clogging of sewer systems.

25 Without human interference, many of the threatened or endangered fauna would reclaim their ecological niches. Unfortunately, household pets would suffer. In addition, the rat, one of the greatest pests in large cities, would not have the waste of humankind to feed off of and would be hunted mercilessly by growing populations of hawks and falcons. And the cockroach, which to many a city dweller seems to symbolize invincibility, would disappear
30 from all but the warmest climes without artificial heat to sustain it.

Within 500 years, again barely a heartbeat in geological time, most of humankind's monuments would be gone, covered over by plants and trees. It's happened before; the

Mayan civilization in Northern Guatemala survived for 2,000 years but was swallowed up by
35 the jungle at its end. And after a few thousand years, if earthquakes and volcanic eruptions
have not obliterated everything made by humans, the glaciers would come, sweeping
down from the mountains, slowly and inexorably destroying everything in their path. Several
times in its history, Earth has been swept clean by these giant sheets of ice. The legacy of
humankind would be wiped from Earth.
40

Of course, not every man-made artifact would be reclaimed by nature. Plastic is a synthetic
material that does not occur in nature. The strong bonds that hold plastic together are
virtually impervious to natural erosion. Long after concrete and glass have turned back into
sand and all processed metals have rusted away, plastics will still be cycling through the
45 Earth's ecosystem, resilient to even the most destructive of natural forces. Some scientists
believe that plastic molecules may eventually break down entirely, but there is no reliable
data on just how long complete re-assimilation into the environment might take. Furthermore,
it is impossible to predict just what sort of resources Mother Nature might develop in the
distant future. There is always the possibility that, given enough time, some microbe or
50 bacteria may evolve the capability to digest plastic. If nature somehow evolved a way to
process plastics, then even humanity's most enduring artifacts might vanish in the space of
a few hundred years.

The question of plastics aside, there is some evidence that Weisman's view may be true.
55 Since 1953, a 150-mile-long tract of land separating North and South Korea has been
declared a no-man's-land. After only a little more than 50 years, there is almost no trace
of the rice paddies that farmers had created and used for almost 5,000 years. Even more
spectacular are the flocks of red-crowned cranes that now inhabit the zone. These birds
are the second rarest of all birds, but they have flourished in this area, free from human
60 interference of all kinds.

Paragraph 1

What? _____

What about it? _____

Paragraph 2

What? _____

What about it? _____

Paragraph 3

What? _____

What about it? _____

Paragraph 4

What? _____

What about it? _____

Paragraph 5

What? _____

What about it? _____

Paragraph 6

What? _____

What about it? _____

Paragraph 7

What? _____

What about it? _____

Paragraph 8

What? _____

What about it? _____

Overall Purpose? _____

Passage C

What causes hallucinations, vivid perceptions of unreal sights or sounds that appear quite real to the person experiencing them? These mystical experiences have long fascinated psychologists, neuroscientists, and anthropologists alike. In many cultures, shamans, prophets, and seers are marked by their susceptibility to hallucinations. Are hallucinations
5 caused by ghosts or spirits? Are they messages from another world? Although researchers don't have all the answers, there is some intriguing information on the topic.

According to surveys, anywhere from 10 to 25 percent of the population has experienced at least one hallucination. Most often, the hallucination comes in the form of some visual
10 experience, but some people report hearing a sound or even voices. Even rarer, but not unheard of, is a hallucination of a particular smell or aroma. It is not known exactly what causes hallucinations, although one commonly accepted theory is that hallucinations occur

when the external stimulus received by the senses no longer matches the level of activity occurring in the brain. Sensory deprivation is one of the surest ways to elicit hallucinations.

15 Hallucinations can also be elicited in a number of other ways. Some of the most common experiences of hallucinations happen when a person is in the throes of an epileptic fit or suffering from a high fever.

20 Other methods of bringing about a hallucination include fasting or sleeplessness. Admiral Richard Byrd reported having hallucinations after spending several months alone in the Antarctic. Hallucinations can be so powerful that members of many cultures seek them out, undertaking "vision quests" in the hopes of having a hallucinatory experience. Usually the participants who go on these quests journey out into the elements without food or shelter.

25 Not all hallucinations are the product of extreme physical conditions. Some very complex hallucinations can be triggered by nothing more unusual than everyday memories. People who have lost limbs often report that they continue to feel physical sensations as if the limb were still there. These "phantom limbs" are most likely the result of the brain interpreting

30 signals it receives from severed nerve endings in the context of its memories of the missing limb. An even stranger phenomenon involves hallucinations produced by the memories of recently departed loved ones. Called grief hallucinations, these vivid visions can be simple visual hallucinations or more complex fantasy interactions. In one reported case, a woman reported receiving multiple visits from her departed children. The woman claimed that she

35 and her "ghosts" regularly held long and involved conversations. Neuroscientists theorize that grief hallucinations may be the product of vivid memories that last in the mind long after a loved one has passed away. As bizarre as grief hallucinations may sound, the experience is quite common. Some researchers estimate that up to 80 percent of people will experience some form of grief hallucination in their lifetime.

40 Although neuroscientists may not be sure of the exact mechanism in the brain that causes hallucinations, they have isolated activity in the left temporal lobe of the brain that appears to play a part in the phenomenon. Certain drugs that affect this region of the brain are known for their ability to cause hallucinations. Drugs such as LSD, psilocybin, and mescaline gained

45 popularity with the 1960s Western youth culture for their ability to provide vivid hallucinatory experiences.

It is also suspected that the brain has its own chemicals designed to produce hallucinations. For example, some patients suffer from delirium tremens, a violent period of hallucinations

50 accompanied by sweating, an increase in heart rate, and a rise in body temperature. Through experience treating episodes such as this, it is also known that certain chemicals can stop hallucinations. The drug Thorazine is often used to treat patients suffering from psychotic disorders that involve hallucinations.

55 Regardless of the causes of hallucinations, the effects they have on their subjects are very real. Hallucinations can cause the aforementioned change in heart rate and body temperature, and they can also lead a person to act on the hallucination. Psychologists have found that the memories created by a hallucination are processed by the same part of the brain that handles normal memories. Thus, for the subject of a hallucination, the experience

60 is as real as any other.

Paragraph 1

What? _____

What about it? _____

Paragraph 2

What? _____

What about it? _____

Paragraph 3

What? _____

What about it? _____

Paragraph 4

What? _____

What about it? _____

Paragraph 5

What? _____

What about it? _____

Paragraph 6

What? _____

What about it? _____

Paragraph 7

What? _____

What about it? _____

Paragraph 8

What? _____

What about it? _____

Overall Purpose? _____

Purpose: _____

Examples: _____

_____

_____

_____

Lecture Analysis

Lectures typically follow the format of reading passages. The speaker will provide an introduction, supporting reasons and examples, and some sort of conclusion. Of course, as you're listening to the lecture, you won't be aware of when a paragraph ends, but you should still know what to expect based on the part of the lecture to which you're listening.

Here's the introduction of the lecture, broken down piece by piece.

> (1) Okay, class, let's get started. (2) Today, um, today we're going to talk about the ah…structural functionalist theory in sociology. (3) You guys remember last week we discussed the interactionist perspective, right? (4) Now that theory, the interactionist theory, focused on how people get along with one another and, uh, the way that interactions um…create behaviors.

Now, let's analyze what's going on in this first part of the introduction.

(1) **Introduction.** On the TOEFL, the lectures and conversations usually start with a greeting of some sort. This greeting is not important to the lecture.

(2) **Topic.** At some point early in the lecture, the professor will probably state what the class is going to talk about "today" or "in this class." This is very important. Note the topic on your scrap paper.

(3) **Background.** Usually, the professor will refer to a prior lecture or topic. The professor will state that the class talked about this topic "last time," "last class," or something along those lines. This information may be important to the lecture or it may be a distraction; it depends on what the purpose of the lecture is.

(4) **More background.** This line provides more background information.

Here's the second part of the introduction.

> (1) This theory…the structural functionalist theory…I'm just going to call it the functionalist theory…is very different. (2) Now, we'll talk about the historical context of this theory a little bit later, (3) but first I would like to just…um, go over the main tenets of the theory.

Let's analyze what's going on in this second part of the introduction.

(1) **Transition:** Speeches and lectures tend to have transitions. These transitions don't add any new information.

(2) **Digression:** You will also notice a digression (an off-topic comment) or two during the lectures. Usually, the professor will refer to something that will be "discussed later" or "at another time." Sometimes the professor will say, "I'm not going to get into this now." This information is unimportant.

(3) **Purpose:** Listen for the statement of purpose early in the lecture. If you figure out the purpose, write it down on your scrap paper.

This is the next part of the lecture.

(1) The basic view of functionalism is that our behaviors and actions can be best explained with...explained by the role...or function, if you will...that they perform for the society as a whole. (2) Now, that may be a little vague. (3) What do I mean by that? (4) Well, let's look at some different behaviors and, uh, see how a functionalist would explain them.

Let's analyze what's happening in this part of the lecture.

(1) **Definition/explanation:** The purpose of many of the lectures is to define or explain a term.

(2, 3) **Digression:** Neither sentence 2 nor sentence 3 adds anything to the lecture. As you're listening, try to focus on the topic and the examples given to support/explain it.

(4) **Transition:** Here's another transition. Note how the speaker is about to discuss examples. Typically, the lecturer will say something such as, "Now, let's look at..." or "Now, I want to talk about...." These words let you know that examples are coming.

Here's the next section.

(1) A good example would be the, uh, drug use. (2) A functionalist wouldn't really um...judge a drug user as a deviant, a bad person. Instead, the functionalist would try to ah...figure out what role the drug user, the person, fills in society. (3) This seems a little strange at first but bear with me. (4) Think about what role a drug user fills in society. (5) You may automatically think that the role, um, the role is always negative—crime, the cost of treatment, maybe more jails—but the functionalist tries to see the positives as well.

And here's the analysis of this section.

(1) **Example:** Once the lecturer begins discussing examples, the structure is very similar to a reading passage. There will be an example followed by specific details.

(2) **Detail:** Many of the questions will ask about details, so try to note some of them.

(3, 4) **Digression:** These two sentences address the class. They emphasize the lecturer's example, but they are relatively unimportant.

(5) **Detail:** This is similar to sentence 2. Don't try to write down or memorize everything the lecturer says. You won't have time.

Here is the next part of the lecture.

(1) I bet you're thinking that drug use doesn't have too many positives, right? (2) Well, here's what a functionalist would say. (3) While a drug user may be harming himself or herself, to be fair, he is also benefiting society. Having drug users means we need to have more police, which means obviously, more jobs.

And also…if you think about it…more doctors, nurses, and social workers. Even drug counselors. All these people would be out of work, probably, if we didn't have a drug problem. Let's keep going…without drug users, we wouldn't need the entire Drug Enforcement Agency, that bureau employs thousands of people, you know, and there's also the border patrol, customs agents, and so on, and so on.

And here's what's happening in this section.

(1) **Transition:** This sentence acts as a bridge from one paragraph (which describes negative factors) to the next sentences (which describe positive factors).

(2) **Detail:** This sentence brings the discussion back to the topic.

(3) **Detail:** The rest of the sentences give details about the topic. Again, you can't possibly note every single part, so just try to note down one or two important points.

Finally, here is the last part of the lecture.

(1) So I think our example has given you a pretty good idea of how a functionalist views behaviors. (2) Again, the important thing is that they don't really judge behaviors as good or bad…they only view them based on their role or function in society.

And I think we can probably guess then, that to a functionalist, all behaviors… no matter how good or bad you may think they are...are necessary to society. (3) It's really a, uh, pretty interesting viewpoint, if you think about it.

Here's what's going on in this last part.

(1) **Conclusion:** Listen for the conclusion of the lecture. The speaker may say something such as, "So…" or "Thus…" or "And so…."

(2) **Summary:** Some lectures will end with a brief summary of the important points.

(3) **Digression:** This sentence contains no new or important information.

As this exercise shows, many of the parts of the lecture are similar to the reading passages. While you listen to the sample lectures, think about their purpose and structure, just as you would with a reading passage.

Summary: Lectures

Try to identify the main parts of the lecture. Listen for the following:

1. **Topic:** This should appear early in the lecture, after the greeting.

2. **Purpose:** Shortly after the topic is introduced, the purpose of the lecture will be stated.

3. **Examples:** The majority of the lecture will be examples and details. Don't try to write down or memorize every single one.

4. **Conclusion:** Note any final points or summaries.

Listening to Conversations

Now let's listen to a conversation similar to what you'll hear on the TOEFL and see how this form works.

Headphones On!

Play Track 2 on the accompanying CD (or listen to it in your Student Tools online). A transcript can be found on page 113.

Conversation Analysis

Conversations have the basic elements of reading passages. There should be some basic purpose to the conversation and reasons or examples related to that purpose. Here is a breakdown of the conversation you just heard.

Computer Lab Monitor: Hi. Do you need help with something?

Student: Yes. I'm supposed to use this program for my statistics class, but I'm not sure how.

Conversations also start with a greeting. Usually, the purpose will appear right at the beginning. Note this purpose on your scrap paper. Let's see what's next.

CLM: Okay. Do you have the program with you?

S: Sure, here it is.

CLM: Okay, let's bring this over to a computer and see how it works.

S: I think there's something wrong with the program. When I tried to run it on my computer, nothing happened.

These lines provide a detail about the problem the student is having. The questions will often ask about this type of detail, so be sure to note it.

CLM: Hmm. That's interesting. Well, let's see what happens here. It looks like it's running fine on this computer.

S: Weird. My computer freezes every time I try to open the program.

CLM: You mean the entire computer locks up? Have you had this type of problem before?

S: Yeah, I guess. Sometimes when I try to use certain programs, they just don't seem to work correctly. I don't know why though.

More specific details are provided about the problem. Note that in a conversation, you'll have to pay attention to the roles of the speakers. In this case, one speaker is describing a problem, and the other is trying to help find a solution.

> *CLM:* You can always use the computers here in the lab, you know. That way you won't have to worry about it.
>
> *S:* I know. But I'd rather figure out what the problem is with my computer. The computer lab can be busy, and I need to work on this project often. It's going to be one-third of our grade.
>
> *CLM:* What class is this for?
>
> *S:* It's for Statistics 101, with Professor Lee.
>
> *CLM:* And this program is required for the course?
>
> *S:* Yep. Professor Lee even got the campus bookstore to stock a bunch of copies. That's where I bought it.
>
> *CLM:* Do you use your computer for a lot of things? Maybe you should clear up some memory before you run the program.
>
> *S:* Yeah, I've tried that actually. I do have a lot of programs on my computer, but I should have enough memory to run this program.

Here, the lab monitor proposes a solution. This is an important part of the conversation, so make sure to note it. Also note the student's response to the solution. Many of the other details, such as the course or the professor's name, are not important. Focus only on details that relate back to the purpose. Let's see how the conversation wraps up.

> *CLM:* Well, I'm not quite sure what the problem could be. But you're welcome to use the program here.
>
> *S:* Okay.
>
> *CLM:* And you should definitely come back later and talk to my supervisor. She's a computer whiz. I bet she can solve your problem.

Conversations should have a fairly definite conclusion. You want to pay attention to how the conversation ends. Has the purpose been achieved? Note this on your scrap paper.

Summary: Conversations

Conversations have a definite structure. When listening to a conversation, pay attention to the following:

1. **Purpose:** What do the people in the conversation hope to achieve? Why are these people having this conversation?
2. **Details:** What specific details or examples are offered? How do these examples relate back to the purpose?
3. **Conclusion:** Is there any resolution? Do the people achieve their purpose?

TRANSCRIPTS

Track 1

Professor: Okay, class, let's get started. Today, um, today we're going to talk about the ah... structural functionalist theory in sociology. You guys remember last week we discussed the interactionist perspective, right? Now that theory, the interactionist theory, focused on how people get along with one another and, uh, the way that interactions um...create behaviors.

This theory...the structural functionalist theory...I'm just going to call it the functionalist theory...is very different. Now, we'll talk about the historical context of this theory a little bit later, but first I would like to just...um, go over the main tenets of the theory.

The basic view of functionalism is that our behaviors and actions can be best explained with...explained by the role...or function, if you will...that they perform for the society as a whole. Now, that may be a little vague. What do I mean by that? Well, let's look at some different behaviors and uh, see how a functionalist would explain them.

A good example would be the, uh, drug use. A functionalist wouldn't really um... judge a drug user as a deviant, a bad person. Instead, the functionalist would try to uh...figure out what role the drug user, the person, fills in society. This seems a little strange at first but bear with me. Think about what role a drug user fills in society. You may automatically think that the role, um the role is always negative— crime, the cost of treatment, maybe more jails—but the functionalist tries to see the positives as well.

I bet you're thinking that drug use doesn't have too many positives, right? Well, here's what a functionalist would say. While a drug user may be harming himself... or herself, to be fair...he is also benefiting society. Having drug users means we need to have more police, which means obviously, more jobs.

And also...if you think about it...more doctors, nurses, and social workers. Even drug counselors. All these people would be out of work, probably, if we didn't have a drug problem. Let's keep going...without drug users, we wouldn't need the entire Drug Enforcement Agency...that bureau employs thousands of people, you know...and there's also the border patrol, customs agents, and so on, and so on.

So I think our example has given you a pretty good idea of how a functionalist views behaviors. Again, the important thing is that they don't really judge behaviors as good or bad...they only view them based on their role or function in society.

And I think we can probably guess then, that to a functionalist, all behaviors...no matter how good or bad you may think they are...are necessary to society. It's really a, uh, pretty interesting viewpoint, if you think about it.

Track 2

Computer Lab Monitor: Hi. Do you need help with something?

Student: Yes. I'm supposed to use this program for my statistics class, but I'm not sure how.

CLM: Okay. Do you have the program with you?

S: Sure, here it is.

CLM: Okay, let's bring this over to a computer and see how it works.

S: I think there's something wrong with the program. When I tried to run it on my computer, nothing happened.

CLM: Hmm. That's interesting. Well, let's see what happens here. It looks like its running fine on this computer.

S: Weird. My computer freezes every time I try to open the program.

CLM: You mean the entire computer locks up? Have you had this type of problem before?

S: Yeah, I guess. Sometimes when I try to use certain programs, they just don't seem to work correctly. I don't know why though.

CLM: You can always use the computers here in the lab, you know. That way you won't have to worry about it.

S: I know. But I'd rather figure out what the problem is with my computer. The computer lab can be busy, and I need to work on this project often. It's going to be one-third of our grade.

CLM: What class is this for?

S: It's for Statistics 101, with Professor Lee.

CLM: And this program is required for the course?

S: Yep. Professor Lee even got the campus bookstore to stock a bunch of copies. That's where I bought it.

CLM: Do you use your computer for a lot of things? Maybe you should clear up some memory before you run the program.

S: Yeah, I've tried that actually. I do have a lot of programs on my computer, but I should have enough memory to run this program.

CLM: Well, I'm not quite sure what the problem could be, but you're welcome to use the program here.

S: Okay.

CLM: And you should definitely come back later and talk to my supervisor. She's a computer whiz. I bet she can solve your problem.

Chapter 4
Core Concept:
Speaking

As mentioned earlier, the TOEFL is an integrated exam, which means that each individual section will measure several abilities. You'll be learning Speaking skills that you will use in concert with the Reading, Listening, and Writing skills.

SCORING FOR THE SPEAKING SECTION

Although the Speaking section is different from the Writing section in some ways, many of the guidelines for scoring it are similar. The Speaking section is graded on a scale of 0 to 4, while the scale for the Writing section is 0 to 5. In both Speaking and Writing, a score of 0 is reserved for a response that simply repeats the prompt, is in a foreign language, or is left blank, whereas a score of 4 on the Speaking section is judged to have accomplished the following:

- The response fulfills the demands of the task.
- The response presents a clear progression of ideas.
- The response includes appropriate details.

These standards conform to our three basic Core Concept Reading skills: *purpose, main idea,* and *structure.*

The main difference on the Speaking section is that the graders will also consider the quality of your speech. While they don't expect perfect English, they expect a top response to

- use speech that is clear, fluid, and sustained, although it may contain minor lapses in pronunciation or intonation. Pace may vary at times, but overall intelligibility remains high.
- demonstrate good control of basic and complex grammatical structures and contain generally effective word choice. Minor errors or imprecise use may be noticeable, but they neither require listener effort nor do they obscure meaning.

The best way to make sure you meet these guidelines is to *practice.* We'll give you suggestions and tips on how to achieve these goals, but there's no substitute for continued repetition.

PART 1: STATING YOUR PURPOSE

You remember that you needed to find a purpose in Reading passages and listen for a purpose in lectures on the Listening section. Well, the best way to succeed on the Speaking section of the TOEFL is to use those skills you've learned in the reading and listening exercises.

Purpose and the Speaking Section

The speaking tasks on the TOEFL usually require you to do one of the following:

- Present your opinion on an issue.
- Explain facts presented in a lecture or reading.
- Summarize someone else's position.
- Describe something of importance to you.

Your speech on the TOEFL will need an introduction, just as you've observed in reading passages. Let's look at some ways to come up with an effective introduction.

Clearly Expressing Purpose on the Speaking Section

Let's look at a sample speaking task.

Describe a job that you've held, and explain why it was important.

Now, here are the steps to follow.

Step 1: Decide What Your Purpose Is

Make sure you take a moment to decide what your purpose is; otherwise, you will not be able to communicate it effectively. As you have seen in the previous bullet points, there are four different types of tasks that you may encounter on the Speaking section of the TOEFL.

Step 2: State the Topic

For speaking tasks that ask you to present your opinion or to describe something personal to you, use the following introductory phrases:

I believe	*I think*	*I feel*
My view is	*My opinion is*	*My preference is*

After each of these statements, you'll need to mention the topic and whatever example you're going to use. For the sample task about a job you've held, your first sentence could be as follows:

I think that the most important job I've had was working at a library.
(introductory statement)   *(topic)*   *(specific example)*

State your topic in a clear, direct way. Also, note that on opinion questions, there is no right or wrong answer. Your purpose is to convince the listener that your position is correct, whatever your position may be.

For speaking tasks that require you to summarize someone else's opinion or to explain facts, the following introductions are appropriate:

This person believes that	*This person holds that*	*This person argues that*
This person's view is that	*This person's point is that*	*The lecture stated*
The reading stated	*The reading presented*	*The lecture offered*

After each statement, fill in what the topic or position is. For example, a TOEFL task may ask you to summarize facts from a reading. Your introduction may sound like the example below.

The reading presented facts on...(topic)

Step 3: State *What* or *Why*

For speaking tasks that ask your opinion, you will have to state *why* you believe something. For speaking tasks that require you to summarize facts or someone else's position, you'll have to say *what* his or her reasons are. Use the following words to indicate *what* and *why*:

Because	*The reason*	*Due to*	*For*

Once you put it all together, your speech may look like the following:

I think that the most important job I've had was working at a library. I believe this because I met many interesting people at this job.

Spoken responses on the TOEFL are only 45 or 60 seconds, so most of your time will be used presenting details or examples. Therefore, your introduction should be brief and to the point.

Drill #1: Practice Speaking an Introduction to a Speech

Practice speaking introductions for each of the following tasks. If possible, record yourself so that you can review and evaluate your responses later.

1. If you could have any job in the world, which job would you choose?

2. Describe a person you admire, and explain why you admire him or her.

3. A university has recently received a large sum of money. The university desperately needs to improve housing on campus, but students have also complained that the library needs to be fixed. Do you think that the money should be spent on housing or the library? Provide examples and reasons for your choice.

4. Read the following short passage:

   > The cane toad, a poisonous species of toad, is causing problems in Australia. The cane toad was brought to Australia in 1935 to help control the population of greyback beetles. Unfortunately, the toads did nothing to reduce the beetle population. Now, however, cane toads number in the millions and are threatening native animal populations.
   >
   > The cane toad has two poisonous sacs located near its head and is so toxic that dingoes, snakes, and even crocodiles die within fifteen minutes of eating a cane toad. Now, conservationists are forced to transport some endangered species of animals to islands free from cane toads so that the endangered species can breed in safety.

   The passage above describes a problem. Explain what the problem is and what steps are being taken to fix it.

5. Read the following conversation between two coworkers:

   Employee A: I'm really swamped at work. I don't know if I'm going to be able to finish all of my projects by the deadline.

   Employee B: I know. We really need to hire some more people around here. What are you going to do?

   Employee A: I don't know. My boss said I have to finish the budget analysis by Friday, but he just gave me a new project that he needs completed right away.

   Employee B: Well, if I were you, I'd tell your boss that there's no way you can finish both in time. I'd ask for more time.

   Employee A: Yeah, I guess I could do that.

   Employee B: Or maybe you can ask your boss to assign the project to someone else. That way you can focus on the budget analysis.

   Employee B offers two possible solutions to Employee A's problems. Describe the problem, and state which of the two solutions you prefer. Explain why.

Sample Responses to Drill #1

Read the following responses and practice speaking them aloud:

1. If I could have any job, I think that I would like to be an ambassador. I think this because I enjoy visiting other countries and meeting and interacting with other people.

2. One person whom I admire very much is Mohandas Gandhi. I admire him for many reasons, especially his strong sense of justice and rightness.

3. In my opinion, the university should spend its money on the library. I think this because a university should be an institution of learning and a good library is essential to that.

4. The passage states that the problem is the poisonous cane toad. The toad is threatening many of the species in Australia.

5. The problem the employee has is that he or she cannot finish his or her work on time. In my opinion, the better solution is to ask the boss to assign the project to someone else. I think this because it is better to get the work done on time than to extend the deadline.

Summary: Stating Your Purpose

Your introduction is the first chance you have to make a good impression on your listener—so make it solid. Since you won't have much time to give your spoken response, make your introduction quick and concise.

The three points you need to convey in your introduction are as follows:

1. **Purpose:** Your task.
2. **Thesis:** Your topic. The thesis is basically a statement of your position or belief on a topic or your main idea. It will be slightly different based on what you are trying to accomplish in your spoken response.
3. **Why:** After introducing the topic, state why you are discussing it. The answer to this *why* question should relate back to the purpose.

In your introduction, don't go into specific details about your examples. You'll get to those later in the body of your speech. Also, avoid repeating the prompt word-for-word.

PART 2: ORGANIZING YOUR IDEAS

Before you begin speaking, take a few seconds to think about how you will organize your response. Make sure to follow the same guidelines that you saw in the Reading passages. You should include the following in every spoken response:

- **Introduction**: State your purpose, which is what we practiced earlier.
- **Body**: Take the majority of your time to give examples and details which refer back to your purpose. (We will focus next on the body of your response.)
- **Conclusion**: Finally, summarize your thoughts. We will take a look at conclusions toward the end of this chapter.

Developing Body Paragraphs When Speaking

Everything you learned about body paragraphs in the Reading section applies to speaking. Body paragraphs are the place where the author, or speaker, develops his or her ideas. While the introduction states the purpose, the body paragraphs provide specific details to support that purpose.

Note that your responses on the Speaking section will be only 45 or 60 seconds, which means you will have a limited amount of time to develop your body paragraphs.

Articulating Your Body Paragraph

As we've seen from the reading exercises, the body paragraphs are where an author attempts to accomplish his or her purpose by presenting facts, arguments, and evidence.

A good body paragraph contains the following elements:

1. A **topic sentence** that introduces the main point of the paragraph
2. **Examples, facts, and evidence** that help the author achieve his or her purpose

Step 1: Provide a Topic Sentence

A good topic sentence does two things: it provides a transition between ideas and clearly states the main idea of the paragraph.

Let's look back at the introduction we established before.

"I think the most important job I've had was working at a library. I believe this because I met many interesting people at this job."

Now, each spoken body paragraph should begin with a topic sentence that supports your introduction.

Therefore, a good topic sentence for the first body paragraph might be this one:

"Working at the library was my most important job because I met Professor Martin, who has become my advisor this semester."

The topic sentence is introducing your idea (the job was important because you met Professor Martin), and then the rest of your body paragraph will give details that support your example. Perhaps Professor Martin convinced you to change your major, suggested you submit an article to the school's literary magazine, or hinted at a promotion on the library staff. These are all details that support your topic sentence.

Another good topic sentence is one that indicates a progression of ideas by using the phrase "One reason..."

In this instance, a good topic sentence might be as follows:

"One reason that my job at the library was important is that I met Professor Martin, who has become my advisor this semester."

Other phrases that accomplish this progression are as follows:

Another reason	*Additionally*	*First*	*Moreover*
Second	*Third*	*Furthermore*	

These are transition statements that help you move from one idea to the next. Each succeeding topic sentence should have a transition statement that connects back to the thesis.

The topic sentence for our next body paragraph might use the following transition:

"Another reason that my job at the library was important is that I met Dr. Lucas, who asked me to edit the book he was writing."

And then the rest of your body paragraph will provide details that support this example.

By writing topic sentences that connect ideas in this way, your response will sound well structured and will be easy to follow.

Step 2: Make Your Case with Examples

To support your thesis statement, you should provide details or information, usually in the form of facts or reasons.

Your examples should be

- **Specific:** They should not be vague or too general.
- **Explained:** Make sure you give details to support your examples.

Use the following template to articulate your examples:

Statement 1: State your example and tie it back to your thesis.
Statement 2: Give one reason why your example is relevant to your thesis.
Statement 3: Add detail to reason #1.
Statement 4: Give another reason why your example is relevant to your thesis.
Statement 5: Add detail to reason #2.
Statement 6 (optional): Provide a summary of your reasons and relate them to your thesis.

Drill #2: Practice Speaking with Examples

For each task, speak aloud using two examples to support your point. Use the template above as a guide while you articulate your thoughts.

Record your answers so you can review and evaluate your responses based on our sample answers.

1. Do you agree or disagree with the following statement?

   It is better for students to gain real-world experience than to spend their time in a classroom.

2. Describe an influential person, and explain why you feel this person is a positive role model.

3. Some schools require first-year students to take the same courses, whereas other schools allow students to select the classes they want. Which policy do you think is better for first-year students and why?

4. Do you agree or disagree with the following statement?

   The most important education occurs not during adulthood but during childhood.

5. Read the following passage about insect behavior:

   > Many insects are social creatures, living in large groups containing literally millions of individuals. Social insects, which include ants, termites, bees, and wasps, are the prime example of unselfish behavior in animals.
   >
   > In any insect social system, each insect performs a specialized duty that is necessary for the survival of the hive as a whole. For example, among ants, there are certain types of ants that are soldiers—large, fearsome creatures with terrible jaws. Other ants, called drones, do not reproduce, instead devoting their time to taking care of the hive and the young of the queen. Each ant selflessly performs its role, not for its own benefit, but for the benefit of all the other ants.
   >
   > Now entomologists have found an interesting case of this sort of cooperation in a nonsocial insect, the cricket. Crickets are a prime example of a "selfish" insect, leading a very isolated existence. They typically interact with other crickets only when mating or fighting over territory. But scientists have observed a species of cricket that undergoes periodic mass migrations. Every so often, the crickets set off to find more favorable living areas. When these migrations occur, the crickets band together into a huge caravan. Surely at a time like this, the crickets realize there is safety in numbers and put aside their selfish instinct for the good of all members.

Now read the following lecture on the same subject:

Professor: One of the biggest misconceptions in biology is the belief that organisms act out of concern for the "greater good" of the species. It is somewhat amazing how people assume that an ant or a mouse has enough sense to figure out how its actions impact all the members of its species!

Still, it is understandable why many people might believe this erroneous view. Many actions can be misinterpreted as being for the "good of the species." A classic example found in many early biology textbooks discussed the behavior of the stag. During mating season, a stag typically battles with other males, and the winner of these contests gains access to the females, while the loser walks away. Some people believed that the loser realizes that his offspring will be weaker, so the defeated stag "allows" the winner to mate to ensure the survival of the stag species.

This couldn't be further from the truth. The defeated stag wants to mate just as much as the winner does; the only problem is that he doesn't want to risk his life for the chance to mate. The stag is better off looking for other females to mate with. Thus, both stags—the winner and the loser—are acting not for the good of the species, but for their own selfish reasons.

Another good example of this is a recent study on the behavior of crickets. Scientists noted that crickets occasionally band together, traveling in huge swarms from location to location. The easy assumption was that the crickets believed in strength in numbers. But a researcher showed this is not the case. He attached tags to a sampling of crickets. Some of the tagged crickets were allowed to travel with the group. But some of them were separated from the rest. All the crickets that were separated were eaten by birds or rodents, whereas the tagged crickets in the group survived.

Apparently, there is safety in numbers, but the crickets aren't looking to help their fellow travelers. They want to avoid being eaten, and what better way is there than to disappear into a group of thousands of other tasty morsels?

Summarize the points in the professor's lecture, and explain how the points cast doubt on the reading.

_____
_____
_____
_____
_____
_____
_____
_____
_____
_____
_____
_____
_____
_____
_____

Sample Responses to Drill #2

See how your responses compared to the suggested answers below. When you review the answers, read them aloud for more practice speaking.

1. Real-world experience is usually better than time spent in a classroom. I believe this because experience is the best teacher.

   One example of a way in which real-world experience is valuable is that students studying auto mechanics cannot just read about an engine. Instead, they have to practice taking that engine apart piece by piece and then put it back together. Only then will students understand the concept.

   A second example of a way in which real-world experience is valuable can be applied to learning a foreign language. If students in a classroom never have a chance to practice the language, they may forget the skills they were taught. In this instance, it would also be helpful to practice their skills in a real-world environment.

2. I believe that Mikhail Gorbachev is both an influential person and a positive role model.

   One reason Mikhail Gorbachev is a role model is because he is willing to work for change. Many people are content to have things stay the same, but he worked hard to change the Communist system. Even though his reforms were not as helpful as he would have liked, his willingness for change makes him a good role model.

   Another reason that Mikhail Gorbachev is a positive role model is because of his devotion to ideals that are larger than himself. For instance, he reached out to Ronald Reagan when he wanted to end the Cold War, instead of just following in the footsteps of Soviet leaders who came before him. Ensuring the future success of the Soviet Union was more important than simply concentrating on his personal power.

3. I would support mandatory classes for freshman instead of allowing the students to pick whatever classes they want.

   First, this will ensure a certain quality of education. With standardized classes, universities can make sure that all of their students are familiar with important intellectual works. That way, all students will have a basic educational level.

   Moreover, required classes will serve to increase the camaraderie of students. Universities are good places for students to meet each other and make connections that will help them later in life. Freshmen can sometimes have difficulty fitting in, so required classes will help them make friends.

4. I agree that the most important education happens when one is a child.

   One reason why I agree with this statement is that younger children are very open to ideas and perceptions. A young child is very impressionable, so the lessons learned at this age can have a great impact.

   Furthermore, childhood is a time when education focuses on the essentials of our society. Although children may not be learning advanced skills, they are learning basic life lessons. At this age, children learn important lessons, such as the difference between right and wrong and how to treat other people.

5. The points made in the professor's lecture cast doubt on the reading.

The first point the professor makes that casts doubt on the reading is his point about the behavior of stags. For example, some people interpret the stag's action as being for the "good of the species," but the professor shows that the stag is actually acting in self-interest. Likewise, the professor talks about how crickets act only in self-interest, which does not support the example in the reading.

The second point the professor makes that casts doubt on the reading is his point about the intelligence of animals and insects. He states that it would require a lot of intelligence for an animal or insect to evaluate how its behavior will affect an entire species. Therefore, his argument is that the cricket is acting only out of self-preservation, which again casts doubt on the reading.

Summary: Choosing Examples and Developing Body Paragraphs When Speaking

Good examples are important for your responses. Make sure your examples and your structure are organized.

Remember to do the following:

- **State** the example.
- **Explain** how the example supports your position.
- **Transitions:** Provide a topic sentence or transition statement to move from one example to the next.
- **Details:** Support each example with details.

Focus on stating just a few examples and explaining their significance. Always provide specific details for each example, and articulate the ways in which your examples relate to your purpose.

PUTTING IT ALL TOGETHER

Now take what you learned about organizing your ideas, stating your purpose, providing topic sentences, and making your case with examples to articulate both an introduction and a full body paragraph for each of the following tasks.

Drill #3: Practice Speaking an Introduction and Body Paragraph

Speak a body paragraph for each of the following tasks. It may help to repeat your introduction statement first. If possible, record your responses and evaluate them when you are finished.

1. If you could have any job in the world, which job would you choose?
2. Describe a person you admire, and explain why you admire him or her.
3. A university has recently received a large sum of money. The university desperately needs to improve housing on campus, but students have complained that the library needs to be fixed. Do you think that the money should be spent on housing or the library? Provide reasons and examples for your choice.
4. Read the following short passage:

The cane toad, a poisonous species of toad, is causing problems in Australia. The cane toad was brought to Australia in 1935 to help control the population of greyback beetles. Unfortunately, the toads did nothing to reduce the beetle population. Now, however, cane toads number in the millions and are threatening native animal populations.

The cane toad has two poisonous sacs located near its head and is so toxic that dingoes, snakes, and even crocodiles die within fifteen minutes of eating a cane toad. Now, conservationists are forced to transport some endangered species of animals to islands free from cane toads so that the endangered species can breed in safety.

The passage above describes a problem. Explain what the problem is and what steps are being taken to fix it.

5. Read the following conversation between two coworkers:

   Employee A: I'm really swamped at work. I don't know if I'm going to be able to finish all of my projects by the deadline.

   Employee B: I know. We really need to hire some more people around here. What are you going to do?

   Employee A: I don't know. My boss said I have to finish the budget analysis by Friday, but he just gave me a new project that he needs completed right away.

   Employee B: Well, if I were you, I'd tell your boss that there's no way you can finish both in time. I'd ask for more time.

   Employee A: Yeah, I guess I could do that.

   Employee B: Or maybe you can ask your boss to assign the project to someone else. That way you can focus on the budget analysis.

Employee B offers two possible solutions to Employee A's problems. Describe the problem, and state which of the two solutions you prefer. Explain why.

Sample Responses to Drill #3

Read the following responses aloud, and practice speaking them until you're comfortable. Pay attention to the use of transitions and direction markers.

1. (Introduction) If I could have any job, I think that I would like to be an ambassador. I think this because I enjoy visiting other countries and meeting and interacting with other people.

   (Body) The primary role of an ambassador is to represent your nation's country in one other country. I would enjoy doing this very much because I love learning about new cultures. I have traveled to many countries already, and I would like the opportunity to visit more.

   (Body) Another reason that I would like to be an ambassador is to have the opportunity to meet and interact with new people. An ambassador's job is to represent his or her country to other people, and I think this would be an exciting role.

2. (Introduction) One person whom I admire very much is Mohandas Gandhi. I admire him for many reasons, especially his strong sense of justice and rightness.

   (Body) The main reason I admire Gandhi is his commitment to his ideas. Gandhi was convinced that his country should be free and devoted his life to that goal. He went on a hunger strike and led many protests.

   (Body) A second reason I admire Gandhi is for his use of nonviolent protest. Even though Gandhi was devoted to his ideas, he realized that there was a right way of achieving them. He rejected violence as a method, and I admire this very much.

3. (Introduction) In my opinion, the university should spend its money on the library. I think this because a university should be an institution of learning, and a good library is important for that.

   (Body) The first reason I would spend money on the library is to benefit the students. It would be a disservice to students if they couldn't perform the type of research required for their classes. To do well in school, students need a good library.

   (Body) Furthermore, I think it is a good idea to spend money on a library to help the reputation of the school. If a university has a top library, it can attract more students. This will bring more money to the university.

4. (Introduction) The passage states that the problem is the poisonous cane toad. The toad is threatening many of the species in Australia.

   (Body) According to the passage, the problem is that the cane toad is very poisonous. The cane toad can kill animals that eat it. This is making it very dangerous for many species in Australia.

   (Body) To fix the problem, conservationists have decided to move some animals to other islands. They think this will allow the animals to breed in safety.

5. (Introduction) The problem the employee has is that he or she cannot finish his or her work on time. In my opinion, the better solution is to ask the boss to assign the project to someone else. I think this because it is better to get the work done on time than to extend the deadline.

(Body) I believe the employee should ask the boss to assign the project to someone else for two reasons. First, it is more important that the job get done on time and correctly. If the employee doesn't have enough time, the job may be finished late or the work may not be of good quality.

(Body) Second, I believe that an employee who can admit when he or she has too much work to do is a very responsible employee. It is better to be honest with your boss about what you can do instead of making him or her think you can do everything.

WRAPPING THINGS UP: THE CONCLUSION

The conclusion is essential to a well-organized speech or essay. Without a conclusion, it will seem to end abruptly, or worse yet, trail off and your score will be lower. Fortunately, the conclusion is probably the easiest part to create. A conclusion has to do one thing and one thing only.

- **Restate** your thesis.

The conclusion is your last chance to make your point to the reader. You want to remind the reader that you accomplished your purpose. As with body paragraphs, conclusions still need to have good transitions. Here are some good words and phrases to use for your final paragraph.

And so	*In conclusion*	*Finally*	*Thus*
Ultimately	*As I've stated*	*Clearly*	*To sum up*
	As this essay has demonstrated		

Here's a sample conclusion from our practice prompt.

In conclusion, if I could have any job, I would choose to be an ambassador. As I mentioned before, I feel this would be a perfect fit for my skill set because I love traveling to other countries and meeting new people.

Drill #4: Develop Conclusions for Speaking

Practice conclusions for your speeches, on the same topics we've practiced before.

1. If you could have any job in the world, which job would you choose?
2. Describe a person you admire, and explain why you admire him or her.
3. A university has recently received a large sum of money. The university desperately needs to improve housing on campus, but students have complained that the library needs to be fixed as well. Do you think that the money should be spent on housing or the library? Provide reasons and examples for your choice.
4. Read the following short passage:

    > The cane toad, a poisonous species of toad, is causing problems in Australia. The cane toad was brought to Australia in 1935 to help control the population of greyback beetles. Unfortunately, the toads did nothing to reduce the beetle population. Now, however, cane toads number in the millions and are threatening native animal populations.

    > The cane toad has two poisonous sacs located near its head and is so toxic that dingoes, snakes, and even crocodiles die within fifteen minutes of eating a cane toad. Now, conservationists are forced to transport some endangered species of animals to islands free from cane toads so that the endangered species can breed in safety.

    The passage above describes a problem. Explain what the problem is and what steps are being taken to fix it.

5. Read the following conversation between two coworkers:

    Employee A: I'm really swamped at work. I don't know if I'm going to be able to finish all of my projects by the deadline.

    Employee B: I know. We really need to hire some more people around here. What are you going to do?

    Employee A: I don't know. My boss said I have to finish the budget analysis by Friday, but he just gave me a new project that he needs completed right away.

    Employee B: Well, if I were you, I'd tell your boss that there's no way you can finish both in time. I'd ask for more time.

    Employee A: Yeah, I guess I could do that.

    Employee B: Or maybe you can ask your boss to assign the project to someone else. That way you can focus on the budget analysis.

Employee B offers two possible solutions to Employee A's problems. Describe the problem, and state which of the two solutions you prefer. Explain why.

Sample Responses to Drill #4

Read the following responses aloud, and practice speaking them until you're comfortable.

1. For all the reasons I have stated, I feel that being an ambassador would be my dream job. I think that it is the perfect match for my interests and skills.

2. As I have stated, there are many reasons that I admire Gandhi. His values and ideas are things that I find very important in a person.

3. So, to conclude, it is my opinion that the money would be best spent on a library. Spending money on a library is the right thing to do for an academic institution.

4. In conclusion, the conservationists think the best solution to the problem of the cane toad is to move the animals to a different place.

5. Ultimately, I believe the best solution is to ask the boss to reassign the project. This is best for the company and is what a responsible employee would do.

Summary: Concluding Your Response

Because you have only 45 or 60 seconds for a spoken response, you won't have a lot of time to wrap up your thoughts. But you always need a concluding sentence so make it short and simply restate your thesis.

One important point to remember is this: don't introduce any new ideas or examples in the conclusion. It will leave your listener or reader feeling as though you should have explained those new examples in more detail.

Now you have all the tools you need to give great spoken responses on the TOEFL!

Chapter 5
Core Concept:
Writing

In the "real" world, speaking and writing are two very different skills. But on the TOEFL, these basic skills are graded on very similar rubrics. Many of the constructions that you used in your speaking can easily be transferred to your writing. Similarly, many of the forms you use when writing can also be used when speaking.

SCORING FOR THE WRITING SECTION

By examining the scoring guidelines for the Writing section, we can gain a better understanding of what our goals should be for this section.

The writing responses will be graded on a scale of 0 to 5. On the TOEFL, according to ETS, an essay receiving a score of 5 has the following characteristics:

- It effectively addresses the topic and the task.
- It is well organized and well developed, using clearly appropriate explanations, exemplifications, and/or details.
- It displays unity, progression, and coherence.
- It displays consistent facility in the use of language, demonstrating syntactic variety, appropriate word choice, and idiomaticity, although it may have minor lexical or grammatical errors. (In essence, it shows that you understand how to use the language, how to use a variety of sentence structures, how to use idioms or common phrases within the language, but it may have minor errors).

At the other end of the scoring scale, an essay receiving a score of 1 suffers from the following difficulties:

- serious disorganization or underdevelopment;
- little or no detail, irrelevant specifics, or questionable responsiveness to the task;
- serious or frequent errors in sentence structure or usage.

An essay receiving a score of 0 is blank, written in a foreign language, identical to the prompt, or consists of random keystrokes.

What the Writing Scoring Guidelines Mean

Each of the first three scoring guidelines relates to one of the skills we've already studied in the Reading section. Here's how.

- **The essay effectively addresses the topic and the task.** This guideline corresponds to the work we've done on *finding the purpose*. An effective written response accomplishes a specific purpose. On the TOEFL, this means responding to one of the prompts. A weak essay has no clear purpose or doesn't achieve its purpose.
- **The essay is well organized and well developed, using clearly appropriate explanations, exemplifications, and/or details.** This guideline matches with the exercises we completed on understanding the *structure*. Good essays demonstrate strong structure, whereas weak essays frequently lack well-developed examples.
- **The essay displays unity, progression, and coherence.** This guideline corresponds to the work we've done on *finding the main idea* of a reading passage. Each paragraph should be connected to the main theme of the passage and contribute to the development of the passage's ideas or argument. An essay receiving a score of 5 stays on topic, whereas an essay receiving a lower score goes off the topic.

The fourth and final guideline will be addressed later in this chapter. However, it is worth noting that on the TOEFL, you don't have to write in perfect English to get a 5. It's acceptable to have some spelling and grammar mistakes in your essay.

Similarities in the Writing and Reading Guidelines

The skills you learned in the Reading section can also help you write a well-structured, organized essay. In fact, the reading passages in this text are great examples for the TOEFL essay! The following techniques from the Reading section are particularly useful:

1. Understand the structure of the passage. Remember, TOEFL passages are always made up of an introduction, several body paragraphs, and a conclusion. Make sure your essays also contain these three key elements and separate them into distinct paragraphs.
2. Use the first sentence of each paragraph to present the main idea. Remember, the first sentence (also known as the topic sentence) should clearly present the main idea of each paragraph.
3. Use the remaining sentences to provide details and examples. Be sure to support each of your points with a reason and a specific idea or an example.
4. Use direction markers to unify your ideas. Use transitions as markers to clearly identify continuations of same-direction ideas or highlight contrasting ideas

PART 1: EXPRESSING YOUR PURPOSE

Our first goal is to make sure your essays have a clear purpose. To do that, we need to look at the types of tasks the TOEFL will feature.

Purpose and the Writing Section

You need to clearly express your purpose in your introductory paragraph. If you recall our earlier discussion of introduction paragraphs (in the Reading and Speaking chapters), you may already have a good idea of how to express your purpose. In general, your introduction needs to accomplish the following tasks:

1. Introduce the topic of your discussion
2. Present your *thesis* statement

Writing an Effective Introduction Paragraph

Here's an example of a writing task similar to one you may encounter on the TOEFL. You would be asked to write an essay explaining whether you agree or disagree with the following topic:

> Parents should select their children's friends carefully to make sure those friends reflect proper values.

Although there are many ways of writing an introduction paragraph, the following strategy will help you write an effective introduction regardless of the topic. Following this strategy will help you write *quickly*.

Step 1: Pick a Side

If the goal of your writing is to have a clear purpose, you must know what that purpose is before you start writing. Otherwise, your essay will lack focus and coherence. On opinion questions, there is no right or wrong answer, as you saw in Core Concept: Speaking. You will be evaluated only on how well you defend your position. Remember that for an opinion essay, your purpose as an author is to convince the reader that your position is correct.

Step 2: State Your Position

Once you've chosen your position, your first job is to state it. Here's an example of a typical first sentence for this type of response.

> I do not believe that parents should select their children's friends.

As you saw in Chapter 4 (Core Concept: Speaking), it's best to make a clear, direct statement of your position. Try using some of the following phrases.

I believe	*I feel that*	*In my opinion*
In my view	*I think that*	*I do not believe*
I do not feel that	*My position is*	*It is my belief that*

Step 3: State the Reason for Your Opinion

Once you've stated your position, you've established for the reader *what* you believe. Now, you must explain *why* you believe your position is correct. Here's an example.

I do not believe that parents should select their children's friends. It would be harmful to children if they were not allowed to choose their own friends. Parents should be interested in their children's friends, but they should let their children pick their own friends.

When stating why you believe your position, it may be helpful to use some of the following phrases:

I believe this because	*I feel this way because*	*The reason I think this is*
This is because	*Since*	

Drill #1: Write an Introduction Paragraph

Write an introduction paragraph explaining whether you agree or disagree with each of the following prompts. Remember to follow the three steps described on the previous pages.

1. It is the teacher's responsibility to make a student learn the material.

_____

_____

_____

_____

_____

2. Material on the Internet should be censored or controlled to protect the public.

_____

_____

_____

_____

_____

3. Colleges and universities should offer more distance learning courses to accommodate the needs of students.

_____

_____

_____

_____

_____

4. When choosing a career, financial gain should be the most important consideration.

_____

_____

_____

_____

_____

5. Schools should have mandatory testing each year to prove they are meeting minimum educational standards.

_____

_____

_____

_____

_____

Sample Responses to Drill #1

The following are sample introduction paragraphs for the prompts. Compare your paragraphs with the ones below and see how well they match up. As always, they do not have to match exactly. As long as your format is similar, you have the right idea.

1. I believe that it is a teacher's responsibility to make a student learn the material. Many students are of a young age and do not realize the value of education. Therefore, it is up to the teacher to help them learn the lessons and realize the value of the material.

2. In my opinion, material on the Internet should not be censored. The Internet is a free zone and it would be wrong for this area to be controlled. Plus, what government or agency would be responsible for censoring the Internet, which is available worldwide?

3. In my view, colleges and universities should offer more distance learning courses. I believe this because in today's world, many people have a lot of demands on their time. Some students are parents or hold part-time jobs. This means that they don't have as much time for school. Distance learning courses would be a good solution to this problem.

4. I do not feel that financial considerations should be the most important ones when choosing a career. If a person is not happy in his or her job, then the money will not be important. A person's happiness should be the number one consideration when choosing a career.

5. I feel that it would be wrong for schools to have mandatory testing each year. I think that each school should be allowed to decide how best to educate its students. Some schools do not focus as much on testing as other schools and use other ways of grading their students, such as projects and final papers. These schools should not be forced to have tests.

These examples are not perfect, and that's acceptable on the TOEFL. But each one is simple, direct, and clearly states the purpose. That's all that is required of an introductory paragraph.

Summary: Expressing Your Purpose

The introduction is your first impression, so make it a good one! To craft an effective introduction, follow these steps.

1. **Decide what your purpose is:** Know what your task is. Are you trying to convince or inform? Are you picking one option over another?
2. **State the thesis:** Always include a simple and direct statement of the topic.
3. **State why:** This is your connection between the task and topic.

For an effective introduction, remember these "don'ts."

- **Don't** go into detail about your examples in your introduction.
- **Don't** repeat the task or assignment word for word.

PART 2: ORGANIZING YOUR IDEAS

Now that we've taken care of the purpose, we need to focus on organization. Organization is one of the most important factors in your writing score. Disjointed or unfocused writing is easy for the graders to spot and will lead to a lower score.

On the TOEFL, each writing task should be organized as follows:

- **Introduction:** We've worked on this already. This is the part in which you state the topic and your purpose.
- **Body:** As with speaking, this is the part in which you should provide the details and examples important to your purpose. We'll examine body paragraphs next.
- **Conclusion:** This is the part in which you summarize your essay. We'll look at written conclusions later in this chapter.

Building the Body

One of the things TOEFL graders look for is your ability to thoroughly provide support for your purpose. The best way to do that is by writing an effective body paragraph.

Writing an Effective Body Paragraph

Good body paragraphs make your writing more effective and more organized, which are both good things on the TOEFL. The first step in creating a good body paragraph is to write a topic sentence.

Step 1: The Topic Sentence

A good topic sentence does two things: it provides a *transition* between ideas and clearly states the main idea of the paragraph. To refresh your memory on how to compose a topic sentence, flip back to Core Concept: Speaking. For writing, we are going to use the same method. A topic sentence should introduce the main point of the paragraph.

Let's continue to work with our previous topic.

> Parents should carefully select their children's friends to make sure those friends reflect proper values.

In our introduction, we stated what our position was and why we believe our opinion was correct. Now, in the body paragraphs, we have to support our position. Here's our introduction.

I do not believe that parents should select their children's friends. It would be harmful to children if they were not allowed to choose their own friends. Parents should be interested in their children's friends, but they should let their children pick their own friends.

To make a clear transition statement, use the topic or thesis of the previous paragraph as a starting point. Look at the following transition:

One reason I believe that **parents should let children pick their friends** is that children need to develop independence.

Notice how the bold portion repeats an idea found in the last sentence of the introduction. Using this technique makes your writing flow better and appear more organized.

Our next paragraph may say

Another reason I think **parents should let children pick their friends** is that children may resent a parent who picks their friends.

And our final body paragraph may say

In addition to the feelings of resentment a child may have, a final reason **parents shouldn't pick their children's friends** is that the children may not get along very well.

This paragraph also uses a link to the main idea of the preceding paragraph. As with the Speaking section, topic sentences and transitions will help your essay appear organized.

Step 2: The Examples

For many of the assignments on the TOEFL, your main goal in the body paragraphs will be to support your opinions. On others, your task will be to report facts stated in either a reading passage or a lecture.

In either case, your model is still the same.

- **State** the example or reason (what the example is).
- **Explain** its significance (why the example is important).

Remember that you've learned how to incorporate examples into your spoken and written responses. The key to making good use of examples is to make sure each example is

- **specific,** not overly general or hypothetical (made up)
- **explained** in sufficient detail

Now let's look at three types of examples that will help make your essay more convincing: examples that *support* your main idea, examples that *summarize* your main idea, and examples that *evaluate* your main idea.

Supporting Examples

Supporting examples are the most familiar type of examples and perhaps the easiest to use. They are used to show the reader why you have a particular viewpoint or position. On the TOEFL, you may see similar tasks that ask the following:

- Do you agree or disagree with the following statement? It is better for students to gain real-world experience than to spend their time in a classroom.
- Describe a book you have read and why that book was important to you.
- Some teachers prefer to lecture to students, whereas others prefer to engage students in a dialogue. Which teaching style do you think is better and why?

For each of these tasks, your mission is to convince your readers that your view is correct by presenting them with facts and evidence.

Summarizing Examples

Some tasks require you to explain or summarize someone else's opinion. For these tasks, you are not trying to *convince* the reader of anything; instead, your purpose is to *report* what you've read or heard. On the TOEFL, summarizing tasks look like the following:

- The professor describes the controversy surrounding a new technique. Explain the technique and what the controversy is.
- In the conversation above, the man presented his opinion on the new budget proposal. State his opinion and explain the reasons he gives for holding that opinion.
- Using details and examples from the piece you just heard, explain how musicians have been influenced by cultural and intellectual movements.

Evaluating Examples

One of the more difficult tasks you may encounter on the TOEFL asks you to evaluate someone else's viewpoint. These tasks require you to judge how valid a position is. The purpose of your examples is to weaken the position. The following is an example of an evaluation task:

Explain how the points in the lecture you've just heard cast doubt on it.

Regardless of the type of example, the way you present your examples remains the same.

Effective Examples

As stated at the beginning of this chapter, you must provide details for each example and an explanation of the meaning or significance of each. The following is a sample response containing poorly used examples:

One reason I believe lecturing is a better teaching method is that teachers can control the content. Also, the teachers are able to organize things better. Finally, lectures let the students focus on only the important parts of the lesson.

This response contains several good ideas, but the problem is that the author failed to provide specific details for each example. You cannot assume that your reader understands exactly what point you are making and why; instead, you must explain each of your examples fully.

For each example you intend to use, ask yourself why the example is appropriate. What makes the example a convincing one?

Let's return to our previous examples and see how they can be made better. Here is the first example from the response above.

1. Lectures allow teachers to control the content.

Now, we need to ask why this example should convince a reader that lecturing is a better teaching method. Here are some reasons.

Example: Lectures allow teachers to control the content.

Why?

1. The teacher is the only one speaking, so there are no digressions.
2. The teacher can plan the lecture beforehand, ensuring all the important information is addressed.

Example: Lectures allow teachers to organize better.

Why?

1. Speaking without planned notes can be difficult.
2. The teacher can practice the lecture numerous times, ensuring it is well organized.

Example: Lectures help students focus on important information.

Why?

1. The teacher can emphasize important information more effectively in a lecture.
2. Students can pay attention to the teacher, not other students.

Now, let's rewrite our earlier paragraph, using the examples more effectively.

One reason I believe lecturing is a better teaching method is that teachers can control the content. When a teacher lectures, all the information presented is supplied by the teacher. There are no digressions because the students are not interrupting the lesson or distracting the teacher. Also, a teacher has the opportunity to plan the lecture beforehand, meaning that the teacher can ensure all the important information is discussed. In a conversation or dialogue, a teacher may never get to some important points because the students may ask too many questions about a certain topic.

Another reason I prefer lecturing to a conversation or a dialogue is that a lecture is much more organized. It can be very difficult to speak without notes or a plan. During a

For more reading and writing practice, be sure to check out *TOEFL Reading & Writing Workout.*

dialogue, the subjects can change very rapidly and can be hard to follow. But a lecture is planned beforehand, so the topics are easier to follow. Also, the teacher can practice the lecture repeatedly and fix any problems in organization.

The final advantage of a lecture is that it helps the students focus on only the most important information. Because the teacher has planned the talk in advance, he or she can let the students know when an important point is being made. This will help the students focus. Additionally, when the students are engaged in a dialogue, a student may pay too much attention to another student's remarks or become distracted by a question or response. In a lecture, this problem is avoided because the student has to pay attention only to the teacher.

Note that when we use examples effectively, we end up having to use more paragraphs. This is necessary to keep our responses organized.

The Example Template

When you use an example in an essay, try to follow this template.

Sentence 1: Introduce the example and tie it back to your thesis.
Sentence 2: State one reason why your example is important or relevant to your thesis.
Sentence 3: Add detail to reason #1.
Sentence 4: State another reason why your example is important or relevant to your thesis.
Sentence 5: Add detail to reason #2.
Sentence 6 (optional): Provide a summary of your reasons, and relate them back to your thesis.

Here's an example of the template in action.

Task: Describe a book you have read and why that book was important to you.

(1) One book that is extremely important to me is *The Suffrage of Elvira* by V. S. Naipaul. (2) One reason I enjoy this book so much is that I like its subject matter. (3) The book provides a humorous look at local politics, and I find politics a fascinating subject. (4) Naipaul is skilled at critically examining his topics, and I think his depiction of politics is very interesting. (5) In this book, he presents a satire of the political process that is both witty and insightful. (6) Because of my interest in politics, *The Suffrage of Elvira* is an important book.

Drill #2: Write Body Paragraphs that Use Examples

Please use the blank spaces below to answer each of the questions presented. Then read the sample responses at the end of the drill to see how your writing compares.

1. Do you agree or disagree with the following statement?

    It is better for students to gain real-world experience than to spend their time in a classroom.

    Example #1: _____

    Why example #1 is important: _____

    _____

    _____

    _____

    Example #2: _____

    Why example #2 is important: _____

    _____

    _____

    _____

    Body paragraph #1: _____

    _____

    _____

    _____

    _____

    _____

    Body paragraph #2: _____

    _____

    _____

    _____

    _____

2. Describe an influential person, and explain why you feel this person is a positive role model.

    Example #1: _____

    Why example #1 is important: _____

    _____

    _____

    _____

Example #2: _____

Why example #2 is important: _____

_____

_____

_____

Body paragraph #1: _____

_____

_____

_____

_____

_____

Body paragraph #2: _____

_____

_____

_____

_____

_____

3. Some colleges require first-year students to take the same courses, whereas other colleges allow students to select the classes they want. Which policy do you think is better for first-year students and why?

Example #1: _____

Why example #1 is important: _____

_____

_____

Example #2: _____

Why example #2 is important: _____

_____

_____

Body paragraph #1: _____

_____

_____

_____

_____

_____

_____

_____

Body paragraph #2: _____

_____

_____

_____

_____

_____

_____

4. Read the following announcement and the conversation that follows it.

Announcement: Due to recent budget cuts, the university will be forced to reduce the library hours. Effective immediately, the library will close at 8:00 P.M. on weekdays and 5:00 P.M. on weekends.

Student A: I can't believe this! Did you hear the announcement about the library?

Student B: Yes. This is terrible. These new hours are going to be a real problem for me.

Student A: What's the problem?

Student B: Well, I work on weekends from noon to 6:00 P.M. at the bookstore. That means I won't be able to get to the library to work on my research project.

Student A: What are you going to do?

Student B: I guess I'm going to have to wake up early and go to the library in the morning, but it's going to be tough. My schedule is so busy. Between the five classes I'm taking and my hours at the bookstore, I don't have much time. These new library hours are really going to hurt me.

Student B expresses her opinion about the announcement. State what her opinion is, and explain the reasons she gives for holding it.

Reason #1: _____

Why reason #1 is important: _____

_____

_____

_____

Reason #2: _____

Why reason #2 is important: _____

_____

_____

Body paragraph #1: _____

_____

_____

_____

_____

_____

_____

Body paragraph #2: _____

_____

_____

_____

_____

_____

_____

5. Do you agree or disagree with the following statement?

The most important education occurs not during adulthood but during childhood.

Example #1: _____

Why example #1 is important: _____

_____

_____

_____

Example #2: _____

Why example #2 is important: _____

_____

_____

_____

Body paragraph #1: _____

_____

_____

_____

_____

_____

_____

_____

Body paragraph #2: _____

_____

_____

_____

_____

_____

6.   Read the following passage about insect behavior:

Many insects are social creatures, living in large groups containing literally millions of individuals. Social insects, which include ants, termites, bees, and wasps, are the prime example of unselfish behavior in animals.

In any insect social system, each insect performs a specialized duty that is necessary for the survival of the hive as a whole. For example, among ants, there are certain types of ants that are soldiers—large, fearsome creatures with terrible jaws. Other ants, called drones, do not reproduce, instead devoting their time to taking care of the hive and the young of the queen. Each ant selflessly performs its role, not for its own benefit, but for the benefit of all the other ants.

Now entomologists have found an interesting case of this sort of cooperation in a nonsocial insect, the cricket. Crickets are a prime example of a "selfish" insect, leading a very isolated existence. They typically interact with other crickets only when mating or fighting over territory. But scientists have observed a species of cricket that undergoes periodic mass migrations. Every so often, the crickets set off to find more favorable living areas. When these migrations occur, the crickets band together into a huge caravan. Surely at a time like this, the crickets realize there is safety in numbers and put aside their selfish instinct for the good of all members.

Now read the following lecture on the same subject:

Professor: One of the biggest misconceptions in biology is the belief that organisms act out of concern for the "greater good" of the species. It is somewhat amazing how people assume that an ant or a mouse has enough sense to figure out how its actions impact all the members of its species!

Still, it is understandable why many people might believe this erroneous view. Many actions can be misinterpreted as being for the "good of the species." A classic example found in many early biology textbooks discussed the behavior of the stag. During mating season, a stag typically battles with other males, and the winner of these contests gains access to the females, while the loser walks away. Some people believed that the loser realizes that his offspring will be weaker, so the defeated stag "allows" the winner to mate to ensure the survival of the stag species.

This couldn't be further from the truth. The defeated stag wants to mate just as much as the winner does; the only problem is that he doesn't want to risk his life for the chance to mate. The stag is better off looking for other females to mate with. Thus, both stags—the winner and the loser—are acting not for the good of the species, but for their own selfish reasons.

Another good example of this is a recent study on the behavior of crickets. Scientists noted that crickets occasionally band together, traveling in huge swarms from location to location. The easy assumption was that the crickets believed in strength in numbers.

But a researcher showed this is not the case. He attached tags to a sampling of crickets. Some of the tagged crickets were allowed to travel with the group. But some of them were separated from the rest. All the crickets that were separated were eaten by birds or rodents, whereas the tagged crickets in the group survived.

Apparently, there is safety in numbers, but the crickets aren't looking to help their fellow travelers. They want to avoid being eaten, and what better way is there than to disappear into a group of thousands of other tasty morsels?

Summarize the points in the professor's lecture, and explain how the points cast doubt on the reading.

Point #1: _____

Why point #1 casts doubt on the reading: _____

_____

_____

_____

Point #2: _____

Why point #2 casts doubt on the reading: _____

_____

_____

Body paragraph #1: _____

_____

_____

_____

_____

_____

Body paragraph #2: _____

_____

_____

_____

_____

_____

Sample Responses to Drill #2

Use the following sample responses as a guide to judge your work. Did your response contain strong topic sentences? Did you relate your examples back to your thesis? Did you explain why your examples are relevant?

1. Do you agree or disagree with the following statement?

   It is better for students to gain real-world experience than to spend their time in a classroom.

   Real-world experience is usually preferable to time spent in a classroom. I believe this because experience is the best teacher. Students will not be able to grasp difficult topics unless they are able to discover them on their own. For example, students who are studying auto mechanics cannot just read about an engine. Instead, for a student to really understand an engine, the student must take it apart piece by piece and put it back together again. Only then will a student truly understand the concept.

   In addition, real-world experience gives a student a chance to apply knowledge. Many times, things learned in a classroom are quickly forgotten if a student does not have a chance to apply them. In some schools, students are required to learn a foreign language. But these classes rarely involve opportunities to apply the new language. If a student never uses the skills learned in class, the skills will quickly become useless. Thus, some real-world experience is necessary.

2. Describe an influential person, and explain why you feel this person is a positive role model.

   One reason I consider Mikhail Gorbachev a positive role model is his willingness to work for change. Many people are content with the status quo and are reluctant to change things. But Gorbachev saw that the Communist system was no longer viable. He worked hard to change the system, instituting new policies to increase the openness of the Soviet system. Even though his reforms were not as helpful as he wished them to be, his willingness to work for change makes him a good role model.

   In addition to his willingness to work for change, I believe Gorbachev is a positive role model because of his devotion to ideals that are larger than himself. Gorbachev came to power at a very tense time in history, the Cold War. Whereas before him, Soviet and American leaders had perpetuated the Cold War, Gorbachev knew that peace was a greater ideal. He reached out to President Ronald Reagan and signed treaties to limit nuclear arms. His devotion to this ideal was so great that he dissolved the Communist Party, of which he was the head. The future success of the Soviet Union was more important than his personal power.

3. Some colleges require first-year students to take the same courses, whereas other colleges allow students to select the classes they want. Which policy do you think is better for first-year students and why?

The first reason I would support mandatory classes for freshmen is to ensure a certain quality of education. Although standardized education is not desirable, a college degree should hold a certain value. It should be the duty of universities to make sure their students are familiar with important intellectual works. That way, all students will have a basic educational level.

Another reason I believe universities should have required classes for freshmen is that required classes will serve to increase the camaraderie of the students. In addition to being institutions of learning, universities also give students an opportunity to meet other people and make connections that may help them later in life. Required classes would make it easy for students to meet one another and interact. Freshmen can sometimes have a hard time fitting in at a school, and required classes would make it easier for them to adapt.

4. Student B expresses her opinion about the announcement. State what her opinion is, and explain the reasons she gives for holding it.

One reason Student B is upset about the new library hours is that she is concerned she won't be able to work on her research paper. Student B works at a bookstore, and her hours on the weekends are from noon to 6:00 P.M.; however, the library closes at 5:00 P.M. This means that she will no longer be able to go to the library after work.

Another reason Student B is upset is because her personal schedule makes it difficult for her to use the library. To go to the library on weekends, she will have to go early in the morning, but she finds that problematic. Student B is taking five classes and has a job, so she is very busy. The new library hours will make things harder for her.

5. Do you agree or disagree with the following statement?

The most important education occurs not during adulthood but during childhood.

There are many reasons why I agree with the statement that the most important education occurs during childhood. One of the most important reasons is that younger children are very open to ideas and perceptions. At a young age, a child has not fully developed his or her personality, so education can have a very powerful effect. A child is very impressionable, and the lessons learned at this age can have a great impact.

Another reason why I believe that the most important education is during childhood is because childhood is a time when education focuses on the very essentials of our society. Although children may not be learning advanced skills or disciplines, they are learning valuable life skills. A child who learns the difference between right and wrong and how to treat other people has learned some of life's most important lessons.

6. Summarize the points in the professor's lecture, and explain how the points cast doubt on the reading.

The first point the professor makes that casts doubt on the reading is his point about the behavior of stags. The professor shows how the actions of an animal can be interpreted in different ways. For example, some people interpret the stag's actions as being for the "good of the species," but the professor shows that the stag is actually acting in self-interest. This casts doubt on the reading because it appears that the crickets' behavior can be interpreted as helping only individual crickets and not the group as a whole. The professor then talks about the results of the experiment, which seem to indicate the crickets are acting only in self-interest.

Another point the professor makes that casts doubt on the reading is his point about the intelligence of animals and insects. As he states, it would seem to require a lot of intelligence to evaluate how a behavior will affect an entire species. This makes the explanation in the reading seem less likely; a cricket is probably unable to think of the consequences of its actions. It is more likely that the cricket is acting only out of self-preservation, as the professor indicates.

Summary: Using Examples Effectively

Proper use of examples is important to your TOEFL score. When using examples, always remember to do the following:

1. **State** the example.
2. **Explain** how the example supports your position or achieves your purpose.

Avoid these common mistakes when using examples.

- **Don't** introduce an example without explaining how it relates to your purpose.
- **Don't** forget to provide specific details for each of your examples.
- **Don't** use more than one example per paragraph.

PART 3: WRITING THE PERFECT BODY PARAGRAPH

Now that you understand the proper structure and ways to use examples in your writing, let's work on writing a perfectly structured paragraph. Here's a body paragraph for our sample topic (Parents should carefully select their children's friends to make sure those friends reflect proper values.). As always, your essay does not need to match our example exactly. Just be sure you're using a structure similar to that of our example.

One reason I believe that parents should let children pick their friends is that children need to develop independence **(topic sentence)**. It is very important for a child to become independent, and the early part of a child's life can affect the level of independence a child has **(statement of example)**. For example, children who are not allowed to pick their friends may believe that their parents will always make important decisions for them **(explanation of significance)**. This belief could make children dependent on their parents, which would have a negative effect on their development **(explanation of significance)**.

That's all there is to it! Now, try to write some body paragraphs for the topics that follow.

Drill #3: Write Body Paragraphs

For each of the following tasks, write a body paragraph (or two). You've already written introductions for these, so it may help to read over what you've written. Before you write, think of one or two examples that support your view.

1. It is the teacher's responsibility to make a student learn the material.

   _____
   _____
   _____
   _____
   _____
   _____
   _____

2. Material on the Internet should be censored or controlled to protect the public.

   _____
   _____
   _____
   _____
   _____
   _____
   _____

3. Colleges and universities should offer more distance learning courses to accommodate the needs of students.

   _____
   _____
   _____
   _____
   _____
   _____
   _____

4. When choosing a career, financial gain should be the most important consideration.

   _____
   _____
   _____
   _____
   _____
   _____
   _____

5. Schools should have mandatory testing each year to prove they are meeting minimum educational standards.

_____

_____

_____

_____

_____

_____

_____

Sample Responses to Drill #3

The following are sample responses. Check your paragraphs against these models. Make sure your body paragraph includes both a topic sentence and an example or reason.

1. One reason I believe it is a teacher's responsibility to help students learn is that many students are of a young age **(topic sentence)**. A first- or second-grade teacher works with children who are only six or seven years old **(statement of example)**. At this age, a student is too young to recognize the value of education **(explanation of example)**. Therefore, it should be the teacher's job to make sure the children learn.

This body paragraph ends by restating the author's main point, which also helps the reader stay focused on the thesis.

2. First of all, material on the Internet should not be censored because the Internet is a free zone **(topic sentence)**. The Internet is not owned by any one government or company **(statement of example)**. This means that no one should have the right to say what can or cannot be posted on it **(explanation of example)**. Companies or governments can control what material shows up on their websites, but they cannot control what private citizens do **(explanation of example)**.

    Second, technology makes it too difficult to censor material on the Internet **(topic sentence)**. Every day, new computer programs are developed that make other programs obsolete **(statement of example)**. As soon as someone figures out how to censor material on the Internet, someone else can figure out how to break the code **(explanation of example)**. This means that a tremendous amount of money would have to be spent on developing new technology, and this expense would not be worth it **(explanation of example)**.

This response includes two body paragraphs. Notice how the second paragraph logically connects to the first through the use of the transition word *second*. Try to make sure your body paragraphs are nicely connected both to the thesis and to each other.

3. One important reason that colleges should offer more distance learning courses is that people are busier than they used to be **(topic sentence)**. In addition to work and hobbies, there are more parents going to college these days **(statement of example)**. All these things make it difficult to attend college **(explanation of example)**. However, education is a valuable thing, and everyone should have access to it **(explanation of example)**. If universities offered more distance learning courses, more people could find time for an education **(explanation of example)**.

Try to use some of the direction marker words and transitions you learned in the reading exercises in Core Concept: Reading and Core Concept: Speaking. For example, this paragraph uses "however" to emphasize the importance of education and how distance learning courses will allow more people to get their education.

4. The most important thing in choosing a career should be the happiness it brings, not the money (**topic sentence**). There is an old saying, "You can't buy happiness," and this statement is very true (**statement of example**). Many people who have lots of money also have strained relationships with their spouses and children (**explanation of example**). Often, they feel they can't trust whether people like them or their money (**explanation of example**). These strains can make a person very unhappy, no matter how much money they have (**explanation of example**).

You should also try to use some emphasis markers in your writing. Stating that something is the "most" important reason or something is "very true" gives your words more of an impact. However, don't overuse these words. Too many of them can distract the reader.

5. Schools should not have mandatory testing each year because tests are not always the best way of measuring education (**topic sentence**). Tests, especially standardized tests, can cover only a limited amount of skills (**statement of example**). There are some things in education that are not easy to test, such as writing and creative thinking (**explanation of example**). For this reason, schools should not be forced to have mandatory testing (**explanation of example**).

   In addition, not all students do well on tests (**topic sentence with statement of example**). Some students are better at writing essays or giving a speech (**explanation of example**). Not all students perform best on standardized tests (**explanation of example**). Therefore, it is unfair for those students to have to take these tests, and schools may not get an accurate view of how successful they are (**explanation of example**).

In the second paragraph, the topic sentence is combined with the statement of the example, which is acceptable.

Summary: Building the Body

The body provides the reader with the key points of your thesis. Build strong body paragraphs by doing the following:

1. **Begin with a topic sentence:** A good topic sentence references the subject you will discuss and also provides a transition to link your ideas together.
2. **Provide details:** The rest of the body should contain important details that help you achieve your purpose.

Build strong body paragraphs by avoiding the following:

- **Don't** try to discuss more than one example per paragraph.
- **Don't** present an example without providing specific details.

PART 4: CONCLUDING YOUR RESPONSE

As you've seen in Core Concepts: Reading, a conclusion is essential to summarizing any argument. In this section, you are going to follow the same approach and simply restate your purpose.

Here's a sample conclusion from our practice prompt.

In conclusion, there are many reasons why parents should not pick friends for their children. Children who are allowed to pick their own friends will be more independent and will get along better with friends they've selected.

That's all there is to it. A conclusion has to be only two or three sentences long. After you restate your thesis, repeat your reasons or make a final statement about the correctness of your views.

Drill #4: Write a Conclusion

For each of the following topics, write a conclusion. Check the sample responses afterward for more ideas on ending your essay.

1. It is the teacher's responsibility to make a student learn the material.

    _____

    _____

    _____

    _____

    _____

2. Material on the Internet should be censored or controlled to protect the public.

    _____

    _____

    _____

    _____

    _____

3. Colleges and universities should offer more distance learning courses to accommodate the needs of students.

    _____

    _____

    _____

    _____

    _____

4. When choosing a career, financial gain should be the most important consideration.

    _____

    _____

    _____

    _____

    _____

5. Schools should have mandatory testing each year to prove they are meeting minimum educational standards.

    _____

    _____

    _____

    _____

    _____

    _____

Sample Responses to Drill #4

1. Ultimately, it is the teacher's responsibility to make students learn the material. Education is too valuable to be left in the hands of students. A good teacher not only teaches the material but also gives students a love of learning.

This conclusion ends by making a general statement about the purpose. This is a good strategy if you don't want to repeat your examples or reasons again.

2. As this essay has demonstrated, material on the Internet should not be censored. The Internet is too big to be controlled, and the technology involved in censoring it would be too expensive.

This conclusion restates both the purpose and the examples.

3. In conclusion, it makes sense for colleges and universities to offer more distance learning courses. It is always better to make education more available, not less.

Here, we end with a strong statement about what we believe. The conclusion is a good time to emphasize a key point or idea, as the following examples show.

4. Clearly, there are many more important considerations than money when choosing a career. Happiness and family are much more important than money.

5. Thus, schools should not be required to have mandatory testing. Testing does not provide students with a fair assessment of their skills, and it makes schools focus more on the tests than on teaching important things.

Summary: Wrapping Things Up

The conclusion is essential to your responses on the TOEFL. It's easy to conclude an essay or speech. All you have to do is

- **Restate:** Tell the reader once more what your purpose is and why you believe it.

Make sure to avoid the following:

- **Don't** introduce new examples or ideas.
- **Don't** leave out the thesis.

GRAMMAR REVIEW

This is a brief summary of the basics of English grammar. Become familiar with these terms so you can avoid common grammatical errors in your written and spoken responses.

Parts of speech

- **Noun**: person, place, or thing
  Example: I just remembered that I need to call my *mother*.

- **Pronoun**: stands in the place of a noun
  Example: *She* asked for a call last night.

- **Verb**: action word
  Example: I *dial* her home phone number.

- **Adverb**: modifies a verb
  Example: *Eagerly,* I wait for her to answer.

- **Adjective**: modifies a noun
  Example: When she picks up, I can tell that she is *happy* to hear my voice.

- **Preposition**: links nouns or pronouns to other words
  Example: I excitedly share the details *of* my new job.

- **Conjunction**: connects words, clauses, or sentences
  Example: She is happy *and* invites me over for dinner.

- **Interjection**: abrupt remark
  Example: *"Oh dear!,"* she exclaimed when I said yes. "I guess I'll have to go to the store."

If you're interested in a more thorough review, The Princeton Review's *Grammar Smart* can be found in most bookstores.

For an intensive vocabulary review, check out our *TOEFL Power Vocab*.

Tenses

- **Present**: an action that is currently happening
  Example: I *walk* to work every day.

- **Past**: an action that already happened
  Example: I *decided* that walking is better than driving.

- **Future**: an action that has not happened yet
  Example: I *will change* my mind later.

Agreement

- **Subject/Verb Agreement**: A singular subject needs a singular verb. A plural subject needs a plural verb.
  Example: The *window is* open.
  Example: The *windows are* closed.

- **Noun/Pronoun Agreement**: A singular noun takes a singular pronoun. A plural noun takes a plural pronoun.
  Example: The *student* wore *his/her* backpack.
  Example: The *students* wore *their* backpacks.

Spelling

- This is not really a point of grammar, but it is a common source of error on the TOEFL. Though it is not necessary for you to have perfect spelling to get a high score, it is important to know how to correctly spell as many words as possible. Many times, words with very simple meanings can be quite difficult to spell. You probably know the meaning of all the words in the following list, but we've included them as examples because they are commonly misspelled by native and non-native English speakers alike.

Commonly misspelled words:

accidentally	easily	hygiene	mathematics	quiet	usage
acknowledge	embarrass	illegal	natural	receipt	usually
average	existence	independent	neighbor	reference	vacuum
bachelor	experience	intelligence	nowadays	relevant	valuable
barbecue	February	khaki	office	rhythm	vicious
bureau	finally	knowledge	often	scissors	weather
celebrity	foreign	knee	original	separate	weird
children	generally	language	parallel	sincerely	whether
calendar	grammar	leisure	prejudice	technique	yacht
definitely	guarantee	luxurious	psychology	tongue	your
disease	happiness	magic	quantity	tragedy	you're
discipline	humorous	maintenance	quite	unfortunately	zoology

Parallelism

- All items in a list must have the same form.
  Example: The professor likes to *read books, grade papers,* and *play guitar.*

Complete sentences versus fragments

- A sentence must express a complete thought. It will always have a subject and a verb within it, in order to be a complete sentence. An incomplete sentence is known as a fragment and should not be used under any circumstances.
  Example of a complete sentence: Wearing a cap and gown, the *student attended* graduation.
  Example of a fragment: Wearing a cap and gown, the *student* at graduation.

Correct punctuation versus run-on sentences

- A run-on sentence is two or more sentences written together without proper punctuation separating them.

  Example of a correct sentence: The girls played volleyball all afternoon; it was not until later that they noticed someone had stolen their car.

  Example of a run-on sentence: The girls played volleyball all afternoon, it was not until later that they noticed someone had stolen their car.

Summary of All Core Concepts:
Reading, Listening, Speaking, and Writing

o   The TOEFL is a standardized test format that evaluates reading, listening, speaking, and writing. All the tasks on the TOEFL require you to work with and identify some basic features common to all of them. The more comfortable you are with these core concepts, the more comfortable you will be taking the TOEFL.

o   For each passage that you read, write on, speak about, or listen to on the TOEFL, you should focus on the purpose, examples, and conclusion. Practice identifying these parts in the sample drills in this book as well as other types of writing you encounter.

Chapter 6
Vocabulary

VOCAB, VOCAB, VOCAB

As you know, the TOEFL is an exam that measures four essential skills: reading, listening, speaking, and writing. Vocabulary is found in all of these areas, and having a strong vocabulary will benefit you throughout the TOEFL. In this chapter, we have assembled some crucial TOEFL vocabulary words along with pronunciation, definition, part of speech, an example sentence, and synonyms. It's a jackpot of useful words!

The TOEFL doesn't have a vocabulary specific section, but the simple fact remains that many of the questions, answer choices, and reading passages contain some difficult vocabulary. You can't improve your score substantially without increasing your vocabulary. You might think that studying vocabulary is the most boring part of preparing for the TOEFL, but it's one of the most important, and it's also one part of TOEFL preparation that's useful to you beyond the confines of the test itself. And the more words that you recognize (and know the meaning of) on the test, the easier it will be. So there's no avoiding the importance of vocabulary to your success on the TOEFL. Fortunately, one thing you have working in your favor is the fact that the same words tend to appear on the TOEFL year after year. The words we've collected for you in this chapter are the words that appear frequently on the TOEFL. So let's get started learning some new words!

Learn to Love the Dictionary

Get used to looking up words. If you see a word you don't know while studying for the TOEFL or elsewhere, it's probably a good TOEFL word. Look it up and make a flash card. Dictionaries will give you the pronunciation, while digital apps can provide quick, handy look-ups for new words. Looking up words is a habit. You may have to force yourself to do it in the beginning, but it becomes more natural over time. Many of the techniques in this book will help you on the TOEFL but don't have much relevance in day-to-day life, but a great vocabulary and good vocabulary habits will add a tremendous amount of value to your career and beyond.

Learning New Words

How will you remember all the new words you should learn for the test? By developing a routine for learning new words. Here are some tips:

- To learn words that you find on your own, get into the habit of reading good books, magazines, and newspapers. Start paying attention to words you come across for which you don't know the definition. You might be tempted to just skip these, as usual, but train yourself to write them down and look them up.
- When you look up the word, say it out loud, being careful to pronounce it correctly. This will help you remember it.
- When you look up a word in the dictionary, don't assume that the first definition is the only one you need to know. The first definition may be an archaic one, or one that applies only in a particular context, so scan through all the definitions.
- Now that you've learned the dictionary's definition of a new word, restate it in your own words. You'll find it much easier to remember a word's meaning if you make it your own.

- Mnemonics—Use your imagination to create a mental image to fix the new word in your mind. For example, if you're trying to remember the word *voracious,* which means having an insatiable appetite for an activity or pursuit, picture an incredibly hungry boar eating huge piles of food. The voracious boar will help you to recall the meaning of the word. The crazier the image, the better.

- Keep a vocabulary notebook, or make a file with a list of new vocabulary words and put it on your desktop. Simply having a notebook with you will remind you to be on the lookout for new words, and using it will help you to remember the ones you encounter. Writing something down also makes it easier to memorize. Jot down the word when you find it, note its pronunciation and definition (in your own words) when you look it up, and jot down your mnemonic or mental image. You might also copy the sentence in which you originally found the word, to remind yourself of how the word looks in context.

- Do the same thing with flash cards. Write the word on one side and the pronunciation, the meaning, and perhaps a mental image on the other. Stick five or six of your flash cards in your pocket every morning and use them whenever you can. Stuck on a delayed subway train? Look at your flash cards. Standing in a long line at the bank? Look at your flash cards. Sick of engaging in small talk with boring acquaintances? Look at your flash cards. (Only kidding about that last one.)

- Use your new word every chance you get. Make it part of your life. Insert it into your speech at every opportunity. Developing a powerful vocabulary requires lots of exercise.

- Learn word roots. Many words share similar origins. By learning these common roots, you'll be better able to work with words you've never seen before. A good dictionary should list the origin and roots of the words in it.

Word	Pronunciation	Part of Speech	Definition	Sentence	Synonyms
absorb	ab SAWRB	verb	to take in or draw up	We are using a sponge to *absorb* most of the liquid that was spilled.	consume; soak up
abundant	uh BUHN duhnt	adjective	possessing a lot of something, often more than what is needed	The food was *abundant* at Thanksgiving dinner; we spent the next two weeks eating leftovers.	plentiful; full
accept	ak SEPT	verb	to receive with pleasure; to agree	The athlete was proud to *accept* his Olympic Gold Medal.	receive; approve
accumulate	uh KYOO myuh leyt	verb	to gather or collect	The geologist was hoping to *accumulate* more rock specimens on his trip out West.	acquire; gain; stockpile
adequate	AD i kwit	adjective	enough for a required purpose	She makes an *adequate* amount of money, but she still can't afford to go on fancy vacations.	unexceptional; acceptable
adjacent	uh JEY suhnt	adjective	located next to something; beside	Our house is *adjacent* to the corner grocery store.	neighboring; bordering
affect	uh FEKT	verb	to produce a change in; to move the emotions of someone	I hope your illness does not *affect* your ability to work.	change; move
analyzing	AN i lahz ing	verb	examining critically	The scientist spent hours *analyzing* the results of the experiment, and still he could not come up with an answer.	studying; investigating; evaluating
ancient	EYN shuhnt	adjective	very old; from the distant past	The *ancient* temple of Angkor Wat is almost 900 hundred years old.	antique; dated
appeal	uh PEEL	verb	to be attractive or pleasing	Eating snails is something that does not *appeal* to me.	attract; charm; interest

Word	Pronunciation	Part of Speech	Definition	Sentence	Synonyms
appropriate	uh PROH pree it	adjective	suitable or fitting to the situation at hand	A business suit is *appropriate* attire for a job interview.	correct; proper
artistic	ahr TIS tik	adjective	exhibiting visual taste or skill	She was so *artistic* that even her fruit bowl was arranged in a beautiful manner.	aesthetic; creative
assumptions	uh SUHMP shuhnz	noun	opinions which are taken for granted or presumed to be true	I made some *assumptions* about Dana's character without really knowing her.	beliefs; judgments
available	uh VEY luh buhl	adjective	able to be used, obtained, or accessed	The shoes I wanted to order from the store are, unfortunately, no longer *available*.	accessible; free
aware	uh WAIR	adjective	possessing knowledge	Soldiers need to be *aware* of potential danger at all times, even when they least expect it.	conscious; informed
beliefs	bih LEEFS	noun	things which are believed; convictions	Many *beliefs*, such as the idea that the world is flat, turn out to be wrong.	opinions; ideas
benefit	BEN uh fit	noun	a positive result or outcome	One *benefit* of exercise is that you will have more energy through-out the day.	advantage; gain
capable	KAY puh buhl	adjective	able to do something; good at a task	Having studied cooking in France for 10 years, she is a very *capable* chef.	skilled; accomplished
cast	kast	verb	threw	The fisherman *cast* his hook into the water, hoping for a bite.	flung; tossed
ceased	seest	verb	ended, stopped, or discontinued	When I lost my job, my expensive nights on the town *ceased*.	concluded; finished

Word	Pronunciation	Part of Speech	Definition	Sentence	Synonyms
certain	SUR tuhn	adjective	without doubt or reservation; particular	Since Rhonda answered only three of the ten questions, she was *certain* she had failed the exam.	confident; definite
circumstances	SUR kuhm stans iz	noun	the state of affairs	Given my financial *circumstances*, I am not sure I should be going on vacation right now.	situations; conditions
classified	KLAS uh fahyd	verb	arranged or organized according to type	The ornithologist *classified* his birds according to color, size, and beak type.	categorized; labeled
compare	kuhm PAIR	verb	to examine the differences and similarities between two things	If you *compare* Paris and New York, Paris is much cheaper.	contrast; evaluate
components	kuhm POH nuhnts	noun	parts of something	Her argument had several *components* I did not agree with.	elements; factors
compromise	KOM pruh mahyz	verb	to settle a disagreement by offering a concession	Since I am an early riser and my wife likes to sleep late, we decided to *compromise* and wake up at 10:00 A.M.	agree; meet halfway; negotiate
concerned	kuhn SURND	adjective	worried or upset	I was *concerned* when you did not show up for work at the usual time.	anxious; troubled; bothered
concrete	KON kreet	adjective	referring to an actual, material thing	Detectives look for *concrete* evidence, such as hairs and fingerprints, when solving a crime.	real; physical; solid
conform	kuhn FAWRM	verb	to act according to set standards	Teenagers often feel the pressure to *conform* in order to be popular.	adapt; follow; comply

Word	Pronunciation	Part of Speech	Definition	Sentence	Synonyms
connection	kuh NEK shuhn	noun	a joining of two things; a closeness or association with someone or something	There is a strong *connection* between wealth and education level.	relation; link; affiliation
considered	kuhn SID erd	adjective	thought of or viewed as	Bach is *considered* one of the greatest composers to have lived.	believed
consistent	kuhn SIS tuhnt	adjective	sticking to the same behavior or principles	Swimming has always been a *consistent* part of my life—I swim three days a week or more.	constant; regular
constant	KON stuhnt	adjective	not changing	Traffic jams are a *constant* source of irritation in modern life.	regular; reliable
constrained	kuhn STREYND	verb	forced or confined	Being a raw-food vegetarian, she has a very *constrained* diet.	limited; restrained
convenient	kuhn VEEN yuhnt	adjective	easy to use or access	We live in a *convenient* location, right next to a 24-hour supermarket.	handy; advantageous
critical	KRIT i kuhl	adjective	tending to find flaws in something; judging harshly	He is a *critical* person with little patience for mistakes.	disapproving; demanding
crude	krood	adjective	rough or lacking refinement	He was a *crude* person who would frequently belch and tell dirty jokes.	unpolished; raw
decision	di SIZH uhn	noun	a choice made after considering something	The quarterback made a quick *decision* to go for a touchdown.	resolution; judgment
deepening	DEE puhn ing	adjective	becoming more intense or profound	There is an ever-*deepening* split forming between the rich and the poor.	increasing; growing

Word	Pronunciation	Part of Speech	Definition	Sentence	Synonyms
define	di FAHYN	verb	to describe precisely	Please *define* your duties as supervisor, so I have a better idea of what your job is.	specify; set
dense	dens	adjective	closely packed	The crowds at the game were so *dense* we could barely move.	thick; heavy
depict	di PIKT	verb	to represent, either in words or visually	In many of his novels, Charles Dickens would *depict* the struggles of poor children living in Victorian England.	show; illustrate
develop	dih VEL uhp	verb	to bring into being; to become affected by	After standing outside in the rain for three hours, it is likely that you will *develop* a cold.	grow; acquire
developing	dih VEL uh ping	adjective	in the process of growth or change, often used with reference to countries	Sudan is still a *developing* country, with few roads and little industry.	nonindustrial; primitive
directly	di REKT lee	adverb	in an honest, straightfor-ward manner	The interrogator asked the witness to answer all questions as *directly* as possible.	candidly; openly
discover	dih SKUHV er	verb	to find out or acquire knowledge of	After Jim left, I was surprised to *discover* that he had left his cell phone at my house.	notice; realize
discuss	dih SKUHSS	verb	to talk over or write about	Janet liked to *discuss* politics with her friends, even though they often ended up in heated debates.	debate; consider
dominant	DOM uh nuhnt	adjective	being the most impor-tant force or component; commanding or controlling	For hundreds of years, the Romans were the *dominant* force in the Mediterranean.	chief; main; principal

Word	Pronunciation	Part of Speech	Definition	Sentence	Synonyms
eager	EE ger	adjective	excited to do something	We were surprised to find out that she was actually quite *eager* to mow the lawn.	excited; ready
eccentric	ik SEN trik	adjective	unusual; different from the normal standard	My aunt is quite an *eccentric* lady, with her bright hats adorned with birds and eggs.	bizarre; strange; weird
effect	i FEKT	noun	the result or end product of an action	Staying out in the sun for too long can have a damaging *effect* on the skin.	result; consequence
emerge	i MURJ	verb	to come into view, often from a hidden place	It is always exciting to watch a plane *emerge* from the clouds and head toward the landing strip.	appear; turn up; arise
engage	in GEYJ	verb	to attract the attention of	The rattle toy was able to *engage* the baby for hours.	interest; captivate
ensure	en SHOOR	verb	to guarantee or make certain	To *ensure* that I would not be late, I set my alarm clock an hour earlier than usual.	assure; secure
environment	en VAHY ruhn muhnt	noun	one's physical or psychological surroundings	Ferns grow best in an *environment* that is moist and full of light.	atmosphere; conditions
essential	uh SEN shuhl	adjective	absolutely necessary or required for something	Yeast is an *essential* ingredient in bread; without it, your dough will never rise.	basic; fundamental
establish	ih STAB lish	verb	to set up permanently; to show to be true	The wealthy industrialist wanted to *establish* a library that would be accessible to all.	create; found
evident	EV i dent	adjective	obvious or clear	It was *evident* that she had gone swimming, in spite of my orders against it.	apparent; plain

Word	Pronunciation	Part of Speech	Definition	Sentence	Synonyms
evolve	ee VOLV	verb	to develop or change gradually	We are hoping this poor neighborhood will *evolve* into a place that is safer.	advance; grow; mature
exist	ig ZIST	verb	to be alive or in existence; to be	Most Giant Pandas *exist* in the mountain regions of China.	live; survive
exposed	ik SPOHZD	adjective	without shelter or protection; laid open to view	In the desert, one is *exposed* to the Sun and heat all day long.	unprotected; open
familiar	fuh MIL yer	adjective	commonly known or experienced; acquainted with	I am not *familiar* with the book you are reading—is it good?	experienced; known
famous	FEY muhs	adjective	being very well known in the world	Michael Phelps is currently the most *famous* swimmer in the world.	renowned; influential
function	FUHNGK shuhn	noun	the purpose or use for something	The *function* of the heart is to pump blood throughout the body.	task; role
fundamental	fuhn duh MEN tuhl	adjective	forming an essential part of something	Dribbling is a *fundamental* skill in basketball—every player must know how to do this.	basic; important
gradual	GRAJ oo uhl	adjective	taking place over a long range of time; little by little	Over the last century, there has been a *gradual* increase in the Earth's temperature.	steady; progressive
habitat	HAB i tat	noun	the natural surroundings of an organism	Snakes prefer a sunny and dry *habitat*.	environment; residence
illustrate	IL uh streyt	verb	to serve as an example of; to make clear	These diagrams *illustrate* the bad effects of smoking on one's health.	prove; demonstrate

Word	Pronunciation	Part of Speech	Definition	Sentence	Synonyms
immediately	i MEE dee it lee	adverb	occurring right away, without any delay	When I found out Maria was in the hospital, I called her *immediately*.	instantly; promptly
indicator	IN di kay ter	noun	something that acts as a sign	A high body temperature can be an *indicator* of illness.	sign; warning; clue
influence	IN floo uhns	verb	to contribute to, change, or modify; to exert power over	My father is a huge *influence* in my life—I have always admired him and sought his advice.	affect; sway
innovations	in uh VEY shunz	noun	new techniques or new things	Several *innovations* in Internet technology have made web surfing faster than ever.	changes; inventions
lack	LAK	verb	to not have; to be without	I am so busy with my new job that I *lack* the time to devote to my book club.	miss; need; want
limited	LIM i tid	adjective	restricted in number or amount; confined within physical boundaries	These days, you can take only a *limited* amount of baggage on airplanes.	fixed; definite
major	MEY jer	adjective	large or great in importance or amount	Fish is a *major* component in the Japanese diet.	big; main
materials	muh TEER ee uhlz	noun	substances which compose an object, or are used to build something	To build a tree house, you need the following *materials*: wood, nails, and glue.	supplies; components
mention	MEN shuhn	verb	to refer to briefly; to speak of	At lunch, Margot failed to *mention* that she had seen Tom the other day.	refer; bring up

Word	Pronunciation	Part of Speech	Definition	Sentence	Synonyms
necessary	NESS uh ser ee	adjective	being essential to or required of something	It's *necessary* to get a job if you want to be able to buy a house.	essential; needed
negative	NEG uh tiv	adjective	lacking positive characteristics; indicating opposition to something	She had a *negative* reaction when I suggested that we move out of the country.	bad; against; unfavorable
nowadays	NOW uh deyz	adverb	of or related to the present time	*Nowadays*, it is rare for a family to live without a television.	today; presently
objective	uhb JEK tiv	noun	the goal of a course of action	The *objective* of the United Nations is to maintain world peace.	aim; purpose
obvious	OB vee uhs	adjective	very clear	As she limped across the field, it was *obvious* that she had been injured.	apparent; evident
occasionally	uh KAY zhuh nuhl ee	adverb	now and then; not often	Though I am a vegetarian, I *occasionally* eat fish.	sometimes; rarely
official	uh FISH uhl	adjective	of an office or position of authority	The *official* position of the apartment building is that no pets are allowed.	authorized; established
opinion	uh PIN yuhn	noun	a personal belief or judgment	After he was late several times, I did not have a good *opinion* of him.	view; estimation
option	OP shuhn	noun	the right to choose something	Prospective buyers have the *option* to buy the car with or without GPS.	choice; privilege
partial	PAHR shuhl	adjective	not complete	We have only a *partial* understanding of our galaxy.	halfway; unfinished
particular	per TIK yuh ler	adjective	related to or associated with a specific group or category	The child was very *particular* about the kinds of foods she ate.	exact; specific

Word	Pronunciation	Part of Speech	Definition	Sentence	Synonyms
pattern	PAT ern	noun	the design, often repeated, of something; a regular and consistent combination of qualities	The *pattern* of the wallpaper consists of flowers and trees.	arrangement; motif
periodic	peer ee OD ik	adjective	occurring at regular time intervals	At *periodic* times through the day, you need to take this medication.	alternate; intermittent
phenomenon	fi NOM uh non	noun	something unusual, significant, or impressive	A solar eclipse is a natural *phenomenon* that some people will never witness in their lifetimes.	wonder; marvel; miracle
physical	FIZ i kuhl	adjective	related to the body or material things	Of all sports, wrestling is the one that involves the most *physical* contact.	real; earthly
portray	pawr TREY	verb	to depict visually or describe in words	The painter always liked to *portray* his subjects next to a window.	represent; draw
possible	POSS uh buhl	adjective	able to exist or occur	Many years ago, people thought it wasn't *possible* for humans to travel to the Moon.	likely; achievable
potential	puh TEN shuhl	noun	possibility; an ability or skill that may be developed in the future	Long legs indicate great *potential* as a runner.	promise; aptitude
prefer	pri FUR	verb	to like something more than another thing	I *prefer* coffee to tea.	choose; favor
primary	PRAHY mer ee	adjective	the most important; the first in a series	The *primary* source of crime in major cities is drug use.	main; principal

Word	Pronunciation	Part of Speech	Definition	Sentence	Synonyms
principal	PRIN suh puhl	adjective	first or most important	My *principal* reason for leaving this job is the low pay.	chief; primary; main
profound	pruh FOUND	adjective	going beyond what is on the surface; deep	Aristotle gave us a *profound* understanding of human life.	thoughtful; weighty
promote	pruh MOHT	verb	to help or encourage	The treaty was designed to *promote* trade relations between the two nations.	boost; nurture; aid
prove	proov	verb	to establish the truth or validity of	There is little evidence to *prove* your claim that you were in the shower during the crime.	verify; confirm
published	PUHB lisht	verb	prepared and distributed a piece of writing for public sale	The writer finally *published* his first novel after years of rejection.	issued; released
qualities	KWOL i teez	noun	the traits or characteristics of someone or something	The house has many desirable *qualities*, including a large lawn and pool.	features; properties
rapid	RAP id	adjective	very fast; occuring with great speed	He is a *rapid* painter who can paint an entire house at record-setting speed.	speedy; quick
rate	reyt	verb	to rank or assess the value of	The study attempted to *rate* cars on the basis of affordability and reliability.	measure; judge
realistic	ree uh LIS tik	adjective	seeming close to reality; resembling what is true or practical	It is not *realistic* to assume that next year I will earn a million dollars.	reasonable; sensible

Word	Pronunciation	Part of Speech	Definition	Sentence	Synonyms
recent	REE suhnt	adjective	not long past; having oc-curred in the near past	*Recent* events in the Middle East have dem-onstrated that peace is unlikely.	current; modern
recommend	rek uh MEND	verb	to suggest as useful or good	I asked my friend to *recommend* a hair-dresser to me.	advise; advocate
reflects	ri FLEKTS	verb	shows an image of; demonstrates	Giving money to that homeless person *reflects* how kind you are.	attests; manifests
relation	ri LEY shuhn	noun	a connection between two things, some-times familial	Bob's facial features are just like mine, but he is no *relation* to me.	association; kinship
reliable	ri LAHY uh buhl	adjective	trustworthy and dependable	The Toyota is one of the most *reliable* cars on the market—it rarely breaks down.	constant; unfailing; predictable
rely	ri LAHY	verb	to depend on or put trust in	You can *rely* on me to pay you back in two weeks' time.	depend; trust
remain	ri MEYN	verb	to stay in the same position or state	If I *remain* at this job for another year, I will be eligible for a signifi-cant pay raise.	continue; last
require	ri KWAHY uhr	verb	have need for; demand or insist upon	A medical degree will *require* many courses of study in the sciences.	necessitate; ask
resistant	ri ZIS tuhnt	adjective	being opposed to or against something	The child was *resistant* to naptime.	contrary; rebellious
result	ri ZUHLT	noun	the outcome of an action or course of events	One *result* of the stock market crash is lower consumer spending.	consequence; outcome

Word	Pronunciation	Part of Speech	Definition	Sentence	Synonyms
ritual	RICH oo uhl	noun	a ceremony or procedure used in a tradition, often religious	One of the *rituals* of Passover is to abstain from eating bread for the week.	tradition; habit
routes	rootz	noun	roads or ways to travel	The map shows several *routes* that will take us from Chicago to Detroit.	paths; passages
sake	SEYK	noun	the purpose or reason for something	For the *sake* of your health, you must quit smoking.	benefit; motive
sense	sens	noun	a mode of perceiving the world; an intuition	Dogs have a very strong *sense* of smell.	feel; impression
significance	sig NIF i kuhns	noun	the meaning or importance of something	The *significance* of the computer is apparent in every aspect of our lives.	importance; meaning
solution	suh LOO shuhn	noun	the answer to a question or problem	If the physics problem is too hard, you can find the *solution* at the back of the book.	resolution; explanation
sophisticated	suh FIS ti kay tid	adjective	in possession of worldly knowledge; complex or advanced	It was such *sophisticated* math that only a skilled mathematician could understand it.	worldly; intricate
specific	spi SIF ik	adjective	clearly defined or exact	The doctor gave the patient *specific* instructions to take the medication only at night.	definite; particular
speculate	SPEK yuh leyt	verb	to think about or reflect on without necessary evidence	Since she refuses to answer my questions, we can only *speculate* as to what her true motives were.	guess; conjecture

Word	Pronunciation	Part of Speech	Definition	Sentence	Synonyms
stages	STEY jiz	noun	steps in a process	There are many *stages* involved in becoming a cop, including basic training and field experience.	degrees; levels
standards	STAN derdz	noun	a level of quality by which others are ranked	The school has such low *standards* that it is virtually impossible to fail.	guidelines; ideals; requirements
subsequent	SUHB si kwuhnt	adjective	occurring after something else	The defeat of Greece and its *subsequent* decline led to the birth of the Roman Empire.	following; succeeding
succeeding	suhk SEE ding	adjective	coming after or following	People today may resent these tax hikes, but *succeeding* generations will thank us for the debt relief.	subsequent; next
sufficient	suh FISH uhnt	adjective	enough for what is needed, but not going beyond that	Fortunately, we found *sufficient* food for the last remaining days of our camping trip.	adequate; decent
suggest	suhg JEST	verb	to mention, hint, or propose	She was hoping the waiter would *suggest* a good dish off the menu.	imply; advise
support	suh POHRT	verb	to encourage or to uphold; to bear weight or financial responsibility	Having known you for many years, I *support* your decision to run for president.	promote; help; back up
survive	ser VAHYV	verb	to stay alive	The stranded hikers were able to *survive* by eating berries and grass for several days.	live; remain; endure
technique	tek NEEK	noun	method of performance; technical skill	The famed chef had a secret *technique* for making great bread.	approach; procedure

Word	Pronunciation	Part of Speech	Definition	Sentence	Synonyms
technological	tek nuh LOJ i kuhl	adjective	related to science and industry	*Technological* innovations such as the vacuum and washing machine have made housework much easier.	industrial; mechanical
tend	tend	verb	to take care of or look after	I am happy to *tend* to your plants while you are away on vacation.	oversee; guard; watch over
topic	TOP ik	noun	a subject of study or discussion	The historian's favorite *topic* of conversation was the Trojan War.	matter; issue
tradition	truh DISH uhn	noun	a custom or belief that has been handed down throughout history	The Christmas *tradition* involves decorating a tree and leaving out cookies for Santa Claus.	convention; practice
traditional	truh DISH uh nuhl	adjective	based on an established custom or convention	In a *traditional* Italian meal, pasta is always served.	conventional; established
typically	TIP i kuh lee	adverb	conforming to regular behavior	In Seattle, it *typically* rains every day.	normally; usually
underneath	uhn der NEETH	preposition	below	I keep my slippers *underneath* my bed.	beneath; under
unifying	YOO nuh fahy ing	adjective	tending to bring together or unite	Attending sports events can have a *unifying* effect on a community.	joining; solidifying
unique	yoo NEEK	adjective	one of a kind; having no equal	New York City is a *unique* place—there is no place like it in the entire world.	unusual; not typical
unpredictable	uhn pri DIK tuh buhl	adjective	unable to be predicted or foreseen	Life as a musician is *unpredictable*—you never know when you'll get your next gig.	uncertain; unreliable

Word	Pronunciation	Part of Speech	Definition	Sentence	Synonyms
unusual	uhn YOO zhoo uhl	adjective	not ordinary or common	Marge's blue hair gave her an *unusual* appearance.	strange; remarkable
value	VAL yoo	verb	to place importance in; to calculate the monetary worth	Of all the traits that a friend could possess, honesty is the one I *value* most.	appreciate; prize
varied	VAIR eed	adjective	characterized by many different qualities	People in my school come from *varied* backgrounds—one student grew up in Kansas, another in Saudi Arabia.	assorted; diverse
vertical	VUR ti kuhl	adjective	in a direction from top to bottom (as opposed to left to right)	At the edge of the cliff was there was a 40-foot *vertical* drop.	upright; perpendicular
visual	VIZH oo uhl	adjective	pertaining to seeing	The film had great *visual* effects, such as fireballs and flying people.	observable; viewable
waste	WEYST	verb	to fail to use, or to use for no good reason	We *waste* electricity every time we leave a lamp on in an unoccupied room.	expend; squander

While the TOEFL does not explicitly test vocabulary, building your vocabulary of English words will help you in many ways. First, it will lessen the chance of seeing or hearing words you don't know in the Reading or Listening sections. Second, it will give you a broader choice of words to use in your Speaking and Writing responses. And third, possibly the most valuable way that learning more vocabulary will help you is to help you to increase your comfort level when communicating with others in English overall.

ROOT WORDS

One of the easiest—and quickest!—ways to build your vocabulary is to learn common roots that are used to form words in the English language. As you may have already guessed, English has "borrowed" from Latin and Greek very heavily over the years. We can see these influences still showing up in our language today.

For example, the root "mal," from Latin, means "bad." So, if you see the word "malaria," you may not know that it describes a disease that is transmitted by mosquitos. But you might be able to take a reasonable guess that it has a negative meaning because it has "mal" in the word.

Now, just because you see "mal" in a word doesn't mean it *must* mean something bad. For example, "male" certainly doesn't have a negative meaning. But, when you're trying to learn a large amount of vocabulary in a reasonably short time (like when you're preparing for the TOEFL!), learning root words can be a great way to accomplish your goal.

Below you'll find a list of a large number of Latin and Greek roots. One of the best ways to study them is to create "Root Cards." (You'll need a couple packs of 3″ × 5″ cards for this exercise, using one card per root word.)

On the front of the card, write the root and its meaning:

> *'mal'*
> *means 'bad'*

And on the back of the card, write as many words as you can think of that use that root.

> *malaria*
> *malicious*
> *malice*
> *malignant*

When you learn a new word, look at the etymology in the dictionary and see if the word uses one of these roots. If it does, add it to your card!

Then, review your cards every few days (or more frequently) so you can commit the roots and their meanings to memory.

Here is a list of many roots that show up in words in English. We've also added a few words for each one to get you started.

Master Root List

Root	Meaning	Example(s)
ab	away from/negative prefix	abnormal, abnegate
ac/acr	sharp	acute, acrid, acrimonious
ad/at	to, toward	adduct, adhere
amb	go/walk	amble, ambulate
ambi	both/mixed	ambidextrous, ambivalent
ami/amo	love	amicable, amorous
an/anti	against	antifreeze, antibiotic
andr/anthr	human	anthropology, android
anim	life, spirit	animated, animal
ante	before	anteroom, anterior
apt/ept	skill, ability	aptitude, adept
arbo	tree	arbor, arboretum
arch	rule, over	archdiocese, archbishop
aud	sound	audible, audio
auto	self	automatic, autonomous
bell/belli	war	belligerent, bellicose
ben/bono	good	benefit, bonus
bi	two	biannual, bipartisan
bio/bios	life	biology, biography
bra	arm	embrace, bracelet
carn	meat, flesh	carnivore, incarnate
cent	hundred	century, centigrade
chron	time	chronology, chronograph
circ/circu	around	circle, circuit, circumference
cis/cise	cut	incisor, scissor, excise
cli	lean	incline, recliner
clu/clo/cla	close, shut	clasp, closure
co/com/con	with, together	community, cooperate
contr-	against	contradict, contrast
cred	believe	incredible, credibility, credo
culp	blame	culprit, exculpate
cur/cour	run (a course)	incur, discourse

Root	Meaning	Example(s)
de	away from/opposite, of	decline, deny
dec/deci	ten	decade, decimal
dent	teeth	dental, denture
derm	skin	dermatologist, dermatitis
desc	down	descent, descendant
dext	ability	ambidextrous, dexterity
di	two, apart, split	diode, dilute
dic/dict	say, tell	edict, dictionary
dign/dain	worth	dignity, disdain
dis	apart from, not	distant, dissipate
domi	rule over	dominant, domicile
dorm	sleep	dormitory, dormant
duc/dul	lead	duct, conductor
dys	faulty, bad	dysfunction, dyslexia
e/ex/ej	out, outward	exit, eject, emote
en/em	into	enter, embolden
epi	upon	epicenter, epilogue
equ/equi	equal	equidistant, equal
esce	becoming	coalesce, evanesce
eu	good, pleasant	euphoria, euphemism
extr	outside, beyond, additional	extraterrestrial, extraneous, extra
fac/fic/fig	do, make	factual, fictional, figurative
fid	faithful	confide, confidential
fort	strong	fortify
fract	break, split	fraction, fracture
frat	brother	fraternal, fraternity
fren	highly energetic	frenzy, frenetic
gen	birth, creation, kind, type	gender, general
geo	earth	geography, geocentric
gno/kno	know	agnostic, knowledge
grand	big	grandeur, grandiose
graph	write	graphic, dysgraphia
grat	grateful	gratitude, ingrate
gress	step	progress, egress
gyn	female	gynecology, androgynous
her/hes	stick (on)	cohesive, adhere
herb	plant	herbal, herbicide
hetero	different, mixed	heterogeneous, heterodox
hex/sex	six	hexagon, sextuplet

More Great Books

Well, not books, but cards. The Princeton Review sells TOEFL flashcards to help you review the top key terms that you absolutely must know. Buy them wherever books are sold or online!

Root	Meaning	Example(s)
homo	same	homogenous, homophone
hyd/hydr	water	hydrate, hydrant
hyper	over, beyond	hyperactive, hyperventilate
hypo	under, insufficient	hypodermic, hypothermia
il	not	illicit, illegal
im	not, into	impotent (not), imported (into)
in	not, into	incapable (not), internal (into)
inter	between	interstate, interlock
intra	within	intramural
itis	inflammation, infection	arthritis, bronchitis
ium	place, building of	stadium, terrarium
jeu/ju	play, youthful	juvenile, junior
lab/labo	work	labor, laboratory
laud	praise	applaud, laudable
lav	wash	lave, lavish
lev	rise	levitate, elevate
loc/log/loqui	to speak	loquacious
lu/luc/lum	light	luminous, lucid
mag/magna	great	magnificent, magnanimous
mal	bad	malicious, malignant
man/manu	hand	manual, maneuver
mar/mer	sea	marine, mermaid
matr	mother	matron, matriarch
met/meter	measure	metric, thermometer
meta	more, beyond	metaphysics, metaphor
mic/micro	tiny	microscope, microchip
mill	thousand	millimeter, millennium
mis	wrong, bad	mistake, misfortune
mit	send	transmit, emit
mob/mobi	moving	mobilize
mor/mort	death	immortal, mortify
morph	change (shape)	amorphous, morphology
mut	change, alter	mutate, transmute
nat/natu	natural, birth	natural, natal
neg	negative	negate, negligent
neo/nov	new	novel, neonatal
noct	night	nocturnal
nom/nym	name	pseudonym, nominal
non/not	negative prefix	nonfat, nonsense

Root	Meaning	Example(s)
nounce	call	announce, pronounce
nox/nec	harmful	noxious, necrosis
ob	against	obstruct, obnoxious
ology	study of	biology, theology
omni	all, every	omniscient, omnipresent
ory	place of	observatory, directory
pac/pax/plac	peace, pleasing	pacific, placid
pan	all, everywhere	pandemic
par	equal	parity, partner
para	beyond, beside	paranormal, paralegal
path	feeling, emotion	empathy, apathetic
patr	father	patron, paternal
pen/pend	weight	pendulum, penury
pent	five	pentagon
peri	around	periscope, peripheral
pet/pec	small	petite, peckish
phil	love, high regard	philanthropy, oenophile
phob	fear	agoraphobic
phon	sound	phonetic, euphonium
pod/ped	foot	pedal, podiatry
pon/pos	place, put	position, ponder
port	carry	transport, portable
post	after	posterity, posterior
poten	power, influence	potent, potential
pre	before	pre-existing, preclude
pro	for	promote, proponent
prox	near	proximity, approximate
pseudo	false	pseudonym
quad	four	quadriceps, quadrant
qui	quiet	acquiesce, quietude
quint	five	quintuple
re	again	restart, regain
sci/scien	knowledge	science, prescient
scop	see	microscope, telescopic
scrib/scrip	write	script, scribe
sec/sequ	follow, come after	sequence, second
sed/sid	sit, be still	sedate, sidle
solo	alone	solitary, soliloquy
son/soni	sound	sonorous, sonic

Root	Meaning	Example(s)
spec/spic	see, look	spectacle, inspect
sta/sti	still, unmoving	stationary, still
sua	smooth	suave, assuage
sub	under	submarine, suboptimal
super	beyond, greater than	supersonic, superficial
syn/sym	bring together	synonym, symbiotic
tact	touch	tactile, intact
tech/techn	tools	technical, technology
tele	at a distance	telephone, teleport
temp	time	temporary, tempo
ten/tend	hold	tender, attend
ter	earth, ground	terrain, territory
tox	harmful, poisonous	toxic, toxemia
tract	pull	traction, tractor
trans	across	transit, transmit
trep	fear, anxiety	intrepid, trepidation
tri	three	triad, trimester
un	not	uncooperative, uncommon
uni	one	unicorn, united
us/ut	use	utility, useful
val/vale	value, feel	valor, validate
vend	sell	vendor
ver/vera/veri	true	aver, veritable, veracity
verd	green	verdant, verdure
verge	boundary, together	converge
verse	turn	reverse, converse
vi/vit/viv	alive	vital, vivacious
vid/vis	see	visual, video
voc	call, talk	vocation, vocalize
vor	eat, consume	voracious, herbivore

If you find that root words are helping you get a better grasp of English vocabulary, here's another exercise that can be incredibly valuable: Word Webs!

Use the collections of words that we've included over the next few pages, like this one:

Synchronize	Chronicle	Anachronism	Amoral
Apathy	Apartheid	Amorphous	Metamorphosis
Sympathy	Empathy	Pathos	Antipathy
Parity	Disparate	Dissociate	Disparity
Disperse	Dissuade	Dissipate	Dignify
Deign	Disdain	Metacognitive	Dismiss

Start with any word right in the middle of your paper. Circle the roots you see in that word:

Then, look for another word in the group that uses one of the same roots as the one you started with. Write the new word on your paper, circle its roots, and connect the same roots together with a line:

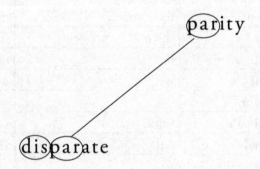

Continue this process until you have used all of the words in the set!

As you go along, make sure to look up the words you don't recognize so you can connect the root words' meanings to the meanings of the actual words.

Word Web #1

Miscreant	Misanthrope	Mistake	Anthropology
Philanthropy	Androgynous	Misogyny	Philosophy
Technophile	Technophobe	Technology	Technique

Word Web #2

Substantiate	Subterranean	Subordinate	Terrestrial
Terrarium	Subvert	Advertise	Extrovert
Traverse	Extraterrestrial	Extrapolate	Supervise
Superimpose	Supersede	Sediment	Sedate
Subside	Subservient	Introvert	

Word Web #3

Voracious	Devour	Carnivorous	Carnage
Incarceration	Infiltrate	Input	Inject
Ingratiate	Incarnate	Intractable	Protract
Tractor	Antecedent	Antebellum	Rebel
Belligerent	Bellicose	Enamored	Amorous
Amity	Amicable	Innate	Nascent
Naïve	Natal	Native	Renaissance
Omnivorous	Omniscient	Omnipotent	Potential
Potent	Potentate	Prescience	Preface
Prefix	Predestine		

Part III
Cracking Each Section of the TOEFL

Chapter 7
Cracking the
Reading Section

The TOEFL Reading section consists of these elements:

> Three to four **passages**, each approximately 700 words long
>
> - Each passage is followed by about 12 to 14 questions.
> - You will have 60 to 80 minutes to complete the entire section.

As mentioned in the introduction, many of the questions are multiple choice and worth one point each, but some questions are worth two or more points. Typically, questions that are worth more appear at the end of the section.

Some of the words and phrases in the reading passages are underlined in blue on the screen; if you click on these phrases, a definition is provided. You can see what the screen will look like in the picture on the opposite page.

In this case, if you click on the words *uranium isotope* or *moniker*, you will see a definition of the word in question. You'll also notice that some of the words appear in gray boxes. These words have a special type of question associated with them, which we'll look at soon.

> During the actual test, some very difficult words will appear underlined in the reading passages. The TOEFL will give you a definition of these words, so don't worry when you see them!

Remember, if you prefer, you are free to skip questions within this section; simply click on the "Next" button on the top right-hand side of the screen. You can return to questions you've skipped when you are ready. You can also click the "Review" button to see a display of all the questions you've answered and all those you've left blank. From this screen, you can return to any question.

As we mentioned in the early part of this book, the Reading scores are subdivided into three sections:

High (22–30). Students who score in the "High" range are usually comfortable reading content that covers a wide range of difficulty. These students usually have a strong command of vocabulary and grammar, and can make inferences easily from the text.

Medium (15–21). Students who score in the "Medium" range are comfortable reading English texts, but sometimes have difficulty with higher-level vocabulary or more complex sentence structures. Generally, their ability to understand is sufficient in most texts, but these students may find harder texts challenging.

Low (0–14). Scores in the "Low" range indicate a limited ability to understand academic texts. Students in this range have a basic command of vocabulary, and have difficulty understanding concepts like main idea and author's purpose in more complex texts.

Use your active reading skills and tackle the passage below.

Adaptive as their shell is, it leaves arthropods with at least one distinct disadvantage: The cuticle cannot expand to accommodate growth. As the animal increases in size, therefore, it must occasionally molt. The existing cuticle separates from newer, more flexible layers being secreted beneath it,
55 gradually splits open, and can be shaken or slipped off. The new chitin and protein will harden and be provided with a fresh lipid coating, but this process can take hours or days after molting occurs. The arthropod must first take in extra air or water to swell its body to greater than its normal size. After the shell has hardened in its expanded form, the arthropod expels the air or
60 water. It then has room for growth. But until it hardens, the new coat is tender and easily penetrated. Accordingly, the arthropod must remain in hiding. Otherwise, it risks being snapped up by a predator clever enough to take advantage of its lowered defenses.

Question Type #5: Paraphrase Questions

Our next group of questions deals with the passage and its structure. Here's one example.

10. Which of the following choices best expresses the essential meaning of the highlighted sentences in paragraph 7? Incorrect choices will change the meaning or leave out important details.

   a. Arthropods are vulnerable to predators only during the period in which their shell is tender and easily penetrated.
   b. Predators typically prefer to eat arthropods that are waiting for their new coats to harden.
   c. While the arthropod's shell is hardening, the arthropod cannot rely on its shell to protect it from predators.
   d. When the arthropod's defenses are lowered, it will use many different strategies to avoid predators.

This type of question is a **paraphrase** question. We usually won't have to rephrase these questions. Instead, we have to worry more about rephrasing the shaded portion of the passage. Let's take a look at the lines in question.

But until it hardens, the new coat is tender and easily penetrated. Accordingly, the arthropod must remain in hiding. Otherwise, it risks being snapped up by a predator clever enough to take advantage of its lowered defenses.

When paraphrasing, you need to *find the essential information*. Thus, trim the fat. Get rid of unnecessary modifiers and descriptive phrases (remember, modifiers and descriptive phrases simply tell you more information about the subject). Look for the subject and the main verb of the sentence or sentences in question. For example, let's break down the sentences into their most basic parts.

See our section on "Trim the fat!" on page 86.

1. ~~But until it hardens~~, the new coat is tender and easily penetrated.

The subject here is *new coat*, and the important thing about it is that it's *tender* and *easily pen-etrated*. Cut out the phrase *but until it hardens*, which is a modifier.

2. ~~Accordingly~~, the arthropod must remain in hiding.

The subject of this sentence is *arthropod*, and the verb is *must remain in hiding*. Cut the rest.

3. ~~Otherwise~~, it risks being snapped up by a predator ~~clever enough to take advantage of its lowered defenses~~.

The important parts here are *it* (the arthropod) *risks being snapped up by a predator.*

Now, our job is to find the answer choice that contains these elements and these elements only. Here are the choices again.

a. Arthropods are vulnerable to predators only during the period in which their shell is tender and easily penetrated.
b. Predators typically prefer to eat arthropods that are waiting for their new coats to harden.
c. While the arthropod's shell is hardening, the arthropod cannot rely on its shell to protect it from predators.
d. When the arthropod's defenses are lowered, it will use many different strategies to avoid predators.

Let's consider each choice.

- Start with (A). It does mention *arthropods* and *predators*, which is good. How-ever, we are missing some information. There is no mention of *hiding*, one of our key elements. Also, (A) states that arthropods are "vulnerable...only during this period...." That is beyond the information in the passage. Eliminate (A).
- Choice (B) is problematic because it makes *predators* the subject. We should have something that talks about arthropods. Eliminate this choice.
- Now look at (C). It first mentions the weakened shell, which matches with sentence 1. Next, it says the arthropod "cannot rely on its shell." At first this doesn't seem to match, but sentence 2 stated that the creature "must remain in hiding"—this is an example of "not relying on its shell." Finally, the choice men-tions the predators from sentence 3. Everything matches, so keep this choice.
- Choice (D) is close, but it has one big problem. It mentions "many different strate-gies," whereas the passage mentions only one. We don't want any choice that adds information, so eliminate (D).
- That leaves (C) as the best answer.

POE Strategies for Paraphrase Questions

If you're having trouble paraphrasing the sentence in question, the easiest POE strategy is to eliminate any answers that introduce new information. These choices will always be *wrong*. Another good strategy is to try to identify the subject of the sentence. One of the choices will usually have a different subject. Eliminate this choice.

Question Type #6: Definition Questions

Let's look at another type of question.

> 12. Click on the highlighted sentence in the passage in which the author gives a definition.

This is a **definition** question. Once again, we don't have to rephrase this type of question. Go to the passage and look for the four sentences in boldface. Here they are.

1. These give the arthropod information about its surroundings, much as the nerve endings in human skin do.
2. Its primary component is chitin, a natural polymer that contains calcium and is very similar in structure to the cellulose in wood.
3. Combined, the endocuticle, exocuticle, and lipid coating form a shell that provides formidable protection.
4. Many species of scorpion, for instance, have cuticles that contain hyaline.

We need to paraphrase each one, looking for the sentence that clarifies the meaning of a word or phrase. Unfortunately, these questions are mostly based on your comprehension. If you are comfortable with the words in the sentences, then go ahead and answer the question. If you are having trouble understanding the sentences, skip the question.

In Core Concept: Reading, we discussed "trimming the fat"—cutting out the nonessential information from the sentence. In a definition question, the definition will usually turn up in the "fat" part of the sentence. Thus, we need to separate the sentence into its different parts and examine them. For definition questions, follow the procedure below.

1. Find the subject, verb, and object.
2. Look at the other parts of the sentence.
3. See if the remaining parts define or clarify the subject, verb, or object.

For example, in sentence 1, the subject is *These*, and the main verb is *give*. The object is *information*. So, the sentence basically reads: These give information.

Now, examine the remaining parts of the sentence. First, we have the phrase *the arthropod*—does this define anything from the basic sentence? No. It only clarifies what is receiving the information. The next phrase is *about its surroundings*. This is not a definition; it is a prepositional phrase. The final part is "much as the nerve endings in human skin do." Does this refer back to the main sentence, defining something from it? No, it does not. Instead, it makes a comparison. Eliminate this choice.

Do the same for the second sentence. The second sentence breaks down as follows: Its component is chitin.

The first word we cut out was *primary*. This is an adjective, a modifier. It doesn't define anything. The rest of the sentence states "a natural polymer that contains calcium and is very similar in structure to the cellulose in wood." Could this define one of the terms from the main sentence? In fact, it does. It provides a definition of *chitin*. Thus, this is our answer.

POE Strategies for Definition Questions

As stated previously, your success on definition questions will be largely based on your comfort level with the sentences. If you're having a hard time figuring out the meaning of a sentence, keep the following in mind:

- Definitions frequently are introduced using the words *which, that,* or *means.* Look for sentences in which the author uses these words.
- Trim away prepositional phrases. These are phrases beginning with words such as *of, on,* and *in.* A definition will *not* be a prepositional phrase.
- Watch out for sentences that merely list or introduce examples. Remember, you need a phrase that tells you what a word or concept means, *not an example* of the word or concept.

Question Type #7: Before/After Questions

It's time to look at yet another type of question.

9. The paragraph following the passage would most logically continue with a discussion of

    a.   different strategies used by predators to capture arthropods

    b.   non-arthropods that have protective shells

    c.   the defense mechanisms of other types of animals

    d.   adaptations arthropods make to survive during molting

Some questions ask about a hypothetical paragraph before or after the passage; thus, we call these **before/after** questions (note that *before* questions are very rare on the TOEFL). First, rephrase the question.

What would a paragraph after the passage discuss?

To answer this type of question, we need to concern ourselves with only the last paragraph. Here it is again.

> Adaptive as their shell is, it leaves arthropods with at least one distinct disadvantage: The cuticle cannot expand to accommodate growth. As the animal increases in size, therefore, it must occasionally molt. The existing cuticle separates from newer, more flexible layers being secreted beneath it, gradually splits open, and can be shaken or slipped off. The new chitin and protein will harden and be provided with a fresh lipid coating, but this process can take hours or days after molting occurs. The arthropod must first take in extra air or water to swell its body to greater than its normal size. After the shell has hardened in its expanded form, the arthropod expels the air or water. It then has room for growth. But until it hardens, the new coat is tender and easily penetrated. Accordingly, the arthropod must remain in hiding. Otherwise, it risks being snapped up by a predator clever enough to take advantage of its lowered defenses.

Use active reading strategies to figure out the basic meaning of the paragraph. The first sentence tells us that we will discuss "disadvantages" of the shell. The body of the paragraph proceeds to give details about the disadvantages but, once again, we don't need to worry too much about these details. The author ends the paragraph by discussing how the arthropod is at a disadvantage while its defenses are lowered.

The correct answer to a before/after question will be related to the *main idea* of the paragraph. In our own words, this final paragraph is about a disadvantage of the shell and the arthropod's vulnerability.

Now use POE on the answer choices.

- Choice (A) discusses the strategies of predators. But the final paragraph—in fact, the entire passage—is about arthropods. Thus, our answer should also be about arthropods. Eliminate this choice.
- Choice (B) has the same problem; it discusses non-arthropods, but our paragraph is specifically about arthropods. Thus, (B) is wrong.
- Choice (C) mentions defense mechanisms, but once again it discusses other animals, not arthropods. That means (C) is wrong as well.
- Finally, we're left with (D). This choice discusses both arthropods and their defenses when they lack shells ("adaptations…during molting"). That is exactly what we need. Choice (D) is our answer.

Let's try another question of this type.

13. Which of the following would most likely be the topic of the paragraph before this passage?

   a. A brief discussion of the different phyla of animals
   b. A scientific examination of human hair and nails
   c. A description of various natural polymers
   d. A listing of some common arthropods

This question asks about the paragraph before the passage, so we'll focus on the first paragraph. Look at the first paragraph, and state its general idea.

> There are more arthropods alive on Earth than there are members of any other phylum of animals. Given that not only insects and spiders but also shrimp, crabs, centipedes, and their numerous relatives are arthropods, this fact should not occasion surprise. For all their diversity, arthropods of any type share two defining characteristics: jointed legs (from which the phylum takes its name) and an exoskeleton (the recognizable hard outer shell).

Here, the basic idea is that there are more arthropods than any other type of animal and that all arthropods share two common characteristics. Our answer should somehow lead into this discussion. Let's go through the answer choices and use POE.

- Choice (A) discusses different phyla of animals. This could be our answer because the first paragraph states that arthropods are more numerous than "any other phylum." Choice (A) could be a good introduction to the topic. We'll leave this choice for now.
- Choice (B) talks about human hair and nails. This doesn't match very well with arthropods and their characteristics. Plus, you may have noticed that this topic appears in the second paragraph. It wouldn't make sense to place a paragraph about this subject before the first paragraph.
- Choice (C) is off topic. Our paragraph is about arthropods, not natural polymers. Eliminate this choice.
- Choice (D) is appealing, but there is one problem with it. The first paragraph already provides a listing of some common arthropods. Thus, it would be repetitive to have a paragraph about this topic preceding the passage.
- Choice (A) is the best answer.

POE Strategies for Before/After Questions

The key to these questions is to stay as close as possible to the main idea of the first or last paragraph, depending on whether you are doing a before or an after question. Eliminate answer choices that do the following:

- **Introduce new information:** The right answer will match the topic of the paragraph. Get rid of any choices that bring in information not mentioned in the paragraph.
- **Interrupt the structure:** Make sure the topic in the answer choice doesn't appear elsewhere in the passage. The ideas in the passage should follow a logical order—don't return to a topic that's been discussed previously (as in after questions) or will be discussed later (as in before questions).
- **Repeat information:** The correct answer will be based on the paragraph, but will not repeat information that has already been mentioned.

Question Type #8: Sentence Insertion Questions

Now we'll look at another structure-based question. Here's the passage again, but notice the placement of four black squares (■).

The Exoskeleton of the Arthropod

There are more arthropods alive on Earth than there are members of any other phylum of animals. Given that not only insects and spiders but also shrimp, crabs, centipedes, and their numerous relatives are arthropods, this fact should not occasion surprise. For all their diversity, arthropods of any type
5 share two defining characteristics: jointed legs (from which the phylum takes its name) and an exoskeleton (the recognizable hard outer shell).

Though the shell itself is made of dead tissue like that of human hair and fingernails, it is dotted with sensory cells. These give the arthropod
10 information about its surroundings, much as the nerve endings in human skin do. Also like human skin, the shell protects fragile internal organs from potentially hazardous contact with the environment. It seals in precious moisture that would otherwise evaporate but permits the exchange of gases.

15 Its primary component is chitin, a natural polymer that contains calcium and is very similar in structure to the cellulose in wood. Chitin and proteins are secreted in the epidermis, the living tissue just below the shell, after which they bond to form a thin sheet. Each new sheet is produced so that its chitin fibers are not parallel with those directly above, which increases their
20 combined strength.

The result is the endocuticle, a mesh of molecules that forms the lowest layer of the shell. The endocuticle is not quite tough enough for daily wear and tear.■ Over time, however, its molecules continue to lock together.■ As

25 the endocuticle is pushed upward by the formation of new sheets by the epidermis, it becomes the middle shell layer called the exocuticle.■ With its molecules bonded so tightly, the exocuticle is very durable.■ There are points on the body where it does not form, since flexibility is needed around joints. This arrangement allows supple movement but provides armor-like protection.

30 Though strong, the chitin and protein exocuticle itself would provide a poor barrier against moisture loss. Therefore, it must be coated with lipids, which are also secreted by the epidermis. These lipids, mostly fatty acids and waxes, form the third, outermost layer of the shell. They spread over the

35 cuticles to form a waterproof seal even in dry weather. This lipid layer gives many arthropods their distinctive luster.

Combined, the endocuticle, exocuticle, and lipid coating form a shell that provides formidable protection. The external shell has other advantages. One

40 is that, because it has far more surface area than the internal skeleton found in vertebrates, it provides more points at which muscles can be attached. This increased number of muscles permits many arthropods to be stronger and more agile for their body size than birds or mammals. The coloration and markings of the exoskeleton can be beneficial as well. Many species

45 of scorpion, for instance, have cuticles that contain hyaline. The hyaline is excited by ultraviolet radiation, so these scorpions glow blue-green when a black light is flashed on them. Scientists are not sure why scorpions have evolved to fluoresce this way, but the reason may be that their glow attracts insects that they can capture and eat.

50 Adaptive as their shell is, it leaves arthropods with at least one distinct disadvantage: The cuticle cannot expand to accommodate growth. As the animal increases in size, therefore, it must occasionally molt. The existing cuticle separates from newer, more flexible layers being secreted beneath it,

55 gradually splits open, and can be shaken or slipped off. The new chitin and protein will harden and be provided with a fresh lipid coating, but this process can take hours or days after molting occurs. The arthropod must first take in extra air or water to swell its body to greater than its normal size. After the shell has hardened in its expanded form, the arthropod expels the air or

60 water. It then has room for growth. But until it hardens, the new coat is tender and easily penetrated. Accordingly, the arthropod must remain in hiding. Otherwise, it risks being snapped up by a predator clever enough to take advantage of its lowered defenses.

The black squares in the fourth paragraph are used for **sentence insertion** questions. Here's an example.

2. Look at the four squares [■] that indicate where the following sentence could be added.

    While this process continues, the endocuticle is gradually shifted.

    Where would the sentence best fit?

To answer this type of question correctly, we need to look at the sentences before and after each black square. The correct answer will join these two sentences together by mentioning an idea from each sentence. Here are the sentences before and after the first black square.

> The endocuticle is not quite tough enough for daily wear and tear. ■ Over time, however, its molecules continue to lock together.

Our task is to try to match the sentence in the question with the ideas in these two sentences. The answer choice mentions a "process." Does this match with anything in these two sentences? It doesn't appear to do so. Let's look at the rest of the sentence in the answer. It also states that the "endocuticle is gradually shifted." Does this match with the details in these two sentences? Although we can match the word *endocuticle*, neither of the sentences discusses a "shift." Therefore, we can't place the sentence here.

Now, let's look at the second pair of sentences:

> Over time, however, its molecules continue to lock together. ■ As the endocuticle is pushed upward by the formation of new sheets by the epidermis, it becomes the middle shell layer called the exocuticle.

Now, we'll try to match our sentence with ideas from this pair of sentences. We need to find something that corresponds to "this process." The first sentence in the pair refers to "molecules...lock together." This seems like a process. Next, we want to match up the part of the sentence that talks about the endocuticle gradually shifting. The second sentence in the pair says "as the endocuticle is pushed upward...." This matches nicely with the "gradually shifting" part in the question. This looks like a likely place to add the new sentence.

Check the other two sentence pairs. Here's the third.

> As the endocuticle is pushed upward by the formation of new sheets by the epidermis, it becomes the middle shell layer called the exocuticle. ■ With its molecules bonded so tightly, the exocuticle is very durable.

As we've already seen, the first sentence in this pair is a good match for the sentence we have to add. However, the problem is the second sentence in the pair. This sentence mentions the *durability* of the exocuticle, which doesn't match with anything in the sentence we have to add. That makes this choice incorrect.

Finally, here's the fourth pair.

> With its molecules bonded so tightly, the exocuticle is very durable. ■ There are points on the body where it does not form, since flexibility is needed around joints.

In this case, it is clear that this pair of sentences does not match at all. The first sentence refers to the *exocuticle*, whereas the sentence we need to add is about the *endocuticle*. Furthermore, the second sentence in the pair is about places where there is no shell because flexibility is needed. These ideas are not part of the sentence we have to add. It looks as if the second black square is the best place to add the sentence, so your answer should look like this.

Over time, however, its molecules continue to lock together. While this process continues, the endocuticle is gradually shifted. As the endocuticle is pushed upward by the formation of new sheets by the epidermis, it becomes the middle shell layer called the exocuticle.

Keep in mind that when you click the black square on the TOEFL, the sentence will appear in the passage. This will make it easier to look for matches.

POE Strategies for Sentence Insertion Questions

Much like other questions in the Reading section of the TOEFL, these questions are all about matching information. The best answer is simply the one that is the closest match to the information in the passage. When doing a sentence insertion question, eliminate choices that don't match or are only half right.

- **Doesn't match:** The sentence you add should form a link between two sentences. If the ideas in the paragraph don't match the ideas in the added sentence, eliminate that choice.
- **Half-right:** Make sure the added sentence matches ideas with *both* the sentence before and the sentence after it. Wrong answers often are only partial matches.

We've looked at several different question types. Let's pause for a brief review before we continue.

Quick Review: Paraphrase, Definition, Before/After, and Sentence Insertion Questions

All of these question types refer you to a specific part of the passage, which is typically highlighted or marked. So there is no difficulty in figuring out where in the passage the answer lies. The difficulty lies in finding the right answer. In general, when answering questions of this type, focus on the following POE guidelines:

- **Doesn't match:** This is one of the easiest ways to eliminate an answer choice. If the information in the choice doesn't match the passage, it's wrong.
- **New information:** Be very suspicious of answer choices that introduce new information. These choices are usually wrong.
- **Half-right:** Read each choice carefully because wrong answers will typically match only half of the information in the passage or answer choice. Make sure *all* the information corresponds.

Questions of this type can be a little more challenging than the question types we've looked at already. Try these questions only after answering the vocabulary in context, reference, lead word, and detail questions.

Question Type #9: EXCEPT/NOT/LEAST Questions

This type of question tends to be one of the most difficult questions in the Reading section. Let's look at these questions and figure out how to crack them.

Once again, here's our practice passage for reference.

The Exoskeleton of the Arthropod

There are more arthropods alive on Earth than there are members of any other phylum of animals. Given that not only insects and spiders but also shrimp, crabs, centipedes, and their numerous relatives are arthropods, this fact should not occasion surprise. For all their diversity, arthropods of any type
5 share two defining characteristics: jointed legs (from which the phylum takes its name) and an exoskeleton (the recognizable hard outer shell).

Though the shell itself is made of dead tissue like that of human hair and fingernails, it is dotted with sensory cells. These give the arthropod
10 information about its surroundings, much as the nerve endings in human skin do. Also like human skin, the shell protects fragile internal organs from potentially hazardous contact with the environment. It seals in precious moisture that would otherwise evaporate but permits the exchange of gases.

15 Its primary component is chitin, a natural polymer that contains calcium and is very similar in structure to the cellulose in wood. Chitin and proteins are secreted in the epidermis, the living tissue just below the shell, after which they bond to form a thin sheet. Each new sheet is produced so that its chitin fibers are not parallel with those directly above, which increases their
20 combined strength.

The result is the endocuticle, a mesh of molecules that forms the lowest layer of the shell. The endocuticle is not quite tough enough for daily wear and tear. Over time, however, its molecules continue to lock together. As
25 the endocuticle is pushed upward by the formation of new sheets by the epidermis, it becomes the middle shell layer called the exocuticle. With its molecules bonded so tightly, the exocuticle is very durable. There are points on the body where it does not form, since flexibility is needed around joints. This arrangement allows supple movement but provides armor-like protection.
30

Though strong, the chitin and protein exocuticle itself would provide a poor barrier against moisture loss. Therefore, it must be coated with lipids, which are also secreted by the epidermis. These lipids, mostly fatty acids and waxes, form the third, outermost layer of the shell. They spread over the
35 cuticles to form a waterproof seal even in dry weather. This lipid layer gives many arthropods their distinctive luster.

Combined, the endocuticle, exocuticle, and lipid coating form a shell that provides formidable protection. The external shell has other advantages. One
40 is that, because it has far more surface area than the internal skeleton found in vertebrates, it provides more points at which muscles can be attached. This increased number of muscles permits many arthropods to be stronger and more agile for their body size than birds or mammals. The coloration

and markings of the exoskeleton can be beneficial as well. Many species
45 of scorpion, for instance, have cuticles that contain hyaline. The hyaline is
excited by ultraviolet radiation, so these scorpions glow blue-green when a
black light is flashed on them. Scientists are not sure why scorpions have
evolved to fluoresce this way, but the reason may be that their glow attracts
insects that they can capture and eat.

50

Adaptive as their shell is, it leaves arthropods with at least one distinct
disadvantage: The cuticle cannot expand to accommodate growth. As the
animal increases in size, therefore, it must occasionally molt. The existing
cuticle separates from newer, more flexible layers being secreted beneath it,
55 gradually splits open, and can be shaken or slipped off. The new chitin and
protein will harden and be provided with a fresh lipid coating, but this process
can take hours or days after molting occurs. The arthropod must first take
in extra air or water to swell its body to greater than its normal size. After
the shell has hardened in its expanded form, the arthropod expels the air or
60 water. It then has room for growth. But until it hardens, the new coat is tender
and easily penetrated. Accordingly, the arthropod must remain in hiding.
Otherwise, it risks being snapped up by a predator clever enough to take
advantage of its lowered defenses.

Now, take a look at a new type of question.

14. All of the following are mentioned as benefits of the
exoskeleton EXCEPT

a. protection against water loss
b. distinctive coloration and markings
c. ability to take in extra air or water
d. armor-like protection

You'll notice this question has the word EXCEPT written in capital letters. Yet, test takers still
often look for the "right" answer. For EXCEPT/NOT/LEAST questions, your task is to find
the answer that is *not* mentioned. Here's how:

1. Rephrase the question, eliminating the EXCEPT/NOT/LEAST part.
2. Use the answer choices like a checklist, returning to the passage to find each one.
3. Mark each answer choice as either TRUE or FALSE based on the passage.
4. Choose the answer that's different from the other three.

Here's how it works. First, we'll rephrase the question, removing the EXCEPT part. Our new
question asks

What are the benefits of an exoskeleton?

Now, we'll go through each choice, looking for evidence in the passage. Think of each choice as a lead word—scan the passage for the word or phrase, and read a few lines before and after to see if it answers the questions.

- The first choice is "protection against water loss." Go back to the passage and try to find the part that talks about "water loss." This topic appears in paragraph 5. It states that the shell forms a "waterproof seal." This means that (A) is true. Mark that on your scratch paper.
  - (A)   True
- Next, check (B). Our lead phrase for this choice is "coloration and markings." Scan through the passage. Where does it mention this topic? Paragraph 6 says that "coloration and markings of the exoskeleton can be beneficial...." So this answer is true as well. Mark it down on your scrap paper.
  - (A)   True
  - (B)   True
- The third choice is "ability to take in extra air or water." Let's look through the passage for these lead words. Find them? These words show up in the final paragraph, but that paragraph is about the *disadvantages* of the shell. So this choice is false. Note this on your scrap paper.
  - (A)   True
  - (B)   True
  - (C)   False
- Finally, let's verify our answer by checking the fourth choice, which is "armor-like protection." A quick scan of our passage reveals this phrase in the fourth paragraph. This statement is true as well. Thus, we're left with the following:
  - (A)   True
  - (B)   True
  - (C)   False
  - (D)   True
- Now all we do is pick the answer choice that is different: (C). It is very important to check all of the choices when doing EXCEPT/NOT/LEAST questions. Many test takers go through the choices too quickly and end up picking the answer that *is* in the passage instead of the one that *isn't*.

POE Strategies for EXCEPT/NOT/LEAST Questions

These questions are similar to detail and lead word questions. However, they are the *opposite* because you are going to *eliminate* answers that are

- **Supported by the passage:** Remember, we want the choice that is *not* supported by the passage.

Additionally, the correct answer may

- **Contain information not mentioned:** Information not found in the passage makes a good answer for these questions.
- **Use extreme language:** Extreme language is usually bad; but for these questions, it's acceptable.

EXCEPT/NOT/LEAST questions can take a little more time to answer than other types of detail or lead word questions, so make sure to do them in your second pass.

Question Type #10: Inference Questions

Here's our next question type.

> 11. It can be inferred from the passage that molting
>
>   a. happens regularly during the life of the arthropod
>   b. always takes days to complete
>   c. leaves the arthropod without its normal defense
>   d. causes the arthropod to grow larger

Inference questions ask for a very specific type of answer. An inference is a conclusion reached based on the available evidence. For example, if a friend of yours walks in and has wet hair, you may infer that it is raining outside. That inference may or may not be true. Perhaps your friend just washed his hair or was sprayed with a hose. However, on the TOEFL, the correct inference is the answer that *must be true* based on the information in the passage.

Our approach to these questions remains the same as many other types. First, restate the question.

> What does the passage suggest about molting?

Next, use a lead word to locate the appropriate part of the passage. For this question, we'll use the word *molting*. This word shows up in the final paragraph. As we've seen with detail and lead word questions, the correct answer should be within four or five lines of the reference. However, for inference questions, you should not attempt to answer in your own words first; this is because you can't be sure which inference will be the correct response, and the answer you predict may not be close to the answer choice.

Instead, we'll follow a process similar to the one we used for EXCEPT/NOT/LEAST questions. We'll look at each answer choice and see if it is true based on the lines about molting. Here's the question again.

> 11. It can be inferred from the passage that molting
>
>   a. happens monthly during the life of the arthropod
>   b. always takes days to complete
>   c. leaves the arthropod without its normal defense
>   d. causes the arthropod to grow larger

- Let's start with the first choice. Go back to the paragraph about molting, and look for any information regarding how regularly it takes place. Remember to read only the lines around our lead word. Because there is no information on the regularity of molting, (A) must be wrong. Eliminate it.
- Now move on to the next choice. Go back to the passage, and look for evidence that molting "always takes days to complete." There is some information about time, but make sure you read carefully. The passage states that "this process can take hours or days...." But that doesn't mean that molting "always" takes days. So, eliminate (B).
- For the third choice, there is some indication that it is true. If you read toward the end of the paragraph, it states that the "new coat is tender and easily penetrated. Accordingly, the arthropod must remain in hiding." It took a little searching, but this is the answer we need.
- Of course, we should still look at the final answer. The fourth choice suggests that molting "causes the arthropod to grow larger." Is there any evidence for this in the passage? Choice (D) is supported in the passage ("As the animal increases in size, therefore, it must occasionally molt."), but the passage doesn't say that molting *causes* growth.
- So (C) is the best answer.

POE Strategies for Inference Questions

Inference questions require a very careful reading of the passage because the wrong answers can be very attractive. When eliminating answers, you should carefully look for the following:

- **Could be true:** Some answers may be true. However, this is not good enough on the TOEFL. You must be able to support the truth of the answer with the passage.
- **Extreme:** The wrong answer on inference questions will often use extreme wording. Watch out for answers that contain the following words:

> *always   never   impossible   all   none   best   worst*

- **Beyond the information:** The wrong answer on an inference question may contain some information found in the passage but make a claim or connection that is not found in the passage.

Inference questions require careful reading of both the passage and the answer choices. The right answer is usually a clever paraphrase of information in the passage. Because these questions can be very tricky, you may want to do them during your second pass.

Question Type #11: Summary Questions

The final question type on the TOEFL is the **summary** question. These questions are typically worth two points and require you to find multiple correct answers.

Here's an example of one.

15. **Directions:** An introductory sentence for a brief summary of the passage is provided below. Complete the summary by selecting the THREE answer choices that express the most important ideas in the passage. Some sentences do not belong in the summary because they express ideas that are not presented in the passage or are minor ideas in the passage. *This question is worth 2 points.*

> **Animals in the phylum called arthropods have shells or exoskeletons with distinctive characteristics.**

> *
> *
> *

Answer Choices	
Insects, spiders, shrimp, crabs, and centipedes are all arthropods.	The chitin in the exoskeleton is similar in chemical composition to the cellulose in wood.
The shell has three layers that protect an arthropod from injury and water loss.	Because the shell is hard, it must be discarded and replaced as the arthropod grows.
The hyaline in a scorpion's shell glows under black light because it is excited by ultraviolet radiation.	The large surface area of the shell makes possible a high number of muscles and a variety of adaptive colorations.

For this type of question, you will click and drag answer choices to add them to the summary. Fortunately, these questions always show up at the end of the section, so by the time you attack a summary question, you should have a pretty good idea of the passage's main points.

Your main task for this question is to separate *details* from *main ideas*. Use your understanding of the structure of a passage to figure out which choice is a detail and which choice is a main point. In general, details will appear in the middle of paragraphs and are often mentioned only once. Main ideas will appear at the beginning or end of paragraphs and show up throughout the passage.

Let's go through each choice and decide if it's a detail or a main idea.

- The first choice is as follows:

  Insects, spiders, shrimp, crabs, and centipedes are all arthropods.

  Is this one of the main ideas of the passage? It's certainly mentioned in the first paragraph, but what is the majority of the passage about? If you said the exoskeleton, you are correct. Our answers should be about the exoskeleton, so let's eliminate this choice.

- Here's the second choice.

  The shell has three layers that protect an arthropod from injury and water loss.

  This choice is more in line with what we need. The passage described the shell, and this answer summarizes the structure of the shell. Let's add it to our summary.

  - **The shell has three layers that protect an arthropod from injury and water loss.**

  -

  -

- The next choice says

  The hyaline in a scorpion's shell glows under black light because it is excited by ultraviolet radiation.

  Is this a main idea or a detail? Where does this fact appear in the passage? Notice how it shows up in a paragraph about the benefits of the shell. That means that this fact is likely just an example of a benefit. The passage even uses the phrase "for instance" when discussing this fact. Plus, the entire passage is not about scorpions. Thus, it's a detail, not a main idea.

- Here's the next choice.

   The chitin in the exoskeleton is similar in chemical composition to the cellulose in wood.

   Although it does talk about the exoskeleton, this choice provides a *very specific* detail about the chitin. We're looking for a *more general* description. Let's look at the other choices and see if they are better answers.

- The next choice reads

   Because the shell is hard, it must be discarded and replaced as the arthropod grows.

   This choice talks about the shell as well. It gives a good summary of the final paragraph of the passage, which talked about the disadvantages of the exoskeleton. Because the entire passage gave information on the benefits and disadvantages of the exoskeleton, we should add this choice to our list.

   - **The shell has three layers that protect an arthropod from injury and water loss.**

   - **Because the shell is hard, it must be discarded and replaced as the arthropod grows.**

   -

- Here's our final option.

   The large surface area of the shell makes possible a high number of muscles and a variety of adaptive colorations.

   This choice is also part of the main idea. Notice how it differs from the previous choice about the scorpion's markings. This choice mentions two benefits, not just one. And it doesn't mention just one type of arthropod. Therefore, it belongs in the summary.

- Here are our final choices.

  o The shell has three layers that protect an arthropod from injury and water loss.

  o Because the shell is hard, it must be discarded and replaced as the arthropod grows.

  o The large surface area of the shell makes possible a high number of muscles and a variety of adaptive colorations.

Notice how this summary matches the summaries we practiced in Core Concept: Reading. We've mentioned each of the important points from the topic sentences of the passage.

POE Strategies for Summary Questions

For these questions, eliminate answers that don't show up as key points during your initial reading of the passage. Use the structure of the passage to help eliminate answers. Remove choices that are

- **Too specific:** Watch out for choices that contain specific facts or details. Make sure you don't include examples! Remember, examples only support the main point; they don't state it.
- **Not mentioned:** Make sure the information in the choice is actually found in the passage. Some answer choices are cleverly worded to distract you.

These questions can be very difficult, but if you've been practicing the active reading strategies in this book, they should be much easier. Still, save these questions for last.

Reading Summary

Congratulations! You've just cracked an entire section of the TOEFL. Before we give you a drill to practice your new skills, let's review some of the key ideas from this chapter.

Basic Ideas

o **It's in there:** No matter how difficult the question may seem, remember that the answer is somewhere in the passage.

o **Two-pass system:** Not all questions are created equal. Do all the questions that you find easier first, and save the killer questions for last. This system is what we call your Personal Order of Difficulty—wherein you get to choose to tackle the questions that feel the easiest to you first and tally those points, then come back around for the more challenging questions.

o **POE:** Sometimes it's easier to find the wrong answer than the right answer. Make sure you know the POE guidelines for the test.

The Approach

o **Actively read the passage,** looking for the purpose, structure, and main idea.

o **Attack the questions** based on question type.

o **Find the answer** to the question in the passage.

o **Use POE** to eliminate bad answers.

Timing Tips

o   For the first few passages, time yourself to see how long it takes you to complete the passage.

o   Once you have a good idea of how long it takes you, time yourself to work a little bit faster each time.

o   Try to maintain your accuracy.

Reading Personal Order of Difficulty (POOD)

o   Which question types do you feel most confident about? _____

o   Which questions have you determined aren't worth your investment of time on test day? _____

o   Which letter will you choose as your Letter of the Day on all questions you determine aren't worth your time?   A   B   C   D

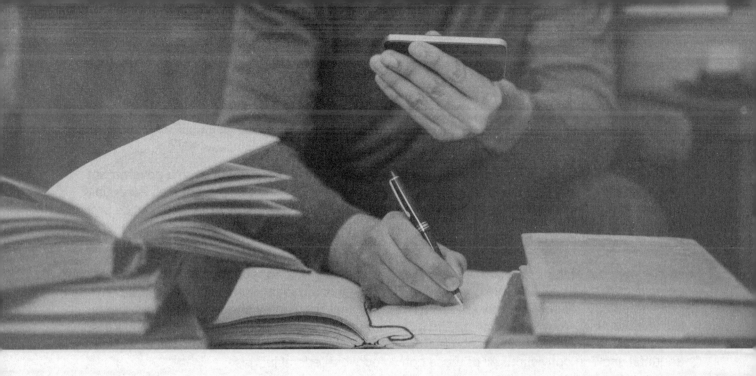

Chapter 8
Reading Practice
Drills

Here are some practice reading passages. Remember to use the two-pass approach you just learned in the previous chapter. At this point, don't worry about time—just focus on getting the right answers and understanding the process. After you've completed these drills, be sure to read through the explanations of the right and wrong answers in the next chapter.

Reading Practice Drill #1

Impeachment

Under the Constitution, the House of Representatives has the power to impeach a government official, in effect serving as prosecutor. The Senate then holds the impeachment trial, essentially serving as jury and judge, except in the impeachment of a president when the chief justice presides. The president, vice president, and all civil officers of the United States are subject to impeachment;
5 conviction means automatic removal from office.

→ The concept of impeachment originated in England and was adopted by many of the American colonial governments and state constitutions. At the Constitutional Convention, the framers considered several possible models before deciding that the Senate should try impeachments.
10 Since 1789, only 17 federal officers have been impeached by the House, 14 of which were tried by the Senate. Three were dismissed before trial because the individual had left office, 7 ended in acquittal and 7 in conviction. All of those convicted were federal judges.

→ Impeachment is a very serious affair. It is perhaps the most awesome power of Congress, the
15 ultimate weapon it wields against officials of the federal government. The House of Representatives is the prosecutor. The Senate chamber is the courtroom. The Senate is the jury and also the judge, except in the case of a presidential impeachment trial when the chief justice presides. The final penalty is removal from office. There is no appeal.

20 → So grave is this power of impeachment, and so conscious is the Congress of this solemn power, that impeachment proceedings have been initiated in the House only sixty-two times since 1789. Only seventeen federal officers have been impeached: two presidents, one cabinet officer, one senator and thirteen federal judges. Sixteen cases have reached the Senate. Of these, two were dismissed before trial because the individuals had left office, seven ended in acquittal, and seven in
25 conviction. Each of the seven Senate convictions has involved a federal judge.

The American colonial governments and early state constitutions followed the British pattern of trial before the upper legislative body on charges brought by the lower house. Despite these precedents, a major controversy arose at the Constitutional Convention about whether the Senate should act
30 as the court of impeachment. Opposing that role for the Senate, James Madison and Charles Cotesworth Pinckney asserted that it would make the president too dependent on the legislative branch. They suggested, as alternative trial bodies, the Supreme Court or the chief justices of the state supreme courts. Hamilton and others argued, however, that such bodies would be too small and susceptible to corruption. In the end, after much wrangling, the framers selected the Senate as
35 the trial forum.

There was also considerable debate at the convention in Philadelphia over the definition of impeachable crimes. In the original proposals, the president was to be removed on impeachment and conviction "for mal or corrupt conduct," or for "malpractice or neglect of duty." Later, the
40 wording was changed to "treason, bribery, or corruption," then to "treason or bribery" alone. A final revision defined impeachable crimes as "treason, bribery, or other high crimes and misdemeanors."

In the Constitution, the House is given the "sole power of impeachment." To the Senate is given "the sole power to try all impeachments." Impeachments may be brought against "the President,
45 Vice President, and all civil officers of the United States." Conviction is automatically followed by "removal from office."

While the framers very clearly envisaged the occasional necessity of initiating impeachment proceedings, they put in place only a very general framework. ■ They left many questions open
50 to differences of opinion and many details to be filled in. ■ Despite the open-endedness, as Peter Charles Hoffer and N.E.H. Hull note in their book *Impeachment in America 1635–1805*, thanks to the framers: a tool used in Parliament to curb kings and punish placemen was molded into an efficient legislative check upon executive and judicial wrongdoing. ■ The power of the English House of Commons to impeach anyone, for almost any alleged offense, was restrained; the threat of death
55 and forfeiture upon conviction was lifted; and the interference of the Commons and the House of Lords with the regular courts of justice was limited. ■ American impeachment law shifted, at first inadvertently and then deliberately, from the orbit of English precedent to a native republican course. Federal constitutional provisions for impeachment reflected indigenous experience and revolutionary tenets instead of English tradition.

1. The word power in the passage is closest in meaning to

    a.   motivation
    b.   desire
    c.   bearing
    d.   authority

2. According to paragraph 3, what three roles do the House of Representatives and Senate play in the impeachment process?

    a.   Government official, jury, judge
    b.   Prosecutor, jury, judge
    c.   President, prosecutor, judge
    d.   Civil officers, jury, prosecutor

    Paragraph 3 is marked with an arrow [➜]

3. In paragraph 2, the author explains that the idea of impeachment began

    a.   at the Constitutional Convention
    b.   in 1789
    c.   in England
    d.   in colonial governments

    Paragraph 2 is marked with an arrow [➜]

4. What can be inferred from paragraph 2 about the decision to impeach a government official?

a. The decision made In the Senate
b. Impeachment results in removal from office
c. Impeachment occurs often
d. Impeachment rarely occurs

Paragraph 2 is marked with an arrow [➔]

5. The word wields in the passage is closest in meaning to

a. uses
b. maintains
c. formulates
d. shapes

6. In paragraph 3, the author explains that during the impeachment of a president

a. a chief justice presides
b. the Senate presides
c. the House of Representatives presides
d. Congress presides

Paragraph 3 is marked with an arrow [➔]

7. According to paragraph 4, how many impeachment proceedings have been initiated since 1789?

a. Seventeen
b. Two
c. Sixty-two
d. Sixteen

Paragraph 4 is marked with an arrow [➔]

8. The word precedents in the passage is closest in meaning to

   a.   charges
   b.   statutes
   c.   examples
   d.   claims

9. According to the passage, the impeachment process incorporates

   a.   the House of Representatives and the Senate
   b.   the Senate and the President
   c.   a Chief Justice and the House of Representatives
   d.   a Chief Justice and the Senate

10. Which of the sentences below best expresses the essential
    information in the highlighted sentence in the passage? Incorrect
    choices change the meaning in important ways or leave out
    essential information.

    There was also considerable debate at the convention in
    Philadelphia over the definition of impeachable crimes.

    a.   Philadelphians debated considerably over the definition of impeachable
         crimes.
    b.   Formidable debate occurred at the convention in Philadelphia concerning
         the meaning of impeachable crimes.
    c.   Impeachable crimes were debated at the convention in Philadelphia.
    d.   The classification of impeachable crimes was a significant debate at the
         Philadelphia convention.

11. ALL of the following are mentioned as part of the final definition of
    impeachment EXCEPT

    a.   corruption
    b.   misdemeanors
    c.   bribery
    d.   treason

12. The word initiating in the passage is closest in meaning to

    a.   concluding
    b.   starting
    c.   deciding
    d.   forming

13. Look at the four squares [■] that indicate where the following sentence could be added to the passage.

    Consequently, the American version of impeachment was clearly quite different than the English version upon which it was based.

    Where would the sentence best fit?

    Click on a square [■] to add the sentence to the passage.

14. Directions: An introductory sentence for a brief summary of the passage is provided below. Complete the summary by selecting the THREE answer choices that express the most important ideas in the passage. Some sentences do not belong in the summary because they express ideas that are not presented in the passage or are minor ideas in the passage.

    The power of impeachment was initiated during the Constitutional Convention as a means to try government officials who do not act according to the law.

    -
    -
    -

Answer Choices	
Sixty-two trials of impeachment have occurred since 1789.	The impeachment process is initially brought forth by the House of Representatives, and it is tried before the Senate.
A chief justice presides over the hearing of presidential impeachment, and this is the only instance in which the Senate is not the judge.	If a government official is convicted subsequent to impeachment, he/she is automatically removed from office.
The power to impeach is taken very seriously by Congress and very few government officials have been impeached.	The definition of impeachable crimes was an important component of the Constitutional Convention; nevertheless, the language defining remains decidedly vague.

Reading Practice Drill #2

Fire Tornadoes

→ Fire tornadoes—also known as fire whirls, firenados, or fire twisters—look like tornadoes but are made up of fire. Therefore, they aren't really tornadoes at all. Tornadoes are formed when just the right weather elements combine: moist, warm air lying close to the ground; an unstable atmosphere; and air fronts that collide and propel moist air vertically into the sky.

5   A fire tornado has two parts: the core, which is actually on fire, and an invisible, rotating air pocket. It can reach temperatures of nearly 2,000°F, which is hot enough to even reignite ashes that have been sucked into the vortex from the ground. While real tornadoes occur as a result of atmospheric conditions high above, fire tornadoes result from hot, dry air rising quickly away from the ground.

10   When hot, strong winds come into contact with an already-burning brushfire, updrafts of hot air catch the fire and surrounding winds and send it whirling into the air. This whirling air forms columns; as more and more hot air is pulled into a column, the column begins to swirl, very much like a real tornado.

15   A fire twister's spinning column creates a vortex thanks to angular momentum. The law of angular momentum states that when an object is inside a spinning column it will move faster and faster the closer it gets to the center of rotation. The fire tornado picks up flaming embers, combustible gases, burning debris, and ash. When sucked up by the firenado, unburned gases travel up the core until they reach an area where there is enough oxygen to ignite them. This ultimately creates a spinning
20   fire tower that can be hundreds of feet tall.

While fire whirls move pretty slowly, they can cause significant damage. Anything—or anyone!—unfortunate enough to be in a fire whirl's path will likely either be set ablaze or flung vigorously from its location. But it's not just the fire that's dangerous—the winds it generates can create
25   wind speeds of more than 100 mph, which is strong enough to knock down trees. Fire whirls also typically don't last very long, but when they do they can wreak havoc and leave disaster in their wakes.

→ There have been numerous major firenados in the last 150 years, many of which have proved
30   lethal. In 1871, the great Peshtigo Fire in Northeastern Wisconsin and Upper Michigan resulted from inauspicious conditions: dry weather during the summer, slash-and-burn farming practices, and a vigorous cold front that brought strong winds. Together, these three contributing factors created firenados that turned a few small prairie fires into a furious conflagration. The town of Peshtigo, with hundreds of wooden structures and lumberyards, sat in the middle of a forest of pine and hardwood.
35   When the fire reached the town, it found abundant fuel. In just minutes, 100-mph winds and ambient temperatures of more than 700°F caused what is still recognized as the worst fire disaster in the history of the United States. As best as anyone could tell, nearly 2,000 people lost their lives.

More recently, a fire twister was recorded in January 2003 on Mount Taylor in Canberra, Australia. It
40   had a diameter of almost 1,600 feet and winds of more than 160 mph. In April 2016, a fire tornado nearly claimed the life of a firefighter in Alberta, Canada. His team was fighting a blaze that started as an out-of-control campfire. The firefighter's teammate yelled at him to watch out. Without thinking, he jumped in the nearby river, saving his own life.

45 Unfortunately, we still don't know much about fire twisters. Because they can arise in any part of a fire, there is no way to predict where one might appear. And because they don't usually last very long, it's reasonable to consider that even firefighters can't identify where a fire twister has touched ground. Even with that information, we would still be left with the question of whether the fire caused the vortex or whether the vortex was helped by the fire. Perhaps someday we'll find out!

1. It can be inferred from paragraph 1 of the passage that fire tornadoes

   a. are truly tornadoes
   b. form easily
   c. look like tornadoes
   d. result only from an unstable atmosphere

   Paragraph 1 is marked with an arrow [➜]

2. The word whirling in the passage is closest in meaning to

   a. spinning
   b. working
   c. flying
   d. jumping

3. The word it in the passage refers to

   a. the fire
   b. the air pocket
   c. the fire tornado
   d. the ashes

4. The word reignite in the passage is closest in meaning to

   a. remove
   b. char
   c. quench
   d. light again

5. Which of the following is NOT mentioned as a characteristic of a fire tornado?

   a. Column
   b. Core
   c. Air pocket
   d. Angular momentum

6. The word vortex in the passage is closest in meaning to

    a.   spinning column
    b.   angular momentum
    c.   unburned gases
    d.   center of rotation

7. Which of the following is an example of angular momentum?

    a.   A runner running faster the further she runs
    b.   A tennis player hitting harder earlier in the game
    c.   An ice skater spinning faster as she pulls her arms in to her body
    d.   A swimmer swimming faster at a higher altitude

8. The phrase flung vigorously in the passage is closest in meaning to

    a.   burned quickly
    b.   moved slowly
    c.   thrown forcefully
    d.   tossed gently

9. The author implies that

    a.   fire whirls don't move quickly
    b.   fire whirls don't cause damage
    c.   fire whirls can't knock down trees
    d.   fire whirls can last for days

10. The phrase wreak havoc in the passage is closest in meaning to

    a.   start sizeable fires
    b.   last forever
    c.   move quickly
    d.   cause significant damage

11. According to paragraph 5 of the passage, firenados

    a.   have happened more than once
    b.   have never been documented
    c.   first occurred in Peshtigo
    d.   are always lethal

Paragraph 5 is marked with an arrow [➔]

12. The word inauspicious in the passage is closest in meaning to

    a.   lucky
    b.   fortunate
    c.   unlucky
    d.   dangerous

13. Directions: An introductory sentence for a brief summary of the passage is provided below. Complete the summary by selecting the THREE answer choices that express the most important ideas in the passage. Some sentences do not belong in the summary because they express ideas that are not presented in the passage or are minor ideas in the passage. This question is worth 2 points.

A firenado is one example of a natural phenomenon that is as uncommon as it is dangerous.

-
-
-

Answer Choices	
Firenados require a unique combination of conditions in order to occur.	A firefighter escaped a firenado by jumping in a river.
Firenados suck up ashes and gases into their core.	Scientists don't know much about firenados because it is hard to predict where or when they will occur.
Firenados can cause significant damage.	The firenado in Peshtigo was the first firenado on record.

Reading Practice Drill #3

Periodical Cicadas

→ Certain cicadas spend most of their lives about 2 feet underground, feeding on fluids from the roots of trees in forests across the eastern United States. These particular species, called periodical cicadas, are developmentally synchronized, meaning they develop into adults all at the same time. There are seven distinct species of periodical cicadas, four of which have 13-year lifecycles and
5   three of which have 17-year lifecycles. After the respective 13 or 17 years of subterranean lifestyle, the almost-mature cicada nymphs emerge at a given place and time in astounding numbers— as many as 1.5 million cicadas per acre. The nymphs wait for a spring evening when the soil temperature about 8 inches below the surface is above 64°F. For the four 13-year-cycle species, which tend to be further to the south and west of the eastern United States, this may be as early
10   as late April or early May. But for the three 17-year-cycle species, which are generally found more toward the northern end of the eastern United States, this may not happen until late May or early June.

Once they emerge they have only about 4–6 weeks to live. First, they find a new home on plants
15   near their emergence location where they complete their transition into full adult cicadas. Next, they molt a final time and then remain in the leaves, where they are protected from most predators, to wait for their exoskeletons to completely harden. Within two months of their emergence, they have laid their eggs and their lifecycle has been completed. Once the mature cicadas die, there will be no more cicadas of that brood for another 13 or 17 years.
20
Periodical cicadas are divided into groups called broods; these broods are based on the calendar year in which they emerge. In 1898, entomologist C. L. Marlatt identified as many as 30 broods, although not all of them have actually been observed since then. He identified 17 broods with a 17-year lifecycle and 13 broods with a 13-year-lifecycle. Brood VI, for example, has a 17-year lifecycle.
25   It is typically found in Eastern Ohio, Western Maryland, Southwestern Pennsylvania, Northwestern Virginia, and West Virginia. Brood VI's last emergence was 2017, so it will emerge again in 2034.

Adult periodical cicadas are small, roughly one inch long, with males growing slightly larger than females. Cicadas do not have specific defense mechanisms: While their mouths are designed to
30   pierce plants and suck out the plants' sap, they don't bite or sting. **Their sole purpose during their adult lives is to reproduce. Male cicadas form "aggregations," or choruses, and "sing" a mating song that is specific to their species in order to attract females to mate.** They don't create sound with vocal chords, like humans do, though. Instead, they produce sounds with their tymbals, corrugated exoskeletal structures that are specifically used to produce sounds. **On the**
35   **male cicada, the pair of tymbals is located on the sides of the abdomen.** The membranes across the "ribs" of the tymbal vibrate quickly, and the cicada's body functions like a resonance chamber and magnifies the sound. The cicadas can adjust the "volume" of their sound by turning their bodies in different directions.

40   ■ **Periodical cicada populations grow to astounding numbers, not only because the only purpose of their adult lives is to reproduce, but also because they tend to escape natural population control by predators.** ■ Because they emerge only once every 13 or 17 years, predators cannot rely upon them as a regular part of the food cycle. ■ As a result, when the cicadas do become prey, their predators can seemingly eat their fill without making a significant impact on
45   the cicada population. ■

Periodical cicadas are fascinating creatures, largely because they don't play a regular role in their environments' ecosystems. In fact, they are so fascinating that scientists named their genus Magicicada. Most interesting, though, is how they keep track of time and know when 13 or 17 years
50 have passed. Alas, researchers don't actually know how they do it, other than knowing that it's some kind of molecular clock. The insects themselves make for difficult research, since researchers have to wait at least 13 years for a brood to reemerge!

1. The word subterranean in the passage is closest in meaning to

    a.   lifecycle
    b.   underground
    c.   species
    d.   cicadas

2. The word nymphs in the passage is closest in meaning to

    a.   immature cicadas
    b.   different species
    c.   roots of trees
    d.   water creatures

3. The word this in the passage refers to

    a.   periodical cicadas
    b.   astounding numbers
    c.   southeastern United States
    d.   ground temperature of 64°F

4. According to paragraph 1, periodical cicadas can be found

    a.   around the world
    b.   throughout the western hemisphere
    c.   across the eastern United States
    d.   in the southeastern United States

Paragraph 1 is marked with an arrow [➜]

5. The word they in the passage refers to

    a.   southeastern United States
    b.   periodical cicadas
    c.   plants
    d.   predators

6. The cicadas are organized into broods according to

    a.   the year in which they emerge
    b.   the length of their lifecycles
    c.   the length of their development cycle
    d.   Marlatt's preferences

7. The word magnifies in the passage is closest in meaning to

    a.   makes louder
    b.   produces
    c.   makes worse
    d.   degrades

8. Click on the sentence (in bold text in the passage and repeated below) in the passage where the author describes how periodical cicadas attract mates.

    a.   Their sole purpose during their adult lives is to reproduce.
    b.   Male cicadas form "aggregations," or choruses, and "sing" a mating song that is specific to their species in order to attract females to mate.
    c.   On the male cicada, the pair of tymbals is located on the sides of the abdomen.
    d.   Periodical cicada populations grow to astounding numbers, not only because the only purpose of their adult lives is to reproduce, but also because they tend to escape natural population control by predators.

9. The word their in the passage refers to

    a.   broods
    b.   cicada populations
    c.   cicada predators
    d.   cicada prey

10. Look at the four squares [■] that indicate where the following sentence can be added to the passage.

This phenomenon is known as "predator satiation," a situation in which prey occur at an incredibly high population that the probability of an individual organism being eaten is drastically reduced.

Where would the sentence best fit?

Click on a square [■] to add the sentence to the passage.

(Here, on this practice test, circle your answer below.)

a. Square 1
b. Square 2
c. Square 3
d. Square 4

11. How do periodical cicadas know when to emerge?

a. They have calendars.
b. They can track the seasons.
c. They have a molecular clock.
d. Scientists don't have any ideas.

12. Directions: An introductory sentence for a brief summary of the passage is provided below. Complete the summary by selecting the THREE answer choices that express the most important ideas in the passage. Some sentences do not belong in the summary because they express ideas that are not presented in the passage or are minor ideas in the passage. This question is worth 2 points.

Periodical cicadas are unique creatures because of their unusual lifecycles and their lack of significant predators.

-
-
-

Answer Choices	
Periodical cicadas have a significant maturation process, emerging only when they are almost ready to lay eggs.	Four species have 13-year lifecycles.
Periodical cicadas do not have many natural predators because their adult life-span is so short.	Once periodical cicadas emerge, they live only 4 to 6 weeks.
Periodical cicadas use their tymbals to make sounds during mating.	The soil temperature must be 64°F before the periodical cicadas will emerge.

Reading Practice Drill #4

MANDALA ART

"Mandala" is a Sanskrit word meaning "circle." While it originated as a spiritual symbol in many Indian religions, the mandala has come to be known generically as a term for any diagram, chart, or geometric pattern that is intended to symbolically or metaphorically represent the cosmos. The typical "circle with a center" pattern represents the foundational structure of life and creation. This
5 pattern is found in many places in our world, including biology, geology, physics, astronomy, and chemistry. For example, even atoms are circular in nature, with evenly balanced protons, neutrons, and electrons. Every cell has a nucleus, which also has a circle at the center. Even the Milky Way galaxy is circular, with our circular solar system within it. One could argue that each of these is a mandala in and of itself.
10
Carl Jung, the founder of analytical psychology, held that "a mandala is the psychological expression of the totality of the self." He sketched a small circular drawing every morning, and felt that whatever came to life in his mandala corresponded to his inner experience at the time. ■ He believed that he could track his internal transformations by looking at the differences in his drawings.
15 ■ Fundamentally, Jung believed that if humans could harness the power of their subconscious—or, as he called it, the Self—then they could grow toward fulfilling their potential for wholeness, and live fully expressed lives. ■ He found that during periods of significant trial and tribulation many of his clients felt compelled to create mandalas. He found that people felt drawn to drawing or painting mandalas simply because it felt right to do so—it seemed that they instinctively turned to creating a
20 mandala as a way to express their experience.■

Why might humans have this instinct? Research into the fields of psychology and child development may shed some light on the subject. It would seem that circles are part of the basic creation of a personal identity. Studies conducted with babies show that as early as one week old, infants
25 prefer to look at curved lines rather than straight lines. Additional research shows that two-month-old infants can discern shapes that look like faces from scrambled patterns. Psychologically, it is believed that simple, closed forms—like circles—are identified more quickly and recognized as meaningful, known, and familiar. Even the shape of an eye is spherical—simply put, it's a three-dimensional circle—and our field of vision is thus also circular.
30
Circles also appear very early in children's art. What begins as random scribbling progresses into drawing circles as early as age two. **By three or four years old, their drawings become more intricate, and without any input from adults they begin drawing suns, flowers, and people whose arms and legs connect to large circular heads.**
35
As adults, when we draw circles—in particular, mandalas—we connect with our inner child—some might say that we connect with our primary sense of self. **Researchers believe that mandalas give us a bridge to our home base, allowing us to recreate our sense of who we are.** Professionals also believe that mandalas help us center psychologically, and they are still used in
40 psychotherapy practice. Drawing a mandala is an organic process—what's most important is the process itself, not the final product. **It may include flowers, shapes, lines, or totally abstract designs. Many therapists believe, as Jung did, that whatever emerges in a mandala matches whatever may be going on in the artist's life; further, if the artist allows their unconscious to come out through the mandala, psychologists believe he or she can align their conscious**
45 **actions and decisions accordingly.**

1. The word it in the passage refers to

   a. Sanskrit
   b. mandala
   c. circle
   d. symbol

2. Atoms, cells, and the Milky Way are mentioned as examples of

   a. circles in nature
   b. patterns
   c. symbols
   d. the cosmos

3. The word held in the passage is closest in meaning to

   a. kept in hand
   b. occupied
   c. believed
   d. guarded

4. The phrase trial and tribulation in the passage is closest in meaning to

   a. ease
   b. difficulty
   c. fun
   d. happiness

5. Look at the four squares [■] that indicate where the following sentence can be added to the passage.

   Based on this belief and his recognition of his own internal evolution through the use of mandalas, he began to use them as a tool in his psychology practice.

   Where would the sentence best fit?

   Click on a square [■] to add the sentence to the passage.

   (Here, on this practice test, circle your answer below.)

   a. Square 1
   b. Square 2
   c. Square 3
   d. Square 4

6. What kinds of shapes are recognized more easily by the human eye?

   a. Circles
   b. Straight lines
   c. Squares
   d. Squiggly lines

7. The word their in the passage refers to

   a. Jung
   b. Jung's clients
   c. children
   d. adults

8. By what age do children begin drawing more detailed and representative pictures?

   a. One week
   b. One year
   c. Two years
   d. Three to four years

9. Click on the sentence (in bold text in the passage and repeated below) in the passage where the author describes how drawing a mandala allows an adult to reestablish a connection with her subconscious.

   a. By three or four years old, their drawings become more intricate, and without any input from adults they begin drawing suns, flowers, and people whose arms and legs connect to large circular heads.
   b. Researchers believe that mandalas give us a bridge to our home base, allowing us to recreate our sense of who we are.
   c. It may include flowers, shapes, lines, or totally abstract designs.
   d. Many therapists believe, as Jung did, that whatever emerges in a mandala matches whatever may be going on in the artist's life; further, if the artist allows their unconscious to come out through the mandala, psychologists believe he or she can align their conscious actions and decisions accordingly.

10. The word they in the passage refers to

   a. Jung's clients
   b. people in general
   c. psychiatric patients
   d. mandalas

11. Which of the following is NOT mentioned in the passage?

    a. The origin of the word "mandala"
    b. Examples of mandalas in nature
    c. Scientists who value mandalas
    d. Friends of people who draw mandalas

12. Directions: An introductory sentence for a brief summary of the passage is provided below. Complete the summary by selecting the THREE answer choices that express the most important ideas in the passage. Some sentences do not belong in the summary because they express ideas that are not presented in the passage or are minor ideas in the passage. This question is worth 2 points.

    Mandala art has ancient roots and can play a therapeutic role for humans.

    *
    *
    *

Answer Choices
The term "mandala" comes from an ancient language and has been passed on for generations.	Many ancient traditions and religions used mandalas in their ceremonies.
Children learn to draw circles before they learn to draw any other shapes.	Carl Jung, the founder of analytical psychology, found value in using mandalas with his patients.
Circles appear in artwork of peoples around the world.	Our solar system is a mandala.

Reading Practice Drill #5

The Olympics

What we call the Olympics—considered the world's premier sports competition—are actually inspired by the ancient Olympic games. These ancient games were a series of athletic competitions that took place in Olympia, Greece, sometime between the 8th century B.C.E. and the 4th century C.E. Free-born, Greek-speaking, male representatives from city-states across Greece gathered
5 every four years to take part in various running, throwing, jumping, and chariot-riding competitions. While the competitions always took place in Olympia, athletes from any city-state or kingdom could compete—they simply had to meet the entrance criteria. Originally, the men wore loincloths during competitions. As time went on, they eventually competed in the nude, in part because the Olympics were a time to recognize and celebrate the strength of the human body. Because the men
10 competed totally nude, though, married women were expressly forbidden to watch—under penalty of death!

Initially, the ancient Olympic games took place for only one day, but as events were added the festival ultimately grew to five days. The initial competition was called the "stadion," which was a
15 fairly short sprint of somewhere in the neighborhood of 200 meters, or the length of one stadium. The second race added sometime later was called the "diaulos," which was the length of one lap of the stadium, or about 400 meters. A few years after the advent of the diaulos, the "dolichos" was added to the races. It was somewhere between eighteen and twenty-four laps around the stadium, roughly three miles total.
20
Not surprisingly, the games also took on political importance, and were used by city-states to establish their dominance over other city-states. City-states maintained an often tenuous balance with each other: the dichotomy between needing each other for political and military alliances while simultaneously competing for limited geographical resources resulted in a frequently-conflicted
25 political environment. The Games, therefore, created an opportunity for the city-states to "compete" peacefully. In fact, these peaceful competitions led politicians to work together to create alliances, much like they do today.

The games didn't only involve athletic pursuits, though. Sculptors, poets, and other artists would
30 gather for competitions and showcase their wares to passers-by, hoping to turn them into patrons. Sculptors liked to highlight the natural body, its muscles, and the way it moved. Poets, too, wanted to honor the athletes and so wrote songs in praise of the victors. These songs often lived on for generations. The Games also had religious importance: They are thought to have first been held in honor of Zeus, and his statue at Olympia was long regarded as one of the seven wonders of the
35 ancient world. The sporting events were frequently accompanied by religious sacrifices to Zeus and other gods, too.

→ Just as historians debate when the first Olympic games were held, it is unclear why the ancient Greek Olympic games came to a halt. Some believe that Roman emperor Theodosius I, in an effort
40 to spread Christianity, decreed that all pagan rituals and cults be eliminated. Others believe that his successor, Theodosius II, later demanded the destruction of all Greek temples, leaving the Olympics with nowhere to take place.

Sometime in the 17th century, interest in the games sprang up anew in several locations. ■ The
45 first stirring of interest came up in England, and then France about a hundred years later. ■ Within another hundred years, in the early to mid-1800s, renewed interest surfaced in Greece, when

6. **A** This is a *vocabulary in context* question. Look at the lines from the passage.

> A fire twister's spinning column creates a _____ thanks to angular momentum. The law of angular momentum states that when an object is inside a spinning column it will move faster and faster the closer it gets to the center of rotation.

The second sentence in the quote above describes what happens to an object in a spinning column thanks to the law of angular momentum. The word in question is created by angular momentum, so the two must be related. Use that to tackle POE. Choice (B) is angular momentum itself, not what it creates, so eliminate it. Choice (C) is unrelated to these sentences, so get rid of it too. Choice (D) may be appealing, but it goes further than necessary—we're just talking about the column that's been created, not its center. Get rid of (D) and go with (A)!

7. **C** This question asks you to understand what the passage says about angular momentum and then find an example that matches that description. Look at the passage.

> The law of angular momentum states that when an object is inside a spinning column it will move faster and faster the closer it gets to the center of rotation.

With that description, go to POE and eliminate answers that don't describe a spinning motion. Choices (A), (B), and (D) have nothing to do with spinning or rotating, so eliminate them.

8. **C** This is a *vocabulary in context* question. Look at the lines from the passage.

> While fire whirls move pretty slowly, they can cause significant damage. Anything—or anyone!—unfortunate enough to be in a fire whirl's path will likely either be set ablaze or _____ from its location. But it's not just the fire that's dangerous—the winds it generates can create wind speeds of more than 100 mph, which is strong enough to knock down trees.

So the fire whirls move slowly and it's the winds that are dangerous. Chances are "flung vigorously" will have something to do with the wind. Try using POE. Choice (A) doesn't have anything to do with wind, so get rid of it. Choice (B) is tricky: the *fire whirl* moves slowly, not the objects in its way so get rid of (B). Choices (C) and (D) both involve throwing something. This may be where a little bit of common sense is required: if the wind speeds are more than 100 mph, will the resulting throw be gentle or forceful? Forceful! So eliminate (D) and go with (C).

9. **A** This is an *inference* question, but it doesn't tell you where to look. Remember that most questions on TOEFL Reading passages are arranged chronologically in order with the passage, so you're probably pretty close to the answer for this question by looking at where you found the answer to the previous question. Take a look at that same paragraph.

> While fire whirls move pretty slowly, they can cause significant damage. Anything—or anyone!—that is unfortunate enough to be in a fire whirl's path will likely either be set ablaze or flung vigorously from its location. But it's not just the fire that's dangerous—the winds it generates can create wind speeds of more than 100 mph, which is strong enough to knock down trees. Fire whirls also typically don't last very long, but when they do they can wreak havoc and leave disaster in their wakes.

Now, look at the answers to see what you can eliminate. Is there anything in the passage that matches what (A) says? Not in exactly the same words, but does "move pretty slowly" mean the same thing as "don't move quickly?" Yes! So leave (A) for now. Choices (B), (C), and (D) are exactly the opposite of what this paragraph is saying, so eliminate them.

10. **D** This is a *vocabulary in context* question. Look at the lines from the passage.

> But it's not just the fire that's dangerous—the winds it generates can create wind speeds of more than 100 mph, which is strong enough to knock down trees. Fire whirls also typically don't last very long, but when they do they can _____ and leave disaster in their wakes.

Anytime you you're not sure what a word or phrase might mean, you can start by asking yourself if it is positive or negative in meaning. In this case, the "and" tells us that the phrase in question will be along the lines of "leave disaster in their wakes." That means it's definitely negative. Use that for POE. Choices (A) and (D) would be negative, and (B) and (C) are neutral or positive, so eliminate them. Then, compare (A) and (D): which one is more negative? Definitely (D)—starting fires is bad, but in turn they cause significant damage, which is worse.

11. **A** This is an *inference* question that guides you to paragraph 5.

> There have been numerous major firenados in the last 150 years, many of which have proved lethal. In 1871, the great Peshtigo Fire in Northeastern Wisconsin and Upper Michigan resulted from inauspicious conditions: dry weather during the summer, slash-and-burn farming practices, and a vigorous cold front that brought strong winds. Together, these three contributing factors created firenados that turned a few small prairie fires into a furious conflagration. The town of Peshtigo, with hundreds of wooden structures and lumberyards, sat in the middle of a forest of pine and hardwood. When the fire reached the town, it found abundant fuel. In just minutes, 100-mph winds and ambient temperatures of more than 700°F caused what is still recognized as the worst fire disaster in the history of the United States. As best as anyone could tell, nearly 2,000 people lost their lives.

Once you've reviewed the paragraph, it's all about POE. Choice (A) is a reasonable match, because the passage says there have been "numerous major firenados in the last 150 years." Choice (B) is out because they *have* been documented—after all, you know they happened long before anyone who's alive today was even born. Choice (C) can be eliminated because nothing says that the fire in Peshtigo was the *first* known occurrence of a firenado. Choice (D) is suspicious because it says "*always* lethal," which you can't prove from the passage.

12. **C** This is a *vocabulary in context* question. Look at the lines from the passage.

> There have been numerous major firenados in the last 150 years, many of which have proved lethal. In 1871, the great Peshtigo Fire in Northeastern Wisconsin and Upper Michigan resulted from inauspicious conditions: dry weather during the summer, slash-and-burn farming practices, and a vigorous cold front that brought strong winds. Together, these three contributing factors created firenados that turned a few small prairie fires into a furious conflagration.

Looking at the sentence after the word in question, you see terms like "vigorous" and "strong" that describe the conditions from which the fire resulted. Together, these tell you that "inauspicious" means something negative. Try using POE. Choices (A) and (B) are positive, so eliminate them. Choice (D), "dangerous," is negative, and while the conditions did clearly prove to be dangerous, they were more (C), "unlucky."

13.   This is a *summary* question that requires you to consider the entire passage. On a summary question, don't choose answers that give specific details that are mentioned only once in the passage. Instead, choose answers that are broader and are supported throughout the passage. This passage has discussed how firenadoes are created and the damage they can cause. Therefore, the three points that show that "A firenado is one example of a natural phenomenon that is as uncommon as it is dangerous" are as follows:

- Firenados require a unique combination of conditions in order to occur.
  This answer shows that they are uncommon, because they require a "unique combination" of conditions.
- Firenados can cause significant damage.
  This answer shows that firenados are dangerous.
- Scientists don't know much about firenados because it is hard to predict where or when they will occur.
  This answer supports the idea that firenados are uncommon.

READING PRACTICE DRILL #3

1.   **B** This is a *vocabulary in context* question. Take a look at the lines in the passage.

> Certain cicadas spend most of their lives about 2 feet underground, feeding on fluids from the roots of trees in forests across the eastern United States. These particular species, called periodical cicadas, are developmentally synchronized, meaning they develop into adults all at the same time. There are seven distinct species of periodical cicadas, four of which have 13-year lifecycles and three of which have 17-year lifecycles. After the respective 13 or 17 years of a _____ lifestyle, the almost-mature cicada nymphs emerge at a given place and time in astounding numbers—as many as 1.5 million cicadas per acre.

Based on the information in the first sentence, a good word for the blank might be "underground." Thanks to POE, only (B) matches!

2.   **A** This is a *vocabulary in context* question. Take a look at the lines in the passage.

> After the respective 13 or 17 years of a subterranean lifestyle, the almost-mature cicada _____ emerge at a given place and time in astounding numbers—as many as 1.5 million cicadas per acre.

This one might feel tougher to fill in the blank. So, ask yourself what the surrounding words talk about: the cicada, which are almost-mature. Take the idea of "almost-mature" to the answers and do some POE: (A) is an almost exact match, so keep it for now. There's no indication in the passage of a "different species," so get rid of (B). The cicadas eat fluids from "roots of trees," which makes (C) sound like a good answer, but it doesn't match in meaning. And (D) is not mentioned at all, so eliminate it.

3. **D** This is a *reference* question: it's asking what noun the pronoun *this* replaces. Look at the passage.

> The nymphs wait for a spring evening when the soil temperature about 8 inches below the surface is above 64°F. For the four 13-year-cycle species, which tend to be further to the south and west of the eastern United Sates, this may be as early as late April or early May. But for the three 17-year-cycle species, which are generally found more toward the northern end of the eastern United States, this may not happen until late May or early June.

Ask yourself, what may be as early as late April or early May? The timing of temperature being just right for the nymphs to emerge. Take a look at the answers. Eliminate (A) because, though the entire passage is about cicadas, that's not what this question is asking about. Choice (B) doesn't match what we predicted, and neither does (C)—get rid of them. Choice (D), though, has to do with the temperature the nymphs need. There you go!

4. **C** This is a *detail* question, asking what the passage says about where periodical cicadas can be found. Go look in the passage for the lines that discuss this topic.

> For the four 13-year-cycle species, which tend to be further to the south and west of the eastern United Sates, this may be as early as late April or early May. But for the three 17-year-cycle species, which are generally found more toward the northern end of the eastern United States, this may not happen until late May or early June.

Now tackle some POE: (A), (B), and (D) don't match the geography mentioned in the passage, so eliminate them. The correct answer is (C). The cicadas can be found in the eastern United States.

5. **B** This is a *reference* question: it's asking what noun the pronoun *they* replaces. Look at the passage.

> Once they emerge they have only about 4–6 weeks to live. First they find a new home on plants near their emergence location where they complete their transition into full adult cicadas.

This question requires you to look back into the previous paragraph, because there is no noun earlier in the same sentence or same paragraph. What was the passage discussing in the preceding paragraph? The cicadas that had emerged. Take that to the answers. Choice (A) references where some of the cicadas emerge, but that's not what the pronoun is referring to, so get rid of it. Choice (B) is exactly what we'd predicted. Choices (C) and (D) haven't even been mentioned, so get rid of them.

6. **A** This is a *detail* question, so go back to the passage and look for the word *broods*.

> Based on the calendar year in which they emerge, periodical cicadas are divided into groups called broods. In 1898, entomologist C. L. Marlatt identified as many as 30 broods, although not all of them have actually been observed since then.

Using the first part of the first sentence, compare the answer choices. Choice (A) is an almost identical match to the passage, so keep it. Choice (B) doesn't match—the passage doesn't discuss the cicadas' lifecycle as the determining factor of their brood organization. Choices (C) and (D) also don't match what the passage says, so eliminate everything except (A).

7. **A** This is a *vocabulary in context* question, so look at the passage and think of a word you could put in place of the word in question.

> The membranes across the "ribs" of the tymbal vibrate quickly, and the cicada's body functions like a resonance chamber and _____ the sound. The cicadas can adjust the "volume" of their sound by turning their bodies in different directions.

If you're not sure what exact word to use, ask yourself what the word relates to. It has something to do with the sound that the cicadas make, and the next sentence says that the cicadas can adjust the "volume" of their sound. So it probably has something to do with adjusting the volume. Take a look at the answers. Would it make sense to "make louder" the sound, as in (A)? Well, it sounds weird when you say it, but the meaning makes sense, so keep it. Is this blank just talking about producing the sound, (B)? Maybe, but that's not as close as (A). Is it likely that the cicadas would do something that makes their sound worse? Probably not, so get rid of (C). And they're also not likely to degrade their own sound, so get rid of (D).

8. **B** This question asks you to find the sentence in the passage that serves a particular purpose, namely to describe how periodical cicadas attract mates. Go directly to the answers and use POE. Choice (A) discusses the purpose of cicadas' adult lives, not their mating habits, so get rid of it. Choice (B) talks about the males forming choruses to attract mates, so keep it. Choice (C) discusses the males' tymbals, not mating habits, so eliminate it. Choice (D) talks about the cicadas' populations, not mating habits, so get rid of that too.

9. **C** This is a *reference* question: it's asking which noun the pronoun *their* refers to. Look at the passage.

> As a result, when the cicadas do become prey, their predators can seemingly eat their fill without making a significant impact on the cicada population.

Ask yourself, who is eating? The predators. Now go take a look at the answers, and eliminate any that don't match. Eliminate (A), (B), and (D), and you're left with (C).

10. **D** This is a *sentence insertion* question. Recall that for this question type, you have to look at the sentences before and after the black squares to try to match the information in those sentences with the new sentence. Here's the sentence we are going to add:

> This phenomenon is known as "predator satiation," a situation in which prey occur at an incredibly high population that the probability of an individual organism being eaten is drastically reduced.

The "this" at the beginning of the sentence has to refer to something else before it, so it can't be inserted at the beginning of the paragraph—eliminate (A). The first and second sentences don't describe an event or phenomenon, so there's nothing for "this" in the inserted sentence to reference in either one. Eliminate (B) and (C). The last sentence, as the paragraph is currently written, describes predators being able to eat their fill without impacting cicada populations, which "this" could definitely reference. Putting the new sentence at the end of the paragraph, therefore, makes the most sense.

11. **C** This is a *detail* question, so go back to the passage for information. Look for the part of the passage that discusses emergence, more or less in the same area where you've already been working. Look at what it says:

> Most interestingly, though, is how they keep track of time and know when 13 or 17 years have passed. Alas, researchers don't actually know how they do it, other than knowing that it's some kind of molecular clock. The insects themselves make for difficult research, since researchers have to wait at least 13 years for a brood to reemerge!

With that information, take a look at the answers and see what matches. It's highly doubtful that insects have calendars, so eliminate (A). There is no evidence in the passage that the cicadas can track seasons, so eliminate (B). There is proof that scientists believe the cicadas have "some kind of molecular clock," which supports (C) and invalidates (D).

12. This *summary* question requires you to consider the entire passage. On a summary question, don't choose answers that give specific details that are mentioned only once in the passage. Instead, choose answers that are broader and are supported throughout the passage. The question asks you to find three points that support the following idea:

Periodical cicadas are unique creatures because of their unusual lifecycles and their lack of significant predators.

The correct answers are as follows:
- Four species have 13-year lifecycles.
    This answer supports the idea that these insects have unusual lifecycles.
- Periodical cicadas do not have many natural predators because their adult lifespan is so short.
    This answer supports the idea that these insects have no significant predators.
- Once periodical cicadas emerge, they live only 4 to 6 weeks.
    This answer supports the idea that these insects have unusual lifecycles.

READING PRACTICE DRILL #4

1.   **B**   This is a *reference* question: it's asking what noun the pronoun *it* replaces. Look at the passage.

> "Mandala" is a Sanskrit word meaning "circle." While it originated as a spiritual symbol in many Indian religions, the mandala has come to be known generically as a term for any diagram, chart, or geometric pattern that is intended to symbolically or metaphorically represent the cosmos.

Just after the comma in the sentence with "it," you can see that the passage says, "the mandala has come to be known…." This tells you that the "it" in question is referring to mandala. Use that as your basis for POE, and eliminate (A), (C), and (D).

2.   **A**   This is a *detail* question, so go back and see what the passage says.

> This pattern is found in many places in our world, including biology, geology, physics, astronomy, and chemistry. For example, even atoms are circular in nature, with evenly balanced protons, neutrons, and electrons. Every cell has a nucleus, which also has a circle at the center. Even the Milky Way galaxy is circular, with our circular solar system within it. One could argue that each of these is a mandala in and of itself.

The "for example" and the last sentence give us the key: …each of these is a mandala in and of itself. That means the author has listed them as examples of mandalas, or circles in our world. Using POE, (A) is a close match, so keep it. Choice (B) may be appealing, but it's not as precise as (A), so get rid of it. There is no mention of symbols or the cosmos in the passage, so eliminate (C) and (D).

3.   **C**   This is a *vocabulary in context* question, so look at the passage and think of a word you could put in place of the word in question.

> Carl Jung, the founder of analytical psychology, _____ that "a mandala is the psychological expression of the totality of the self." He sketched a small circular drawing every morning, and felt that whatever came to life in his mandala corresponded to his inner experience at the time.

A reasonable word to replace the word in question might be "believed" or "thought." POE gets rid of (A), (B), and (D).

4.   **B**   This is a *vocabulary in context* question, so look at the passage and think of a word you could put in place of the word in question.

> He found that during periods of significant _____ many of his clients felt compelled to create mandalas. He found that people felt drawn to drawing or painting mandalas simply because it felt right to do so—it seemed that they instinctively turned to creating a mandala as a way to express their challenging experiences.

The passage indicates that people felt compelled to create mandalas as a way to express their challenging experiences. So, replacing the word in question with "challenging experiences" could work. Now try some POE. Choices (A), (C), and (D) are all positive words that don't match "challenging experiences," so eliminate them. Choice (B) matches exactly.

5. **C** This is a *sentence insertion* question. Recall that for this question type, you have to look at the sentences before and after the black squares to try to match the information in those sentences with the new sentence. Here's the sentence we are going to add:

> Based on this belief and his recognition of his own internal evolution through the use of mandalas, he began to use them as a tool in his psychology practice.

This sentence uses pronouns like "this," "his," and "them," so ask yourself what these might refer back to. "His" likely refers to Carl Jung, and "them" refers to mandalas. Since the sentence describes how Jung used mandalas in his practice, which isn't mentioned until after the second square, eliminate (A) and (B). The last sentence describes the results of using mandalas in his practice, so it doesn't make sense to put this sentence at the end of the paragraph. Eliminate (D).

6. **A** This is a *detail* question, so go back to the passage, around the area where you looked to find support for the last question. Here's what it says.

> Why might humans have this instinct? Research into the fields of psychology and child development may shed some light on the subject. It would seem that circles are part of the basic creation of a personal identity. Studies conducted with babies show that as early as one week old, infants prefer to look at curved lines rather than straight lines. Additional research shows that two-month-old infants can discern shapes that look like faces from scrambled patterns. Psychologically, it is believed that simple, closed forms—like circles—are identified more quickly and recognized as meaningful, known, and familiar. Even the shape of an eye is spherical—simply put, it's a three-dimensional circle—and our field of vision is thus also circular.

The second to last sentence says "…closed forms—like circles—are identified more quickly…." As you use POE, eliminate any answers that are not "closed forms," which includes (B) and (D). Both circles, (A), and squares, (C), are closed forms, so now use the other part of the sentence that says "like circles" to eliminate (C).

7. **B** This is a *reference* question: it's asking what noun the pronoun *their* replaces. Look at the passage.

> He found that during periods of significant trial and tribulation many of his clients felt compelled to create mandalas. He found that people felt drawn to drawing or painting mandalas simply because it felt right to do so—it seemed that they instinctively turned to creating a mandala as a way to express their challenging experiences.

Ask yourself "whose challenging experiences is the author discussing?" It makes sense that the author is discussing the people who are drawing the mandalas, or his clients. Use POE to get rid of anything that doesn't match this idea, so get rid of (A), (C), and (D).

8. **D** This is a *detail* question, so go back to the passage, around the area where you looked to find support for the last question. Here's what it says.

> Circles also appear very early in children's art. What begins as random scribbling progresses into drawing circles as early as age two. By three or four years old, their drawings become more intricate, and without any input from adults they begin drawing suns, flowers, and people whose arms and legs connect to large circular heads.

The passage indicates that the detailed, representative pictures—suns, flowers, and people whose arms and legs connect to large circular heads—come about when children are three to four years old. This allows you to eliminate (A), (B), and (C).

9. **D** This question asks you to find a sentence that serves a particular purpose. In this case, it's asking you to find a sentence that "describes how drawing a mandala allows an adult to reestablish a connection with his or her subconscious." Go straight to POE and eliminate answers that don't serve that purpose.

Choice (A) discusses children's drawing, so eliminate it. Choice (B) discusses researchers' perspectives, so get rid of it. Choice (C) doesn't clearly state what it's describing, so get rid of it. Choice (D) discusses therapists' beliefs that mandalas are representative of internal issues and allow patients to align their conscious and unconscious actions and decisions, which matches the goal set forth by the question.

10. **D** This is a *reference* question: it's asking what noun the pronoun *they* replaces. Look at the passage.

> Professionals also believe that mandalas help us center psychologically, and they are still used in psychotherapy practice.

Ask yourself "what is used in psychotherapy practice?" Most likely, the mandalas. POE allows you to eliminate (A), (B), and (C). It's not likely that *people* are used in the psychotherapy practice!

11. **D** This is a NOT question, so be sure to eliminate answers that *are* mentioned in the passage.

Choice (A) is mentioned in the beginning of the first paragraph, so get rid of it. Choice (B) is mentioned at the end of the first paragraph, so it can also be eliminated. Choice (C) is discussed in the second and third paragraphs. Choice (D), however, is never mentioned.

12. This is a *summary* question that requires you to consider the entire passage. On a summary question, don't choose answers that give specific details that are mentioned only once in the passage. Instead, choose answers that are broader and are supported throughout the passage. The question asks you to find three points that support the following idea:

Mandala art has ancient roots and can play a therapeutic role for humans.

The correct answers are as follows:

- The term "mandala" comes from an ancient language and has been passed on for generations.

   This answer shows that mandala art has ancient roots.

- Many ancient traditions and religions used mandalas in their ceremonies.

   This answer shows that mandala art has ancient roots.

- Carl Jung, the founder of analytical psychology, found value in using mandalas with his patients.

   This answer shows that mandala art can play a therapeutic role for humans.

READING PRACTICE DRILL #5

1. **B** This is a *vocabulary in context* question, so look at the passage and think of a word you could put in place of the word in question.

   > What we call the Olympics—considered the world's _____ sports competition —are actually inspired by the ancient Olympic games. These ancient games were a series of athletic competitions that took place in Olympia, Greece, sometime between the 8th century B.C.E. and the 4th century C.E.

   There isn't really much in the passage to tell you exactly what word could go here, so try looking at the answers to see if any of them make sense. The passage says that the Olympics we know today were inspired by games from long ago. This would help to eliminate (A), because they're not the *first* games, and also (C), because they're not the *only* games to have ever existed. That at least brings you to a fifty-fifty shot at guessing. Then compare the two remaining choices. Is it more likely that the author would describe the Olympics as the world's "leading" sports competition, or as the "chief officer" sports competition? Choice (D) doesn't make sense, so get rid of it.

2. **C** This is a *detail* question, so go back to the passage, around the area where you looked to find support for the last question. Here's what it says.

   > These ancient games were a series of athletic competitions that took place in Olympia, Greece, sometime between the 8th century B.C.E. and the 4th century C.E. Free-born, Greek-speaking, male representatives from city-states across Greece gathered every four years to take part in various running, throwing, jumping, and chariot-riding competitions. While the competitions always took place in Olympia, athletes from any city-state or kingdom could compete—they simply had to meet the entrance criteria. Originally, the men wore loincloths during competitions. As time went on, they eventually competed in the nude, in part because the Olympics were a time to recognize and celebrate the strength of the human body. Because the men competed totally nude, though, married women were expressly forbidden to watch— under penalty of death!

   That is a *lot* of information to take in, so go to the answers and POE. The passage says the games started sometime around the 8th century B.C.E., so eliminate (A). It also indicates that they ended sometime around the 4th century C.E., so eliminate (B). There is proof that they took place in Olympia, Greece, so leave (C). Eliminate (D) because the passage says the games were open only to men, not to men and women.

3.   **A**   This is a *reference* question: it's asking what noun the pronoun *they* replaces. Look at the passage.

> Originally, the men wore loincloths during competitions. As time went on, they eventually competed in the nude, in part because the Olympics were a time to recognize and celebrate the strength of the human body.

Ask yourself, "who eventually competed in the nude?" Well, the competitors are the men. POE allows you to eliminate (B), (C), and (D).

4.   **B**   This is a *vocabulary in context* question, so look at the passage and think of a word you could put in place of the word in question.

> Because the men competed totally nude, though, married women were _____ forbidden to watch—under penalty of death!

What word could you put in the blank? Well, the word has to describe the way that married women were forbidden to watch the men compete nude. They were forbidden "under the penalty of death." That means it was a major deal for them to not watch. So something like "harshly" or "clearly" might make sense.

The women were not "quickly" forbidden—that wouldn't make sense, so eliminate (A). If you're not sure what "explicitly" means, leave (B) in. If it was such a big deal that married women were threatened with death for watching men compete, it's not likely that they were "gradually" forbidden, so eliminate (C). It's also not likely that they were forbidden "emotionally," so get rid of (D). All that's left is "explicitly," (B), which is a synonym for "clearly."

5.   **D**   This is a *vocabulary in context* question, so look at the passage and think of a word you could put in place of the word in question.

> Initially, the ancient Olympic games took place for only one day, but as events were added the festival _____ grew to five days. The initial competition was called the "stadion," which was a fairly short sprint of somewhere in the neighborhood of 200 meters, or the length of one stadium. The second race added sometime later was called the "diaulos," which was the length of one lap of the stadium, or about 400 meters. A few years after the advent of the diaulos, the "dolichos" was added to the races. It was somewhere between eighteen and twenty-four laps around the stadium, roughly three miles total.

The paragraph begins by describing the Olympic games "initially," and the "but" shifts the direction of the sentence. So, you might put something like "final" or "later" into the blank. With those definitions, POE allows you to eliminate (A), (B), and (C) because they do not match your prediction.

6. **A** This is a *detail* question, so go back to the passage, around the area where you looked to find support for the last question. Here's what it says.

> The Games, therefore, created an opportunity for the city-states to "compete" peacefully. In fact, these peaceful competitions led politicians to work together to create alliances, much like they do today.

The passage clearly states that the Games "created an opportunity for the city-states to 'compete' peacefully." This is an exact match to (A), so eliminate the other three.

7. **B** This is a *reference* question: it's asking what noun the pronoun *they* replaces. Look at the passage.

> The Games, therefore, created an opportunity for the city-states to "compete" peacefully. In fact, these peaceful competitions led politicians to work together to create alliances, much like they do today.

Ask yourself, "who creates alliances today?" Politicians. This is an exact match to (B), so eliminate the other three.

8. **D** This is a *vocabulary in context* question, so look at the passage and think of a word you could put in place of the word in question.

> The games didn't only involve athletic pursuits, though. Sculptors, poets, and other artists would gather for competitions and showcase their wares to passers-by, hoping to sell them art and turn them into _____.

What word could go in the blank? The passage indicates that the artists wanted to sell their wares to passers-by, hoping to turn them into _____. You could put "buyers" or "purchasers" in the blank. This directly matches (D), and it doesn't match (A), (B), or (C).

9. **C** This is a *detail* question, so go back to the passage, around the area where you looked to find support for the last question. Here's what it says.

> Just as historians debate when the first Olympic games were held, it is unclear why the ancient Greek Olympic games came to a halt.

So, historians are unclear about when the games began, and why they ended. Walk through POE. There is no question about where the first ancient Games took place, so eliminate (A). The passage also states that "the games also took on political importance, and were used by city-states to establish their dominance over other city-states," so eliminate (B). Historians are also clear that it was only men who took part in the ancient Games, so eliminate (D). That leaves (C), which is directly supported by the passage.

10. **C** This is a *sentence insertion* question. Recall that for this question type, you have to look at the sentences before and after the black squares to try to match the information in those sentences with the new sentence. Here's the sentence that may be inserted:

> He also paid for the entire restoration of the Panathenaic Stadium so it could be used to host future Games.

Ask yourself who might have paid for this? The only people mentioned in the paragraph are Evangelos Zappas and King Otto. It would make sense that Evangelos Zappas might want to pay, because he offered to underwrite, or pay for, a revival of the games. So it would then make sense to put this sentence somewhere close to this information. Eliminate (A) and (B)—they are too early in the paragraph. The question then is whether to put this sentence before or after the sentence about the first modern Games. Since he was paying for a revival, including the restoration of the stadium, it would make sense to put the new sentence in before the discussion of the modern Games taking place in the stadium. Eliminate (D)—it is too late in the paragraph.

11. **B** This is a *vocabulary in context* question, so look at the passage and think of a word you could put in place of the word in question.

> Some believe that Roman emperor Theodosius I, in an effort to spread Christianity, decreed that all pagan rituals and cults be eliminated. Others believe that his _____, Theodosius II, later demanded the destruction of all Greek temples, leaving the Olympics with nowhere to take place.

The sentence indicates that Theodosius II came "later,'" after Theodosius I. This gives insight that the word in the blank has something to do with "coming later" or "coming after." Take a look at the answers. Choice (A) can be eliminated because it's the exact opposite, but (B) matches, so leave it. A "contemporary," as in (C), is someone who lived in the same time, which doesn't match, so eliminate that answer. While the passage discusses competitors, that meaning doesn't fit here, so eliminate (D).

12. **A** This is a *vocabulary in context* question, so look at the passage and think of a word you could put in place of the word in question.

> Within another hundred years, in the early to mid-1800s, renewed interest also surfaced in Greece, when the Greek War of Independence _____ the country from Ottoman Rule in 1821.

Ask yourself, "what result would come from a War of Independence?" "Independence" or "freedom" would be perfect words for the blank. Choice (A) is a very close match, so leave it. Choices (B), (C), and (D), though, have nothing to do with independence or freedom, so eliminate all of them.

13. **B** This question asks you to identify what "their" is referring to. In this case, "their" means (B) the modern games, which have come a long way from their humble origins.

14.   This question asks you to match statements with the appropriate category. This type of question may not be worth your time on test day—it's going to take a LOT of time and energy. While it is worth 4 points, you may find that going to another passage, if you have one left to do, will give you the opportunity to get more points in the same amount of time you'd invest on this question.

To answer this question, you have to go back to many places in the passage to find proof for the answers. You may recall where to go based on where you looked for preceding questions. Here are the answers:

Ancient Games
- Had few competitions
- Women couldn't watch
- Held in honor of gods
- Attended by artists

Modern Games
- Interest began in London
- Elite sports competition
- Inspired by other games
- Were paid for by a philanthropist

READING PRACTICE DRILL #6

1. **C**
2. **A**
3. **B**
4. **D**
5. **B**
6. **D**
7. **A**
8. **A**
9. **C**
10. **B**
11. **C**
12. **D**

READING PRACTICE DRILL #7

1. **B**
2. **D**
3. **D**
4. **C**
5. **C**
6. **D**
7. **A**
8. **A**
9. **B**
10. **C**
11. **D**

12.
- The introduction of electric rail lines made it easier for people to travel long distances between work and home.
- Open land outside urban cores allowed for the development of affordable and attractive tract housing.
- The automobile has made it possible for people to travel quickly even without relying on public transportation networks.

READING PRACTICE DRILL #8

1. **A**
2. **B**
3. **D**
4. **B**
5. **C**
6. **D**
7. **A**
8. But the Harlem cabaret life of the period was definitely an important by-product of the new interest in Afro-American culture created by the movement, and this life strongly influenced the early poetry of Langston Hughes.
9. **B**
10. **D**
11. **C**
12. **A**

Chapter 10
Cracking the
Listening Section

The Listening section of the TOEFL consists of the following tasks:

- Four to six **academic lectures,** at least two of which contain classroom dialogue
  - Each lecture is three to five minutes long.
  - A lecture may involve one speaker or multiple speakers.
  - Each lecture is followed by six questions.
- Two to three **conversations** involving two or more speakers
  - Each conversation is three to four minutes long.
  - A conversation has 12–25 exchanges.
  - Each conversation is followed by five questions.
- You will have 60–90 minutes to complete the entire Listening section.

The Listening section measures your ability to follow and understand lectures and conversations that are typical of an American educational setting. You will hear each lecture or conversation only once, but you are allowed to take notes while you are listening.

As we mentioned in the early part of this book, the Listening scores are subdivided into three sections:

High (22–30). Students who score in the "High" range are able to understand a wide variety of conversation and lecture topics in both formal and informal settings. They are able to identify the most important concepts in a conversation or lecture, and understand how speakers use figurative language.

Medium (15–21). Students who score in the "Medium" range are able to understand most lectures and everyday conversations, but can find complex grammatical structures or colloquialisms occasionally confusing. These students can generally identify important points, but can become confused if contradictory ideas are presented.

Low (0–14). Scores in the "Low" range indicate basic ability to understand conversations and lectures, but will find abstract/complex topics and conversations with complex vocabulary or grammatical structures more difficult. These students are able to identify clearly stated main ideas, but may have difficulty connecting the dots on less obvious points.

At the beginning of the Listening section, you'll be instructed to put on your headset. An example of the screen is shown on the next page.

You'll also receive instructions on how to adjust the volume of the headset. Make sure the volume is at a comfortable level before the section begins.

LISTENING SECTION DIRECTIONS

You should be aware of a few special aspects of the Listening section before you take the TOEFL. First, unlike the Reading section, you are not allowed to skip questions and return to them later. *You must answer each question before you can proceed to the next one.* Second, some of the questions in the Listening section are heard, not read. These questions are indicated by a special headset icon, similar to what you've seen in this book.

It is important to be prepared for these audio questions. In this book, we use the headset icon to indicate when you should listen to the accompanying CD. On the actual test, you will only hear this material; it will *not* appear on your screen.

CRACKING THE LISTENING SECTION: BASIC PRINCIPLES

One of the most common mistakes students make in the Listening section is to try to do too much. Some students try to take notes on every detail offered, and they end up not hearing important information. Other students try to understand every single word in the lecture, and they panic when they miss a word or phrase. Neither of these approaches is very helpful on the test.

Instead, you must do your best to think of the lectures and conversations as being similar to the reading passages on which we've worked. Each lecture or conversation will have a purpose, a main idea, and supporting details. Your goal for the Listening section will be to find these items in each selection. Because there are only five or six questions per listening task, there is no need to memorize or comprehend every single detail.

The Listening section requires you to do the following:

1. **Find the main idea or purpose.** Each lecture or conversation will have a main idea or purpose. Find and note this theme, which is usually stated at the beginning of the discussion or talk.
2. **Focus on the structure.** Pay attention to how the main idea develops. Look for examples, comparisons, and cause-and-effect relationships.
3. **Listen for tone and attitude.** Try to figure out if the speakers are positive, negative, or neutral toward the topic.
4. **Pay attention to transitions.** Make sure you are listening for transition words and phrases. These help you follow the logic of the lecture or conversation.

We'll look at all of these points in more detail in a moment, but there are two other important things to keep in mind when you approach the Listening section.

- **Don't memorize.** As we said earlier, there is far too much information to try to memorize or retain. So, don't even bother trying. Keep in mind that the TOEFL is testing you on your ability to follow a logical flow of ideas, not on your ability to memorize information. Just relax and try to focus on the big issues, not the minor ones.

- **Don't take too many notes.** One easy way to get sidetracked on the Listening section is to write down too many notes. Writing requires your concentration, and if you're concentrating on writing, you're probably not concentrating on listening. Focus on listening; in fact, if you are not comfortable taking notes, don't take any at all.

Basic Principle #1: Find the Main Idea or Purpose

We've spent a lot of time practicing this step with reading passages. Now we will apply our understanding of the main idea or purpose to a listening task. Fortunately, the patterns in the Listening section are very similar to the patterns in the Reading section. Lectures are designed around a main idea, whereas conversations are centered on a purpose.

In **lectures,** the speaker will typically introduce the main idea at the very beginning of the talk. Listen for phrases similar to the following:

- "Okay, today I want to talk about...."
- "What we're going to talk about today is...."
- "Today, we're going to look at...."
- "Tonight, I wanted to look at...."

The professor will then follow with the topic of discussion. If you're taking notes, you should write the topic down. Once you have the main topic, you can expect the lecturer to provide a purpose, explanation, or more information.

In a **conversation,** the beginning sentences will reveal the speaker's purpose. Listen for the purpose to appear after an initial greeting, as in the following examples:

- "Hi, what can I do for you?"
- "Hello, how can I help you?"
- "What can I do for you today?"
- "Is there something I can do for you?"

After this initial question, the other speaker will state his or her purpose. Usually this involves asking for some sort of help or assistance. If you are taking notes, you should write down what the purpose of the conversation is.

Basic Principle #2: Focus on the Structure

After finding the main idea or purpose, focus on the structure of the talk. Lectures and conversations each have standard structures. Listen for them as you take the TOEFL.

Types of Lecture Structures

Most lectures will have one of the following basic structures.

Lecture Structure #1: Compare/Contrast This type of lecture involves finding similarities and differences between two or more things. Listen for the speaker to introduce this framework by using one of the following phrases:

- "several theories"
- "possible explanations"
- "many different views"

After the framework is introduced, the speaker will list each item to be discussed and mention its characteristics. Listen for words that indicate compare/contrast, such as the following:

- "in contrast"
- "on the other hand"
- "similarly"
- "however"
- "additionally"
- "also"

Lecture Structure #2: Cause-and-Effect Relationships   Some lectures attempt to explain why a certain situation occurs. Listen for the speaker to introduce this type of framework with the following phrases:

- "Why would this happen?"
- "What is the reason for this?"
- "How could this happen?"
- "What leads to this?"

If it seems that the speaker is describing a cause-and-effect situation, listen for the cause. A speaker will often use the following phrases to introduce the cause:

- "x causes y"
- "x results in y"
- "x produces y"
- "x leads to y"
- "x brings about y"
- "x is responsible for y"

After identifying the cause, look for the speaker to detail the effects with a phrase similar to the following:

- "y is caused by x"
- "y results from x"
- "y is due to x"
- "y can be blamed on x"
- "y is attributable to x"
- "y happens because of x"

Lecture Structure #3: Abstract Category/Specific Examples   Another common lecture structure involves moving from an abstract category to a specific example. A lecture may also sometimes begin with specific examples and end with a more general interpretation of the examples. A speaker may introduce an abstract concept with one of the following phrases:

- "one approach..."
- "one theory..."
- "the idea is..."
- "the concept..."
- "the basic premise is..."

Next, the speaker will move to the examples, typically using the following phrases:

- "for example..."
- "one instance of this is..."
- "consider..."
- "we see this in/with..."
- "this is illustrated by/with..."

Even if you have difficulty understanding the abstract idea, you can usually figure it out by paying close attention to the examples used.

Lecture Structure #4: Sequences   A lecture may present a series of steps or stages. Listen for the lecturer to mention the following clues:

- "process"
- "development"
- "stages"
- "transition"

The steps or parts will typically be introduced with clear transitions, such as

- "first...second...third..."
- "next..."
- "then..."
- "initially..."
- "finally..."

Types of Conversation Structures
Conversations on the TOEFL also fall into some predictable patterns. Try to identify the pattern when listening to the people speak.

Conversation Structure #1: Problem/Solution   This is a typical conversation type on the TOEFL. One student has a problem, and another student offers advice or a possible solution. Listen for the first student to introduce the problem by mentioning one of the following:

- "problem"
- "issue"
- "difficulty"
- "trouble"

After describing the problem, the other person will offer some sort of advice or solution. Listen for the following phrases:

- "why don't you..."
- "if I were you, I'd..."
- "maybe you should..."
- "have you tried/thought of..."

For this structure, it is important to listen for what the problem is and what steps or solutions the speaker may take to solve it.

Conversation Structure #2: Service Encounter   Another common conversation on the TOEFL is the service encounter. In this encounter, a student will discuss a problem with a professional—usually a professor, a librarian, or an office worker. The problem will be introduced in the same way as in the previous conversation type, but the response may differ. The service professional will usually explain *exactly* what the student needs to do to solve the problem. The solution may involve several parts. If so, listen for the following words to indicate the steps the student must take:

- "requirement"
- "application"
- "form"
- "recommendation"
- "prohibited"

Conversation Structure #3: Significant Event   Some conversations on the TOEFL revolve around a significant event. This could be a meeting, an announcement, or a social event. Usually, the first speaker will introduce the event with one of the following phrases:

- "have you heard about..."
- "did you see..."
- "let you know about..."
- "program/event/opportunity/chance"

After noting the event, listen to any details about it. Also note what the speaker's plans are concerning the event. Listen for the following key words:

- "participate"
- "plans"
- "open to"
- "free" or "busy"

Basic Principle #3: Listen for Tone and Attitude

Although you are unlikely to be asked a tone question in the Listening section, an understanding of the speaker's tone or attitude is helpful on many types of questions. Speakers on the TOEFL often use phrases or words that can have more than one interpretation. However, if you are aware of the speaker's tone, you are less likely to misinterpret the phrase.

For example, lecturers on the TOEFL often say something like the following:

> "...and after the war, the country experienced a prolonged period of economic growth, right?"

Even though the speaker *appears* to be asking a question, he or she is actually just *emphasizing his or her point*. Being aware of the tone will help you interpret statements such as this one.

The tone of most lectures is fairly straightforward. Because the speaker is teaching a class, the tone will usually be similar to one of the following types:

- **Objective:** The speaker is simply listing facts or providing information. The speaker is an authority on his or her subject and so will not be unsure or uncertain about the topic. This type of tone can appear in any of the four common lecture types.
- **Subjective:** In some cases, the speaker will be presenting a position or making an argument. The speaker will try to convince the listeners about a certain view. This type of tone is more likely to appear in *compare/contrast* and *cause-and-effect* lectures.
- **Inquisitive:** There are also classroom discussions on the TOEFL. During a discussion, the professor leads the class through a number of questions, so the tone is inquisitive. The professor considers and responds to the students' questions as the lecture progresses. *Abstract category/specific example* lectures typically involve discussion, although other lecture types may as well.

Conversations tend to have slightly more personal tones. You can expect the tone to be similar to one of the following types:

- **Excited:** This tone is typical of the *significant event* conversation. The speaker is interested in the event and may be trying to influence others about it.
- **Disappointed/upset:** In this case, the speaker is not happy about the situation. He or she may express dissatisfaction with things or events. This usually occurs during the *problem/solution* encounter, although it can appear in other conversations too.
- **Uncertain or confused:** Sometimes the speaker is uncertain or confused, especially in *service encounters*. The speaker will be unsure of what action to take or how to proceed.

Of course, you don't have to spend valuable time during your test trying to figure out the exact tone. However, having a basic idea of the tone—as well as of the purpose of the lecture or conversation—will aid you when you are eliminating answers.

Basic Principle #4: Pay Attention to Transitions

From your work on the Reading section of the TOEFL, you should have a pretty good understanding of the common transitions used in writing. These transitions show up in lectures and conversations as well, and it is good to note them. However, two other types of transitions to be especially alert for are *reversals* and *negations*.

Reversal Transitions

Often, speakers on the TOEFL will reverse the direction or logic of the conversation or lecture. If you're not listening carefully, you may misunderstand the speaker. For example, look at the following lines:

"First, I want to look at the mechanism by which single-celled organisms roproduoc...um, actually, let's come back to that in a moment. We need to talk about..."

In this situation, the speaker abruptly changes the topic. These reversals happen occasionally during lectures and somewhat more frequently during conversations. Here are some phrases to listen for.

- "you know what?"
- "we'll come back to that in a moment"
- "actually, let's"
- "instead"
- "better yet"
- "I don't want to get into that now"

Negation Transitions

Also, speakers will sometimes use a positive word to indicate a negation. Look for phrases like the following, where the negation words are italicized:

- "I don't have to explain that, *right*?"
- "You guys are okay with this, *correct*?"
- "We don't need to go into that now, *okay*?"

In each case, the speaker uses a positive word to express a negative statement. When used in this way, the positive words indicate that the speaker assumes the listener knows what the speaker is talking about and no further discussion or explanation is needed.

Reversals and negations can be tricky, but if you're on the lookout for them, they'll be easier to handle.

CRACKING THE LISTENING SECTION: BASIC APPROACH

Now we're ready to crack the Listening section. Here are the steps.

1. **Actively listen to the selection,** noting the main idea or purpose, structure, and tone.
2. **Attack the question.** There's no skipping in the Listening section, so you'll have to do each question as it appears.
3. **Use POE aggressively,** using your understanding of the main idea, previous questions, and any notes you've taken to help you.

Let's try the steps on a practice passage. Use your CD or online audio files to follow along.

Step 1: Actively Listen to the Selection

If you intend to take notes, take a moment to organize your scrap paper. Remember, you don't want to try to write down everything. Instead, as we've discussed, focus on the main topic, structure, and tone. Listen carefully for these parts and be sure to write them down.

Keep in mind the basic principles you have learned throughout this book. You should expect to hear the main idea or purpose at the very beginning of the speech and the majority of the details and supporting examples throughout the rest. A lecture or conversation usually will have a conclusion as well. Screens similar to the ones that follow will introduce each passage.

Headphones On!

When you are ready, play Track 3 on the accompanying CD or audio files online. After you are finished listening to the lecture and questions that follow, try to answer the questions below. If you are having difficulty answering the questions, replay the selection. A transcript of the lecture is also included on the next two pages for your reference. (But don't cheat and read along as you listen to the track!)

What is the *main idea* of the lecture?

_____
_____
_____

What is the *structure* of the lecture?

_____
_____
_____

What is the lecturer's *tone*?

_____
_____
_____

Let's look at a transcript of the lecture and find the important points.

Narrator: Listen to a biology professor give a talk on an environmental issue.

Professor: There's been a lot of talk over the last few decades about greenhouse gases—those gases in the atmosphere that trap radiation from the Sun so that after it passes into the atmosphere it doesn't pass out. People are increasingly conscious of the environmental effects of their daily activities, which is a good thing. But all the publicity can be confusing too. I think writing for the general public about science is a real service, but...well, it's not nice to say, but...I wish some of these people would verify things with real scientists more often. They'd save themselves some embarrassment.

With that in mind, I'd like to clear up some things about that hot topic: carbon dioxide. Carbon dioxide is a greenhouse gas; it absorbs energy from the Sun. In that respect, it's like water vapor and methane, two other naturally occurring greenhouse gases. You all know that carbon dioxide is produced when we burn fossil fuels—coal, petroleum products, natural gas—and that those fuels run a lot of the machines and manufacturing processes that drive modern life.

Those are the sources that get all the public attention, but, of course, we produce carbon dioxide as a waste product too. It's one of the by-products of respiration. We breathe in air, use up some of the oxygen, and breathe out air that contains carbon dioxide. So do other animals. Because carbon dioxide is part of the natural life cycle, nature has a way of dealing with it. How does nature control the amount of carbon dioxide floating around in the atmosphere?

Male Student: I thought the ocean soaked it up.

Professor: Yes, that's one way. Carbon dioxide is very soluble in water. Soluble...uh, I don't have to explain that one to you because the root's related to the word *dissolve,* right? So carbon dioxide is pulled readily out of the air and into the water. Now, the oceans also release some of their carbon dioxide, but on balance, they absorb more; so that means that, if we produce artificially more than would naturally be emitted through life processes, the ocean could, as Jason put it, soak it up.

Unfortunately, if we're looking for a solution to carbon dioxide pollution, the ocean isn't it, and that's because the ocean absorbs gases from the atmosphere very, very slowly. If we suddenly increased the amount of carbon dioxide we produced, current models suggest that it would take 1,000 years for it to mix into seawater. And even then, there would still be a small amount left. So over the short and medium term, we can't rely on the ocean to take up the slack for us.

Okay, so that's one way nature deals with carbon dioxide. What's the other?

Female Student: Plants, isn't it? I mean, plants breathe carbon dioxide the way we breathe air.

Professor: Sure—I was actually kind of surprised that wasn't the one mentioned first. Yes, plants require carbon dioxide for photosynthesis. The more dense the growth of large plants, the more carbon dioxide is absorbed. Such an area—including forests of large, old-growth trees, and also the ocean—where carbon dioxide is absorbed in large quantities, is called a carbon sink. The carbon dioxide gas is sucked in kind of the way water is sucked down the drain in your sink after you wash the dishes. In fact, in the ocean, there are algae, seaweed...um, other kinds of marine plants too that rely on carbon dioxide to perform photosynthesis, just like the green plants on land. It's just that algae are far, far smaller.

Now, here's something interesting: Like the ocean, green plants release carbon dioxide into the atmosphere as well as absorb it—uh, when a plant dies...you know, if it burns in a forest fire or just dies of old age and decays, then its carbon dioxide is back in the air. So it only holds it in over its lifetime. However—this is the interesting part—unlike the ocean, green plants soak up carbon dioxide to use it—to make the energy they need to live and grow. So what they've found in some regions...populated, industrialized regions...is that increased levels of carbon dioxide can stimulate plant growth. There's more of the fuel the plants need for energy, so they grow more green and dense and lush and use more of it—in other words, the amount of carbon dioxide used up by plants can increase quickly in response to the environment. Some people have suggested that we can use that natural phenomenon to help deal with increased levels of greenhouse gases in the atmosphere.

Narrator: What is the discussion mainly about?

What is the problem with relying on the oceans to solve the problem of excess amounts of carbon dioxide? Why does the professor mention that carbon dioxide is a by-product of respiration? What did the professor call areas where carbon dioxide is absorbed in large quantities? What did the professor mean by this?

As stated earlier, expect the main idea to show up early in the lecture. The very first sentence of the lecture gives us the topic.

"There's been a lot of talk over the last few decades about greenhouse gases—those gases in the atmosphere that trap radiation from the Sun so that after it passes into the atmosphere it doesn't pass out."

A little later on, the professor specifies exactly what aspect of greenhouse gases the lecture will discuss.

"With that in mind, I'd like to clear up some things about that hot topic: carbon dioxide."

From these lines, we have the *basic purpose* of the lecture. Hopefully, you are now on the lookout for the things the professor wants to clear up. The professor continues to talk about two major areas. The first is in the following lines:

Professor: How does nature control the amount of carbon dioxide floating around in the atmosphere?

Male Student: I thought the ocean soaked it up.

Professor: Yes, that's one way.

This is the first important *detail* in the lecture. You may have noticed that the professor also mentioned the following:

"Unfortunately, if we're looking for a solution to carbon dioxide pollution, the ocean isn't it, and that's because the ocean absorbs gases from the atmosphere very, very slowly."

These lines have a good *tone* indicator ("unfortunately") and a good *transition* ("and that's because"). You should also note that the professor repeats the fact about the ocean not being suitable for absorbing carbon dioxide in the next four lines as well, so you have a few opportunities to pick up this important point.

The next major detail occurs here.

> *Professor:* Okay, so that's one way nature deals with carbon dioxide. What's the other?
>
> *Female Student:* Plants, isn't it? I mean, plants breathe carbon dioxide the way we breathe air.

The professor continues with the following, which you may have noted:

> However—this is the interesting part—unlike the ocean, green plants soak up carbon dioxide to use it—to make the energy they need to live and grow.

Once again, the lecturer uses strong *transitions,* such as "however," and *tone* words, such as "interesting part," to alert you to important details. If you were able to pick up on these parts of the lecture, chances are you'll be in pretty good shape for the Listening section. As we've mentioned before, you're *not* expected to memorize or comprehend every detail of the lecture.

Here are some possible responses to the earlier questions.

- What is the *main idea* of the lecture? <u>Oceans and plants are nature's way of controlling carbon dioxide.</u>
- What is the *structure* of the lecture? <u>It's mostly compare and contrast. Two methods are looked at.</u>
- What is the lecturer's *tone*? <u>Mostly neutral, with occasional positive ("here's the interesting part") and negative ("unfortunately") digressions.</u>

You'll find that a basic understanding of these major points will help you to answer most of the questions following the lecture or conversation. The important thing is not to become stressed or worried that you didn't understand every single part of the talk.

Step 2: Attack the Questions

The questions in the Listening section are very similar to the questions in the Reading section. Of course, the major differences are that you will hear the lecture or conversation only *once* and that you will *not* be able to skip questions and come back to them later.

The following types of questions appear most often in the Listening section:

1. **Main idea questions:** The first question of the set will typically be a main idea question. Considering the work you've done up to this point, the main idea question shouldn't be too difficult for you to answer. However, we'll go over some POE strategies just in case.
2. **Detail questions:** The majority of the questions following the lectures or conversations will ask about facts from the selections. The details will not be about minor points, but rather about major points.

3. **Purpose questions:** Some questions will ask you *why* the speaker mentioned a particular detail or fact. For these questions, it is helpful to think about the overall structure of the selection.

4. **Definition questions:** Often, during a lecture (definitions rarely, if ever, show up in conversations), the lecturer will define a particular term for his or her students. Pay attention if you hear the speaker signal a definition with one of the following expressions:
   - "A *caucus* **is** a secret party meeting."
   - "A *caucus* **is defined as** a secret party meeting."
   - "A *caucus* **is the word used for** a secret party meeting."

   Sometimes the speaker will reverse the order of the term and the definition.
   - "A secret party meeting **is known as** a *caucus.*"
   - "A secret party meeting **is called** a *caucus.*"
   - "A secret party meeting **is referred to as** a *caucus.*"

   Finally the definition may be placed in the middle of a larger phrase.
   - "A *caucus*—a secret party meeting—is usually held in emergencies."
   - "A *caucus,* **that is,** a secret party meeting, is usually held in emergencies."
   - "A *caucus,* **or** a secret party meeting, is usually held in emergencies."

5. **Inference or suggestion questions:** The TOEFL will often test your ability to "read between the lines" (or more precisely, "listen between the lines"). There will often be questions asking what the speaker is suggesting or what he or she really means by a particular phrase. A person will often suggest something by using one of the following phrases:
   - "**Why not** come back later?"
   - "**How about** coming back later?"
   - "**What about** coming back later?"
   - "**Why don't you** come back later?"
   - "**If I were you, I'd** come back later."
   - "**You should** come back later."
   - "**You could always** come back later."
   - "**Maybe you could** come back later."
   - "**It may not be a bad idea** to come back later."

   Each of these constructions is a way of expressing the same basic idea that someone may return later.

6. **Multiple-multiple-choice questions:** Some questions in the Listening section require you to select more than one example. Many times, these questions ask you to list the main details or points made in the lecture.

Step 3: Use POE Aggressively

Because you are unable to listen to the lecture or conversation more than once, you'll have to focus on using good POE strategies when answering the questions. If you've missed a key point of the lecture or conversation, you can still increase your chances of getting a question correct by eliminating answers that aren't likely to be correct.

Before we go through the question types and the POE strategies, you may want to listen to Track 3 on the accompanying CD or online one more time. We'll identify the question types and apply test-taking techniques to work through the questions that follow.

Main Idea Questions

Question 1 is a typical main idea question on the TOEFL.

As we saw earlier in our active listening section, the speaker began by talking about carbon dioxide and mentioned two major ways that carbon dioxide is absorbed by nature—by oceans and by plants. Thus, (C) is the best answer.

Here's why the other answer choices are incorrect.

- For main idea questions, wrong answer choices may be *too specific*. For example, (B) talks only about plants. Even if you weren't sure exactly what the lecture was about, you may have noticed that plants did not appear until the end of the lecture. Any details that you hear mentioned only toward the *end* of the lecture will *never* be the main idea.

- Of course, some answers will contain information that is *not mentioned* at all. Choice (A) states that the lecture was about a "solution" for pollution. But no solution was offered. Even if you feel that you missed something important during the lecture, be aggressive. The lecture mentioned two key points: the ocean and plants. Choice (A) states there is "one solution." The great thing about a multiple-choice test is that there are usually a few ways to look at wrong answers.

- Questions on the TOEFL will also typically contain a *trap* answer, which uses words or phrases from the lecture or conversation in a deceptive manner. Choice (D) is a good example of a trap answer. The first part of the choice talks about "two ways." This matches up with the two key examples used in the lecture. Next, the choice talks about "carbon dioxide," which obviously is part of the lecture also. Finally, the choice contains "the ocean," a match with one of the examples in the lecture. Unfortunately, the lecture is about two ways *nature* absorbs carbon dioxide, not two ways the ocean absorbs it. The lesson here is that if you are uncertain of the right answer, and if one of the choices seems too good to be true, it's a trap.

Still, be careful to use this advice only when you're stuck; otherwise, you'll drive yourself crazy over-analyzing the answer choices.

- One other wrong answer type that may appear on a main idea question is a choice that is *too broad*. This is the opposite of an overly specific answer choice. For example, suppose there had been the following answer choice:

(E) The effect of environmental issues on everyday life

This answer is too general. The lecture does have an environmental theme, but the correct answer has to reflect more of the details of the talk, not just the basic idea.

POE Strategies for Main Idea Questions   When answering a main idea question, make sure you avoid the following answer types:

- **Answers that are *too specific*:** Remember that the main idea should be something that ties into the entire lecture. If the answer choice focuses on a detail that you remember hearing only once, it is too specific. Similarly, an answer choice that focuses on something that is mentioned only toward the end of the lecture will not be correct.

- **Answers that are *too broad*:** If the answer choice deals with a topic or theme mentioned early in the lecture but doesn't address the *details* of the talk, it is too broad and therefore incorrect.

- **Answers that are *not mentioned*:** The TOEFL is not a memorization test. If you don't recall hearing anything about the focus of a particular answer choice, then that choice is most likely incorrect. The selections on the TOEFL are centered on a topic and continually refer back to it; thus, it is unlikely that you somehow missed the main idea.

- **Answers that are *traps*:** Use this only as a last resort. If you are really stuck on a question, avoid answers that seem too good to be true.

Once you've answered the main idea question, keep the answer you've selected in mind. It can help you on some of the other questions.

Detail Questions

As you know from the Reading section, detail questions ask you about specific facts from the discussion. Fortunately, the wrong answers to detail questions in the Listening section tend to be a little more obviously wrong. Question 2 is a typical detail question.

The answer to this question was one of the key points in the lecture. Recall that the professor alerted us to an important point by saying the following:

"Unfortunately, if we're looking for a solution to carbon dioxide pollution, the ocean isn't it, and that's because the ocean absorbs gases from the atmosphere very, very slowly."

We noted this because of the speaker's use of the important tone indicator word *unfortunately*. Thus, the correct answer is (B).

If you are having trouble identifying the incorrect answer, you may still be able to eliminate some answers. *Extreme* answers, for example, are usually incorrect. You've seen these answers in the Reading section, and they appear in the Listening section as well. Choice (C) is a good example of an extreme choice. It makes a pretty absolute statement: that oceans have "absorbed their limit" of carbon dioxide. Many extreme answers use words such as the following:

always	*never*	*all*
none	*every*	*everything*
nothing	*only*	*impossible*

Another way of eliminating answers on detail questions is to cross off choices that are *contrary to the main idea*. For example, in this lecture, if you were able to figure out that the speaker gave oceans and plants as the two main examples, you should eliminate (D) because that focuses on marine plants, which was a separate example in the lecture.

If you keep your eyes out for these two common types of wrong answers, you will have a 50 percent chance of getting the question right; those odds aren't so bad!

POE Strategies for Detail Questions   When you are stumped on a detail question, don't give up. Look for the following types of answers and eliminate them:

- *Extreme* answers: Compare the answers. Eliminate any with extreme wording and go with the safe answer. Correct answers on the TOEFL often use fairly bland language.
- Answers that are *contrary to the main idea*: Even if you are uncertain of a specific detail from the selection, you may be able to use your understanding of the main idea to eliminate choices.

Detail questions may also have *trap answers*. Unfortunately, these answers are harder to identify than those on main idea questions. But again, if all else fails, try not to pick answers that seem too obvious or easy.

Purpose Questions

It is important to try to pay attention to the structure of the selection as you listen. If you grasp the structure, it will make purpose questions, like the following one, easier.

3. Why does the professor mention that carbon dioxide is a by-product of respiration?

   a. To emphasize the importance of carbon dioxide to life on Earth

   b. To explain the need for more scientific writings about the environment

   c. To provide some background information for a discussion of carbon dioxide

   d. To give an example of the dangers of environmental pollution

Before trying to answer this question, think about the structure of the lecture. We saw earlier that the professor looks at two key examples (oceans and plants) and compares and contrasts them. Although the lectures on the TOEFL may have some minor digressions, most of the information should in some way relate to the big picture. That means you can safely eliminate answers that seem to introduce *new ideas*. For example, (B) should be eliminated. The lecture is not about scientific writings (although they are mentioned once, they never appear again). Similarly, (D) can be eliminated as well: the lecture doesn't focus on environmental pollution or its dangers.

That leaves (A) and (C). Once again, think about the big picture and look for the answer containing information that is *contrary to the main idea*. Choice (A) talks about "life on Earth." But half of the lecture is about the ocean, which is not alive, so eliminate (A). That leaves us with (C) as the correct answer.

POE Strategies for Purpose Questions   Keep the main idea in mind as you attack purpose questions. Get rid of answers that contain the following:

- **New ideas:** The purpose of examples and details is to support the main idea. Answer choices that contain new information not related to the main idea are wrong.
- **Information contrary to the main idea:** You should also eliminate any answers that seem to go against the main idea of the lecture.

Definition Questions

Definition questions require you to recall a very specific part of the lecture. Thus, they can be very difficult. Question 4 is an example of one.

Unfortunately, if you didn't catch this part of the lecture, POE won't help you much. You can use your knowledge of the words and common sense to eliminate choices, but if you're unsure of the words, you'll have to take a blind guess.

The professor defined the word at this point in the lecture:

"Such an area—including forests of large, old-growth trees, and also the ocean—where carbon dioxide is absorbed in large quantities, is called a carbon sink. The carbon dioxide gas is sucked in kind of the way water is sucked down the drain in your sink after you wash the dishes."

Therefore, the correct answer is (A).

POE Strategies for Definition Questions   Your best option when trying to use POE on definition questions is to

- **Use your vocabulary:** If you happen to know one or more of the words in the answer choices, see if any of the words will work. It is unlikely that the correct definition for a question on the TOEFL will be radically different from the standard definition of the word.

Inference/Suggestion Questions

For inference and suggestion questions, you will often hear a portion of the speech replayed before you answer the questions. When a portion of the lecture is going to be repeated, you will always see a screen similar to the one below.

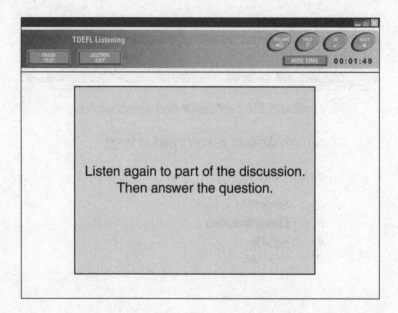

On the actual test, the excerpt from the selection will not appear on the screen; you will only hear it.

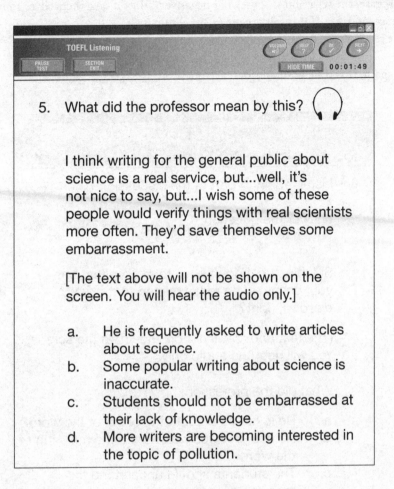

For these types of questions, we have to figure out what the speaker is *really* saying.

The phrase in question contains a suggestion.

"I wish some of these people would verify things with real scientists more often."

Thus, the speaker is indicating that she thinks the writers need to verify their work. The next part of the selection clarifies this suggestion further.

"They'd save themselves some embarrassment."

Let's start eliminating some answers.

- Choice (A) is on the *wrong topic*. The speaker is stating his wish for other people's writing, not making a suggestion to himself; that wouldn't make sense. Eliminate it.
- Choice (C) has the same problem. The professor is talking about *writers*, not students.

- Choice (D) has the *wrong tone*. Even if you're not exactly sure what the speaker is trying to say, you may be able to identify the selection as positive or negative. In this case, the selection is somewhat negative ("They'd save themselves some embarrassment"), but (D) is fairly *positive*. So eliminate it.
- We're left with (B) as the correct answer.

Let's try it again, this time with an inference question.

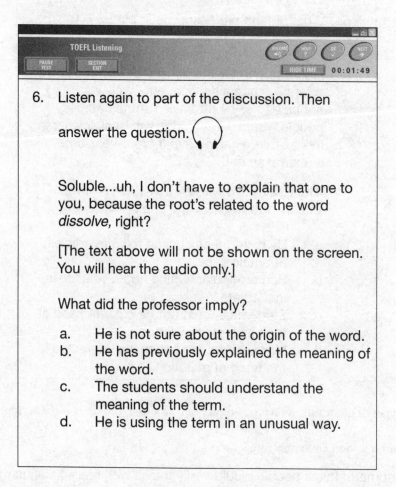

This selection contains a good example of the negations we mentioned earlier when discussing transitions. As used in this context, the word *right* means that the speaker assumes the students understand the topic without needing any further explanation. We also have some POE options on this question.

- Choice (A) is on the *wrong topic*. The professor is addressing the students, not himself. Eliminate this choice.
- Choice (D) has the *wrong tone*. The professor is indicating that he doesn't "have to explain" the term, so it doesn't make sense for him to use the term in an unusual way and not explain it.
- That leaves (B) and (C). Choice (B) is tempting, but we have no way of knowing whether it's true; remember that on the TOEFL, we should be able to support our inferences.
- Therefore, (C) is the best answer.

POE Strategies for Inference or Suggestion Questions The three most important POE strategies for these questions are to pay attention to the following types of answers:

- **Wrong topic:** Stick to the topic. Think about the main idea, and eliminate answers that don't relate to it. Also, eliminate answers that don't make sense based on your understanding of the selection.
- **Wrong tone:** Even if you're unsure of what the speaker is saying, you may be able to figure out the tone. Decide if the speaker views the subject as positive or negative, and eliminate answers that don't work.
- **Extreme:** Inference and suggestion questions often have extreme answer choices as well. If you see one, eliminate it.

Multiple-Multiple-Choice Questions

These questions ask you to select more than one answer. You must rely on your knowledge of the main idea and the structure of the selection to answer them correctly. Question 7 is an example of this type.

As you can see, it's important while you're listening to try to understand the structure of the lecture. This lecture involved a *comparison and contrast* between two ways in which carbon dioxide is absorbed by nature. You may remember that the professor hinted that some important information was about to come when he made the following statement:

"However—this is the interesting part—unlike the ocean, green plants soak up carbon dioxide to use it—to make the energy they need to live and grow."

Thus, we know that plants use the carbon dioxide they absorb. Now, let's use POE. You may have noticed that both (A) and (C) contain *extreme* language: the words "never" and "immediately." Thus, in this instance as well as with other questions on the TOEFL, they're wrong. So, even if you didn't remember the exact differences mentioned in the talk, you can still get the question right.

POE Strategies for Multiple-Multiple-Choice Questions Multiple-multiple-choice questions are typically either *detail* questions or *main idea* questions, so use the same POE strategies provided earlier in this chapter.

FINAL TIPS FOR THE LISTENING SECTION

Tip 1: Know the Test, and You're Halfway There!

Because the New Generation TOEFL iBT Test is given on such a grand scale, just like any standardized test, appropriations have been made so that every official ETS iBT test you take essentially looks the same. This includes everything from the instructions on the screen to test day procedures. And, since ETS has done their utmost to make sure there are no major changes made to the test to throw you off or trip you up, knowing the test will only help YOU save precious moments on the test. Remember, "Knowing is half the battle."

Tip 2: Scratch Paper—Use it WISELY

As you probably already know, scratch paper is provided to you on all sections of the New Generation TOEFL iBT Test. While this fact can help you keep things in order on the Reading section and help you brainstorm on the Writing section, scratch paper should be your staple weapon of choice on the Listening and Speaking sections. "Why," you ask?

The answer is simple. On the Reading section, the reading passages are always there as a veritable safety net for you to fall back on and check your answers with as you go along. Because you have only ONE chance to listen to the conversations and lectures in the Listening and Speaking sections, your notes must be thorough enough that you catch as many details as possible. (This does NOT mean, however, that you have to write down the conversations and lectures verbatim, because NO ONE on Earth writes that fast!) These excellent notes will be yours to look at for as long as you need to during the test (The notes are collected and destroyed at the end of every test.) Remember, if you think it's important, WRITE IT DOWN!

Tip 3: Know Your Vocabulary!

The English language is vast, and while the exact number of words in the English language is a hotly debated topic, it never hurts to know more vocabulary words. Because the topics covered on the TOEFL iBT do not range out of a certain scope of academic topics, knowing the jargon used in those fields will benefit you greatly. Since seeing a word in context is the fastest way to improve your working vocabulary—a vocabulary that you can readily use—read as much as you can and watch your vocabulary soar to new heights! Check out Chapter 6 for a helpful vocabulary list with terms, definitions, pronunciation, and more.

Tip 4: Do What You Can To Prepare

Tip 3 told you to read as much as you can as a way to improve your working vocabulary. However, doing this alone will not improve your English ability. You also need to hear how the words are spoken. In English, as in other languages, HOW something is said is just as important as WHAT is said. Thus, intonation plays a role in how what you say gets received. You should not only listen to English, but REPEAT what you hear, as well. If imitation is the best form of flattery, then why not imitate NATIVE speakers of English?

NOTE TAKING

The Ten Commandments of Note Taking

1. Don't write everything you hear. When listening, be alert and attentive. Pay attention to the main points. Concentrate on the meat of the material, not the fat.
2. USE KEY WORDS! Notes should NEVER be in full sentences.
3. Take accurate notes. Paraphrase what the speaker says using your own words, but do not change the meaning. If you are going to quote directly, quote correctly.
4. Think BEFORE you start writing. Write down only things that are important. Do not take notes just to take notes.
5. Have a uniform system of abbreviations or shortcuts that make sense to you. Use an outline with indentations to show importance. Leave space for additional notes.
6. BE CONCISE! Keep your notes short and to the point.
7. Don't worry if you miss a point.
8. Don't keep notes on oddly shaped pieces of paper. You don't want to take notes on a napkin and accidentally throw your notes away!
9. Shortly after finishing your notes, go back and fill in spots you missed and spell out words you wrote only parts of the first time.
10. Review your notes regularly.

THE FIVE R'S OF NOTE TAKING

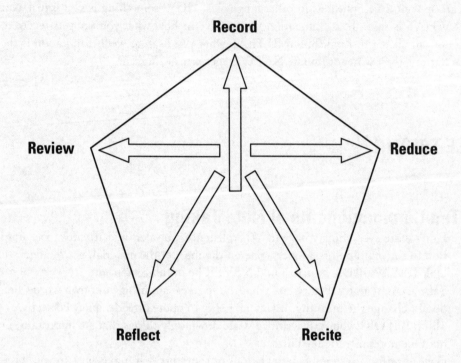

Record	During the lecture, write down as many meaningful facts as possible. Write legibly.
Reduce	Don't try to write everything. Listen to part of the lecture and paraphrase what the speaker has said. Summarizing clarifies meaning, strengthens relationships between ideas, and strengthens memory.
Recite	Cover the details of your notes and attempt to summarize what you have just heard using only the keywords. This will help you internalize the material faster.
Reflect	The best students will look back on their notes and categorize them in their mind. Putting things into categories, outlines, or other structures will help when trying to access the information at a later date.
Review	If you spend ten minutes a day reviewing your notes, you will spend less time cramming for tests. You will feel more relaxed going into a test and score better as well!

6 HABITS OF BAD LISTENERS

1. Thinking the Subject Matter is Boring

Everyone has subjects they don't like. Most people have a favorite subject in school. Have you noticed that you pay more attention in the classes you like?

All you have to do is remember one tiny word and you'll be okay: USE. Good listeners will try to find SOMETHING practical in what the speaker is saying so the listener may use it later on.

2. Criticizing the Speaker

Have you also noticed that school subjects and whether or not you like them also affects what you think about the teacher? Many students feel the teachers of the classes they like are prettier or more handsome, smile more, and are nicer! This is WRONG!

Since you will not be tested on HOW the speaker speaks, whether he or she speaks with an accent, or speaking speed, DO NOT CRITICIZE these things!

Even though the speaker's style might be annoying, good listeners soon become oblivious to the speaker's mannerisms and pay attention to the speaker's content. Good listeners know that WHAT the speaker is saying is ten times more important than HOW he or she says it.

3. Pay Attention

Too many times, we let little things about a speaker bother us. Sometimes it can be as simple as how a certain word is said, or the speaker's accent. Either way, if we pay attention to these kinds of things and not to what the speaker is saying, we will miss the important points the speaker is trying to make.

Sometimes, the problem is that what the speaker is saying comes in conflict with our own opinions and because that bothers us, we tune the speaker out because we don't like hearing about things we don't agree with. This can be especially dangerous, because whether or not we agree with what is being said, we should be paying attention. After all, it could be on the test!

4. Organization

We mentioned earlier that organization while taking notes is very important. While your personal organization is very important, understanding the speaker's organization is equally, if not more, important. If you know what the speaker's main purpose is and you are able to figure out the organization (sometimes this is given in the opening statements of the speaker's lecture), you will be better able to anticipate what the speaker is going to say. Expecting someone to say something is one of the tactics of successful active listeners.

5. Main Ideas vs. Details

The more things you listen to, as well as the more often you are required to take notes, the better you will get at each of these practices. You must be able to distinguish between main ideas and minor details quickly. The quicker you are able to do this well, the better organized your notes will be. This will allow you to find information easier when the time comes to access your notes.

6. Take Notes While You Listen

While you are listening, make sure you are writing things down, not getting lost in the speaker's lecture. Sometimes what the speaker is saying can be overwhelming, but just as Rome wasn't built in a day, you won't get better at note taking unless you practice a lot. The more often you take notes while you listen to something, the more information you will retain.

Listening Summary

Good job! You are halfway through your TOEFL preparation. Here are some important points to remember that will help you crack the Listening section.

- **Don't memorize; understand!** The most common mistake on the Listening section is to try to do too much. Look for the big picture: main idea, structure, and tone. Don't get lost in the details.

- **Taking notes is optional:** If taking notes interferes with your ability to comprehend what you're listening to, then don't do it. Take notes only if you are able to write and maintain your focus on the selection.

- **If you do choose to take notes, remember the Five R's of note taking:** record, reduce, recite, reflect, review.

- **Know what bad answers look like:** Make sure you're familiar with the kinds of bad answers that appear most frequently on the TOEFL.

- **Stay aggressive!** If you don't catch an important detail, don't panic. Stay aggressive and eliminate answers based on your knowledge of the main idea, structure, tone, and previous questions.

Now that we've worked with the passages and lectures on the TOEFL, it's time to create some passages and speeches of our own. Let's practice the Listening section with some drills, and then move on to the Speaking and Writing sections.

4. **A** As with any colloquial expression, pay attention to the way the ideas are connected: the first sentence presents a question, and the second one includes an answer to that question. Find the answer that comes closest to describing that relationship, like (A).

5. **A, C** Hopefully this is in your recent memory, because Louis Armstrong was the last major topic discussed. Use Process of Elimination as effectively as you can, and you should at least be able to get rid of (D). Bringing in a bit of common sense, you could likely get rid of (B): yes, he was an accomplished musician, but that doesn't necessarily address why he appealed to both White American and African American audiences. This would leave you with (A) and (C).

6. **A** Once again, keep the main idea of the lecture in mind: ethnic/national identity. Eliminate answers that aren't in line with that idea. This will lead you directly to (A), since it's the only that deals with identity.

LISTENING PRACTICE DRILL #4: A LECTURE

Here is a transcript of the second lecture. Try to use the active reading strategies you learned to identify the key parts.

Obesity. Pretty much everyone recognizes it's a serious problem. Recent statistics indicate that nearly 78 million adults and 13 million children in the United States alone deal with the physical and emotional effects of obesity every day. It would seem like the solution is easy, wouldn't it? Eat less and move more. Or in other words, consume fewer calories and increase the number of calories burned through physical activity. And yet, more than 90 million Americans continue to battle the bulge. What makes it so difficult to lose weight? Experts believe there are a number of contributing factors.

One consideration is that for some folks, the system that sends signals back and forth between organs such as the stomach and the brain is out of whack. So what can happen is that when the stomach sends a signal to the brain to stop taking in food, the brain doesn't recognize it and so the person just keeps eating. And as if that alone wasn't bad enough, at the end of a meal the "reward system" can come in to play. How so? Well, think about the last time you were at a restaurant and you were convinced that you were absolutely stuffed, and then the waitress brought over the dessert tray. Those desserts looked pretty tempting, didn't they? Turns out that's because of your "reward system." It can make you want to eat whether you're hungry or not when you see or smell appetizing food. No wonder reducing the number of calories consumed can be so challenging!

So, we're eating too much. But, experts also believe we're eating too much of the wrong foods, too. Most folks eat more than they should of red meat, unhealthy fats, refined grains, and processed food—never mind fast food options! What that ends up meaning is that we're eating fewer healthy foods, like fruits and vegetables, whole grains and nuts. Without these foods in our diets, we're not getting all of the nutrition our body needs. Some experts believe this causes us to eat even more of those same unhealthy foods in a desperate attempt to get all of the nutrients it craves.

Experts also believe that societal factors may contribute to difficulty losing weight. Think back to that last dinner at a restaurant again. Think about the size of your meal. Would you be surprised to learn that in the last 50 years restaurant portions have quadrupled in size?! And we haven't even talked about the increase in the size of beverages. Serving sizes of beverages have actually increased by a factor of 6 in the same time frame!

But wait, there's more! It's not all about calories in—it's also about calories out. Today's Americans move a whole lot less than those of 50 years ago did. Our jobs require us to sit behind desks more. We spend more of our 'down time' behind a screen of some variety—surfing the web or streaming a show on a laptop or tablet, watching TV, or playing games on a phone. We meet friends for coffee instead of going for a hike. We commute to work and school in cars, rather than on bicycles or by using our own two feet.

And then there's also speculation that our lifestyles, themselves, are contributing to our weight gain. Our stress levels are higher than ever before, so we're not sleeping, which knocks more than just our eating systems off course. We're tired, so we reach for sugary, caffeinated drinks. Then we race through our fast food lunches because we have to get back to our desks. We have to spend extra time at our desks doing our work because we're not as productive as we'd like to be. And we're not as productive as we'd like to be because we're tired…and so it begins all over again.

So what's the solution? Well, experts disagree there, too. From my experience, it starts with small changes that can help knock you out of your rut. Something as simple as committing to walking 15 minutes a day at lunchtime or drinking a full glass of water for every glass of soda you drink can be the starting point. For some folks, that's all it takes. For others, there's more involved to ultimately regain a healthy weight. But one thing's for sure: there's no single formula that works for everyone.

Just as with a reading passage, a lecture will state its main purpose first. However, since the lectures are spoken, you will probably hear a brief introduction or greeting before the main idea is introduced. Here's an example:

Obesity. Pretty much everyone recognizes it's a serious problem. Recent statistics indicate that nearly 78 million adults and 13 million children in the United States alone deal with the physical and emotional effects of obesity every day. It would seem like the solution is easy, wouldn't it? Eat less and move more. Or in other words, consume fewer calories and increase the number of calories burned through physical activity. And yet, more than 90 million Americans continue to battle the bulge. What makes it so difficult to lose weight? Experts believe there are a number of contributing factors.

The first part of the excerpt is a brief introduction ("Obesity…battle the bulge."), after which the professor states the main purpose—"What makes it so difficult to lose weight? Experts believe there are a number of contributing factors."

Based on this statement, the lecture is most likely going to fit into the cause-and-effect category of lectures. That means we have to look for the causes of obesity mentioned in the lecture. Here's the first.

> One consideration is that for some folks, the system that sends signals back and forth between organs such as the stomach and the brain is out of whack.

Other potential causes are also mentioned:

> But, experts also believe we're eating too much of the wrong foods, too.
>
> Experts also believe that societal factors may contribute to difficulty losing weight.
>
> But wait, there's more! It's not all about calories in—it's also about calories out. Today's Americans move a whole lot less than those of 50 years ago did.
>
> And then there's also speculation that our lifestyles, themselves, are contributing to our weight gain.

So those are the main points the professor is making. Now let's take a look at the questions.

1. **B** While there is a bit of commentary toward the end about potential solutions to the issue of obesity, the passage as a whole is primarily dedicated to discussing the factors that contribute to obesity, or why people have a hard time losing weight. This matches (B).

2. **D** It's certainly challenging to remember all the details about every point the professor made, so use your understanding of the structure of the passage and a bit of common sense to at least eliminate answers that you're fairly certain don't match the professor's thinking. Choice (A) is certainly not in line with what the professor believes—after all, we just said in the previous question that the passage is about the difficulty of losing weight, not the ease of doing so! Choice (B) might be a "maybe" at first glance, so if you're not sure, leave it for now. Choice (C) is definitely out—the professor was clear that portion sizes have increased, not decreased, in the last half century. Choice (D), though, is pretty close to what the entire passage was about: multiple causes that affect weight gain. If you still have (B) in, it's easily eliminated because (D) is much more in line with the content of the passage.

3. **C** A common question topic on the TOEFL Listening section is the use of colloquial phrases, like this one. Use the context of the passage to determine the intended meaning of phrases like these.

> One consideration is that for some folks, the system that sends signals back and forth between organs such as the stomach and the brain is out of whack. So what can happen is that when the stomach sends a signal to the brain to stop taking in food, the brain doesn't recognize it and so the person just keeps eating.

The professor is describing a system that isn't working correctly, which matches (C).

4. **B** When the professor discusses a problem, be sure to pay attention to possible solutions. The only one mentioned by the professor is exercise, (B). If you don't recall the details, eliminate anything you don't remember hearing about and guess!

5. **A** When a lecture is about cause and effect, definitely remember to at least note the primary causes and primary effects. Of the answer choices presented, the only one that is close to anything the professor discussed is (A). Also remember to keep a bit of common sense involved: (B) doesn't have anything to

do with weight gain, and (D) is commonly accepted as a way to decrease weight gain. That means you should at least be able to eliminate two answers and then guess between (A) and (C).

6. **B, D** On multiple answer questions, remember that Process of Elimination is key to choosing the right answers. While (A) might make sense as a contributing factor, it was never mentioned by the professor. Choice (C) is also not likely to be a cause of overeating. That leaves you with the two causes the professor did identify, (B) and (D).

LISTENING PRACTICE DRILL #5: A LECTURE

Read the transcript of the lecture, noting the main idea, structure, and tone. How do the students' questions relate to the main idea?

Male Professor: Since yesterday's brief introduction on the origin of banking confused some of you, today I would like to review it a little bit. Banking the way we know it today is a convenience. The money used in banking represents a certain amount of value, but the money itself isn't valuable; it's just paper. To see how we got here...suppose we think about a society far, far back in history—what would it have used before the paper money we have today?

Female Student: Didn't they trade with the goods themselves?

MP: Sure. The system of exchanging one good for another of equal value is called *bartering*. Bartering was common in early societies, first with essential goods, then with nonessential goods. By nonessential, I mean, for example, art or cultural objects. You might trade a curtain that had been dyed in a decorative pattern for some wheat. The curtain's decorative value isn't essential to survival the way the food value of the grain is. That's the first step toward a money economy: recognizing trade-worthy value in something that isn't essential to survival.

Of course, you may see a hitch. Different cultures don't value the same decorations, so something could be worth a lot to one tribe and nothing to another. With food, that's not a problem—everyone has to eat—but with nonessential items, you're going to use something with cross-cultural value. Can anyone think of anything that would work?

Male Student: How about gold? It's durable...easy to shape...and it's beautiful. Is that why cultures started using it as money?

MP: Well, you can't refer to the earliest trade with gold as a money economy, but yes. Gold is a perfect example. As societies grew more stable and trade flourished, gold, usually molded into small ingots, gradually replaced the system of bartering. There were problems with gold, though.

FS: Yeah, I was going to say, gold is heavy, isn't it? How did people carry enough of it around to buy things? And wasn't it dangerous—like, you'd get robbed if people knew you had money with you?

MP: Definitely. Hauling all your gold around was a real risk in early societies, when there were bandits roaming around and no police to help you. And as you say, gold is heavy and unwieldy. One advantage it has, though, is that, unlike livestock or food, it doesn't go bad, so you don't have to use it up immediately.

That combination of characteristics gave people an idea. They started leaving their gold ingots with gold specialists for safekeeping. The specialists stored the gold for a small fee, and they gave their customers receipts, the way you'd get today. So you'd get something that said that, you know, you were the owner of such-and-such an amount of gold stored at this particular shop. The quality of gold from different mines varies, so the purity and density of your gold ingots—you know, how heavy they were for their size—determined their value and would also be recorded.

Then, when you wanted to use it, you just went back, gave the shopkeeper the receipt, and he gave you your gold.

MS: So if you were storing 500 ounces of gold of whatever percent purity, you'd give the receipt back, and get your 500 ounces of gold back? They kept it for you in your own little drawer or something?

MP: Whoops! I guess I did make it sound that way—thanks for catching that! No, you'd get 500 ounces of gold of the same purity back. They would have equal value, but would not necessarily be the exact same pile of ingots that you originally gave to the shopkeeper.

FS: The shopkeeper would use the gold or lend it out while you were storing it?

MP: Sure, and you can see how that's another of the beginnings of banking as we know it. You wouldn't get back your very own pile of gold; you'd get back a pile of equal value. It was the value itself that was important.

MS: So how did it become like money? I mean, we're still talking about big, heavy stacks of things, and—

MP: Well, that's the last point. Eventually, people figured out that they could use their receipts from storing gold to trade with one another. If they wanted to buy something, instead of running to the gold shop, withdrawing gold, and bringing it to another shop to pay for food or clay pots or whatever, they just gave the food merchant a receipt for the appropriate amount of gold. The merchant could then cash it in for gold, and the trade would be complete. And that's the last major step: The receipts became the first real ancestor of the money we use today because they stood for value actually attached to goods somewhere else.

Some of the academic lectures will include questions from the students and other forms of discussion. While this may appear to make the lectures more confusing, the student questions actually help you to follow the lecture and figure out the main idea.

First, let's figure out what the main topic is. As always, the professor mentions it at the very beginning of the lecture.

MP: Banking the way we know it today is a convenience. The money used in banking represents a certain amount of value, but the money itself isn't valuable; it's just paper. To see how we got here...suppose we think about a society far, far back in history—what would it have used before the paper money we have today?

Now that we know the lecture will be about the beginnings of banking, we should look for a sequence of ideas. The first student question introduces a key point.

>*FS:* Didn't they trade with the goods themselves?

As we said earlier, the students' comments and questions provide an easy way to follow the development of the lecture. Now the professor will explain the important idea below.

>*MP:* Sure. The system of exchanging one good for another of equal value is called *bartering*. Bartering was common in early societies, first with essential goods, then with nonessential goods....Of course, you may see a hitch. Different cultures don't value the same decorations, so something could be worth a lot to one tribe and nothing to another.

A student now asks a question, which again helps us understand the progression of ideas in the lecture.

>*MS:* How about gold? It's durable...easy to shape...and it's beautiful. Is that why cultures started using it as money?

>*MP:* Well, you can't refer to the earliest trade with gold as a money economy, but yes. Gold is a perfect example. As societies grew more stable and trade flourished, gold, usually molded into small ingots, gradually replaced the system of bartering. There were problems with gold, though.

This exchange brings us to another key part of the lecture. The professor details the problems.

>*MP:* Definitely. Hauling all your gold around was a real risk in early societies, when there were bandits roaming around and no police to help you. And as you say, gold is heavy and unwieldy. One advantage it has, though, is that, unlike livestock or food, it doesn't go bad, so you don't have to use it up immediately.

The lecture then continues with a longer explanation of how the problems with gold led to a new idea. But even if you missed some of that discussion, notice how the next student comment helps you figure out the key point.

>*MS:* So if you were storing 500 ounces of gold of whatever percent purity, you'd give the receipt back, and get your 500 ounces of gold back? They kept it for you in your own little drawer or something?

This comment gives us some clue as to what the professor was talking about before—the ability to store gold. Now the professor continues with the sequence.

>*MP:* Sure, and you can see how that's another of the beginnings of banking as we know it.

>*MS:* So how did it become like money? I mean, we're still talking about big, heavy stacks of things, and—

>*MP:* Well, that's the last point. Eventually, people figured out that they could use their receipts from storing gold to trade with one another.

As you can see, in each case the discussion between student and professor helped to clarify the major points of the lecture. So, make sure to be aware of this when dealing with an academic discussion on the TOEFL.

Now let's take care of the questions.

1. **C** This question was answered when the professor talked about bartering and the point was introduced with the use of a direction marker: "of course...." The answer choices in this question are very good candidates for POE. The first choice is extreme. It says that societies "cannot" devote resources. This is an absolute statement and should be eliminated. Choice (D) is another type of extreme answer, one that shows up every once in a while. The problem with this answer is that it can be seen as somewhat offensive. It judges the decorations as "too simple." The TOEFL will never have a correct answer that makes a negative value judgment. The characteristics in (B) refer to gold.

2. **A, B, D** Get rid of (C), which is extreme because it states that "only" specialists could determine the value of gold.

3. **B** Once again, (C) is extreme, so eliminate it. Choice (D) never appears in the lecture, so eliminate it as well. Choice (A) is certainly tempting, but the lecture said that "the quality of gold from different mines varies, so the purity and density of your gold ingots—you know, how heavy they were for their size—determined their value and would also be recorded." Thus, (B) is best.

4. **B** Here's a transcription of the excerpt to which you're asked to listen for this question.

> *MS:* So if you were storing 500 ounces of gold of whatever percent purity, you'd give the receipt back, and get your 500 ounces of gold back? They kept it for you in your own little drawer or something?
>
> *MP:* Whoops! I guess I did make it sound that way—thanks for catching that!

The professor's use of the word *whoops* indicates a mistake of some sort. Eliminate (A) and (D) because the line in question is about the professor ("I guess I did make it sound that way..."), not the student. And no point is introduced in this line, so (C) is incorrect.

5. **C** The professor mentions the answer to this question at the end of the lecture. Alternatively, use POE. Choice (A) is extreme; it says "all" gold shops used the same format. Choice (D) refers to bartering, which was mentioned in the beginning of the sequence as something that came before money. Eliminate it. Choice (B) is not mentioned.

6. **A** This is a definition question. These can be tough because if you miss the definition during the lecture it's hard to use POE. If you recalled that the word *ingot* appeared during the discussion of gold, you may be able to eliminate (C) and (D) because they don't refer to gold. The professor gives a sufficient clue as to the definition of the term here.

> *MP:* The quality of gold from different mines varies, so the purity and density of your gold ingots—you know, how heavy they were for their size—determined their value and would also be recorded.

Chapter 13
Cracking the
Speaking Section

Of all the sections on the TOEFL, the Speaking section often causes the most anxiety in test takers. Of course, we're going to talk about some ways to help you crack this section, but first let's look at what you can expect in the Speaking section.

- **Two Independent Tasks:** One question asks for your personal preference and one asks you to choose between two options. For each task, you'll have
  - 15 seconds preparation time
  - 45 seconds speaking time
- **Two Reading, Listening, and Speaking Integrated Tasks:** You will read a passage, listen to a conversation or lecture, and respond. For each task, you'll have
  - 45 seconds reading time
  - 60- to 90-second conversation/lecture
  - 30 seconds preparation time
  - 60 seconds speaking time
- **Two Listening and Speaking Integrated Tasks:** You will listen to a conversation or lecture and respond. For each task, you'll have
  - 1- to 2-minute conversation/lecture
  - 20 seconds preparation time
  - 60 seconds speaking time
- The entire Speaking section will take about 20 minutes.

As you can see, one of the challenges of the Speaking section is the way in which the questions require you to apply a variety of different skills—reading, listening, and, of course, speaking.

The six Speaking responses you'll have to provide will each be graded on a scale from 0 to 5. As we mentioned in the early part of this book, the Speaking scores are subdivided into four sections:

Good (3.5–4.0). A score in the "Good" range tells schools that you can speak comfortably about personal experiences and about content you've read and listened to. Your speech is fairly fluid, pronunciation is clear, and vocabulary is used appropriately.

Fair (2.5–3.0). A "Fair" score tells schools that you can generally speak about personal experiences and about content you've read and listened to. However, you may have some challenges when it comes to pronunciation and intonation, which makes it more challenging for a listener to understand what you're trying to say. You also may have some difficulty with grammatical structures and vocabulary.

Limited (1.5–2.0). A "Limited" score indicates to schools that you can handle basic conversations in English, but may have difficulty with grammatical structures. You can offer broad responses, but may lack the vocabulary to present well-developed responses to questions.

Weak (0–1.0). A "Weak" score indicates that you didn't finish your response, or that your speech is difficult for listeners to understand.

SPEAKING SECTION DIRECTIONS

The Speaking section has a fairly unique format, so it is helpful to familiarize yourself with the directions before you take the test. That way, you'll feel prepared and more comfortable when you actually take the TOEFL.

The Speaking section begins with a microphone test. At the beginning of the section, you'll be asked to answer a sample question. **This question does not affect your TOEFL score, so don't worry about it**. Your response is used simply to adjust the microphone volume, which will be done automatically at the conclusion of your response. The microphone test screen will look similar to the one shown below.

As you speak, the computer will adjust the volume of the microphone. When a message appears on the screen that tells you to stop speaking, the adjustment has finished.

After the adjustment is finished, the directions appear.

The first two questions will ask you to respond to familiar topics—you will first be asked to state your personal preference and then to choose between two options. For each task you will have 15 seconds to organize your thoughts and then 45 seconds to respond.

The next two questions will give you 45 seconds to read a short text after which the text is removed from the screen and the audio will begin immediately. You will listen to a talk on the same topic as the reading and combine information from both the talk and the reading in your spoken response.

The final two questions ask you to listen to a conversation or lecture that lasts between 1 and 2 minutes and then respond to it. After you hear the lecture you will have 20 seconds to prepare your response and then 60 seconds to speak.

Remember, it is much more important to speak clearly than quickly. You have only a short time. You will not lose points for having an accent, but the graders must be able to easily understand what you are saying in your answer.

You can take notes during all readings, conversations, and lectures, if you find that doing so is helpful. However, the directions for each question will not appear on the screen; you'll be able to listen to them only once, so be sure to listen carefully.

HOW THE SPEAKING SECTION IS SCORED

Each of your spoken responses will be evaluated on a scale of 0–4 by 3–6 different graders. The average of all six scores is then converted to the 0–30 scaled score. The graders consider three major areas when judging the quality of your response—let's look at each in detail.

1. **Delivery:** On the TOEFL, delivery refers to both the flow and clarity of your speech. A higher-scoring response will be well-paced and free of long pauses and unnecessary interjections. Although the speech may contain minor pronunciation errors or problems with intonation, these errors do not detract from understanding the speech.

2. **Language use:** The scorers are looking for effective use of grammar and vocabulary. Complexity of sentence structure will also be considered. A higher-scoring response generally contains a variety of sentence structures, a range of vocabulary, and few grammatical errors. Once again, a top response doesn't have to be perfect, but the errors shouldn't affect the listener's ability to understand the speech.

3. **Topic development:** This includes how well your response addresses the task as well as the development of your ideas. Thus, the graders are judging you not only on *how* you speak, but also on *what* you say. This is an important point because test takers who are comfortable speaking in English may not achieve a top score if they do not structure their responses appropriately.

CRACKING THE SPEAKING SECTION: BASIC PRINCIPLES

The Speaking section of the TOEFL can be very intimidating, but it doesn't have to be. The first important point about the Speaking section is that although there are six different questions, the *types* of responses you will give are all fairly similar. Basically, your goal is to use the skills you've learned throughout the Reading and Listening sections, and use them together with standard templates for responses on the Speaking section. If you are comfortable with the work we've done in the Reading and Listening sections, then your primary focus will be on learning the templates for each Speaking task.

Another important point to consider is the *score range* of the programs to which you're applying. The top score on the Speaking section is 30 (although there are only six questions and the top score on each is a 4, the TOEFL converts your 0–24 points to a 0–30 scaled score); however, many programs are looking for scores far lower than 30. So before you devote too much time to worrying about this section, check the requirements of the schools in which you're interested.

Finally, realize that you *do not* have to sound like a native speaker to score well. It is perfectly acceptable to speak with an accent and make some mistakes in grammar and word use. What ultimately matters is how *understandable* your speech is.

Thus, cracking the Speaking section requires you to be aware of the following:

1. **How you sound.** When speaking, you must try to avoid unnecessary pauses and try to speak at an even pace.
2. **Your command of English grammar and vocabulary.** A top-scoring response uses a variety of words and contains some complex sentence structures.
3. **What you say.** Good responses have a clear flow of ideas and use appropriate transitions to link topics.

Let's examine each of these requirements in more detail.

Basic Principle #1: How You Sound

As mentioned earlier, this does NOT mean you have to sound like a native speaker. It means that you should speak confidently and clearly. The two biggest mistakes you can make are

- pausing often and breaking up the flow of your speech with unnecessary words such as *um* and *uh*
- delivering your speech in a mechanical "robot" voice, as if you were reading the response from a page

The best way to avoid the first challenge is to use the speaking templates you'll learn in this chapter. These are basic patterns that you can use to organize your response. If you master these templates, you'll know exactly what you need to say for each task, which should help you avoid too many pauses in your speech.

As for the second issue, the best way to avoid a mechanical delivery is to practice. Once you familiarize yourself with the templates, practice using them with a variety of different topics. The more you practice using the templates, the more natural your speech will sound. It's also a good idea to remind yourself to smile when you respond, because it makes your response more pleasant to listen to, which is certainly not going to hurt your score! Practice smiling when you speak on the phone or to your friends, and see how they react!

Basic Principle #2: Your Command of English Grammar and Vocabulary

This book is not intended to be a comprehensive grammar handbook; however, we will give you some basic grammatical structures to follow, and you should make sure to memorize the Grammar Review at the end of Chapter 5. (Check out The Princeton Review's *Grammar Smart* if you need more work with grammar.) Similarly, although working on your vocabulary is a worthwhile goal, we're going to focus on only some of the words that will be useful to you on the TOEFL. The Princeton Review also publishes *TOEFL Power Vocab* for additional vocabulary practice.

Improving and Varying Sentence Structure

Let's start with some common sentence structures. Here is the most basic type of sentence.

>   Ichiro hit the ball.

This sentence has a simple pattern: *subject* (Ichiro), *verb* (hit), *object* (the ball). Although many of your constructions will follow this simple pattern, you'll have to vary your sentence structure somewhat to achieve a higher score on the TOEFL. For example, here's another way we can express the same idea.

>   The ball was hit by Ichiro.

This sentence moves the words around and creates a different emphasis. By using "the ball" as the *subject,* we give it more emphasis. Furthermore, by moving "Ichiro" to the *object* of the sentence, we de-emphasize him. If we add some more information to the sentence, we can use the following construction:

>   After hitting the ball, Ichiro ran to first base.

This sentence structure allows us to express two different actions, "hitting the ball" and "ran." And as you've seen, we can use *transitions* to make our sentences even more complex.

>   Although Ichiro hit the ball, he was unable to reach first base safely.
>   Ichiro hit the ball, but he was unable to reach first base safely.
>   Ichiro hit the ball and reached first base safely.

All of these are types of sentences that you can use to increase your TOEFL Speaking score. Let's practice some of them.

Practice Using Complex Sentence Structures   Rewrite each of the following sentences by first switching the subject and the object. Next, add in the new information by using one of the complex structures discussed earlier. Don't forget to use transitions.

Here's an example:

>   Maria bought a picture frame.
>   Rewrite: <u>A picture frame was bought by Maria.</u>

Now add in this new information: "She needed it for her house."

Combine and rewrite: <u>Needing a picture frame for her house, Maria bought one. Also: A picture frame was bought by Maria because she needed it for her house.</u>

Now try it.

1. Steve attended class.
    Rewrite: _____
    Add new information: "Steve did not do his homework."
    Combine and rewrite: _____

2. Ellen chose the black shirt.
    Rewrite: _____
    Add new information: "Ellen prefers the color black."
    Combine and rewrite: _____

3. The professor gave two reasons for the behavior.
    Rewrite: _____
    Add new information: "The professor described the behavior first."
    Combine and rewrite: _____

4. The class required both a midterm and final exam.
    Rewrite: _____
    Add new information: "A student cannot pass the class without passing the midterm and final exam."
    Combine and rewrite: _____

5. The firm hired Ivan.
    Rewrite: _____
    Add new information: "Ivan was the most qualified candidate."
    Combine and rewrite: _____

6. Soccer is Andrew's favorite sport.
    Rewrite: _____
    Add new information: "Andrew started playing soccer when he was very young."
    Combine and rewrite: _____

7. Jaime asked a question.
    Rewrite: _____
    Add new information: "Jaime needed directions to the student center."
    Combine and rewrite: _____

8. Guillermo read the book.
    Rewrite: _____
    Add new information: "Guillermo wrote a paper on the book."
    Combine and rewrite: _____

9. Heather forgot her book.
    Rewrite: _____
    Add new information: "She needed it for class."
    Combine and rewrite: _____

10. Dennis plays the guitar.
    Rewrite: _____
    Add new information: "Dennis is learning to play the piano."
    Combine and rewrite: _____

Answers to Practice Using Complex Sentence Structures

Here are the rewritten versions of the sentence and some suggested ways of combining the sentences with the new information provided.

1. Steve attended class.
    Rewrite: The class was attended by Steve.
    Add new information: "Steve did not do his homework."
    Possible responses: Although he did not do his homework, Steve attended the class.

                              Despite not doing his homework, Steve attended the class.

                              Steve attended the class even though he did not do his homework.

2. Ellen chose the black shirt.
    Rewrite: The black shirt was chosen by Ellen.
    Add new information: "Ellen prefers black."
    Possible responses: Preferring black, Ellen chose that shirt.

                              Because she preferred black, Ellen chose that shirt.

                              Ellen chose that shirt because she prefers black.

3. The professor gave two reasons for the behavior.
    Rewrite: Two reasons for the behavior were given by the professor.
    Add new information: "The professor described the behavior first."
    Possible responses: After describing the behavior first, the professor gave two reasons for it.

                              The professor first described the behavior and gave two reasons for it.

                              The professor gave two reasons for the behavior after first describing it.

4. The class required both a midterm and final exam.
    Rewrite: A midterm and final exam were both required by the class.
    Add new information: "A student cannot pass the class without passing the midterm and final exam."

Possible responses: Because the class requires both a midterm and final exam, a student cannot pass the class without passing both exams.

Requiring a midterm and final exam, the class cannot be passed unless a student passes the exams.

The class requires a midterm and final exam, and a student cannot pass the class unless he or she passes both exams.

5. The firm hired Ivan.
    Rewrite: Ivan was hired by the firm.
    Add new information: "Ivan was the most qualified candidate."
    Possible responses: Being the most qualified candidate, Ivan was hired by the firm.

    Because he was the most qualified candidate, Ivan was hired by the firm.

    The firm hired Ivan because he was the most qualified candidate.

6. Soccer is Andrew's favorite sport.
    Rewrite: Andrew's favorite sport is soccer.
    Add new information: "Andrew started playing soccer when he was very young."
    Possible responses: Andrew's favorite sport is soccer because he started playing it when he was very young.

    Because he started playing it when he was very young, Andrew's favorite sport is soccer.

    Having played since he was very young, Andrew's favorite sport is soccer.

7. Jaime asked a question.
    Rewrite: A question was asked by Jaime.
    Add new information: "Jaime needed directions to the student center."
    Possible responses: Needing directions to the student center, Jaime asked a question.

    Jaime asked a question because she needed directions to the student center.

    Because she needed directions to the student center, Jaime asked a question.

8. Guillermo read the book.
    Rewrite: <u>The book was read by Guillermo.</u>
    Add new information: "Guillermo wrote a paper on the book."
    Possible responses: <u>Guillermo read the book and also wrote a paper on it.</u>

                                <u>Guillermo read the book because he had to write a paper on it.</u>

                                <u>The book was read by Guillermo so that he could write a paper on it.</u>

9. Heather forgot her book.
    Rewrite: <u>The book was forgotten by Heather.</u>
    Add new information: "She needed it for class."
    Possible responses: <u>Although she needed it for class, Heather forgot her book.</u>

                                <u>Heather forgot her book although she needed it for class.</u>

                                <u>Heather forgot her book even though she needed it for class.</u>

10. Dennis plays the guitar.
    Rewrite: <u>The guitar was played by Dennis.</u>
    Add new information: "Dennis is learning to play the piano."
    Possible responses: <u>Dennis plays the guitar and is also learning to play the piano.</u>

                                <u>Dennis is learning to play the piano, although he can play the guitar already.</u>

                                <u>Although he plays the guitar, Dennis is learning to play the piano.</u>

The important lesson to learn from this exercise is to see that there are many ways of expressing the same idea. You'll need to use a variety of sentence structures to score well on the TOEFL. You can practice this exercise on your own also. Take sentences from a book, magazine, or newspaper article and practice rewriting them in a variety of different ways.

Improving and Building Your Vocabulary

The Speaking section asks to you do the following tasks:

*   Describe
*   Summarize
*   Contrast

Let's look at each task and the types of words and phrases that are appropriate to fulfill each one.

Descriptions Some tasks ask you to describe a problem, an opinion, or a personal preference. If you are describing details, you can use the following phrases:

- one **aspect** of...
- one **characteristic** of...
- one **quality** of...
- one **issue** (for describing a problem)...
- one **feature**...
- one **attribute**...
- one **element**...
- one **thing**...

For example, you may be asked to do the following on the TOEFL:

Describe a friend of yours, and explain why you consider this person a friend.
Use details and examples to support your view.

For this task, we are asked to describe our friend. Our response may look like the sample below (note the descriptions are in boldface type).

One of my best friends is Joel. He is my friend for many reasons. One **characteristic** of Joel's that I really admire is his honesty. He always tells the truth to me. Another **quality** of Joel's that I like is his optimistic attitude. Joel always has a positive word for everyone. Joel's sense of humor is a final **aspect** of his personality that I admire. He is always able to make me laugh. For these reasons, I consider Joel a great friend.

As you can see, each word above can be used when describing a specific detail. Now it's your turn to answer the question above, using as many of the descriptive phrases as possible.

_____

_____

_____

_____

Summaries Another common task on the TOEFL Speaking section involves summarizing a reading or lecture. When summarizing, try using some of the following phrases:

- **according to** the reading/lecture/speaker...
- the reading/lecture/speaker **states that**...
- the reading/lecture/speaker **argues that**...
- the reading/lecture/speaker **holds that**...
- the reading/lecture/speaker **asserts that**...
- one reason/explanation **presented by** the reading/lecture/speaker...
- the reading/lecture/speaker **claims that**...
- the reading/lecture/speaker **expresses** the point/reason/opinion...
- the reading/lecture/speaker **indicates that**...
- the reading/lecture/speaker **believes**...

Here's an example of a reading passage that you will be asked to summarize.

Read the following passage and then summarize the points made by the author.

New research in the field of neuroscience is leading some researchers to change their beliefs about how the brain forms. An early view of the brain held that intelligence was primarily determined by genes. Now, however, a new study casts doubt on that view. Researchers have discovered that the neurons in the brain develop in the early stages of infancy. The more stimulation these neurons receive, the more connections the neurons make with other neurons. Cognitive scientists believe that intelligence is partly based on the number of connections between neurons in the brain.

Now, summarize the important parts of the passage. One response might look like this (again, with the summarizing terms shown in boldface):

According to the reading, some scientists have to change their views about the brain. The reading **states that** the early view of the brain is wrong. One reason given, according to the reading, is that there is a new study. The reading **claims that** the new study shows that brain development occurs during childhood. It also **argues that** the amount of stimulation a child receives leads to a higher intelligence.

Now try your own summary of this same paragraph. In addition, practice by using parts of some of the other reading passages in this book.

_____

_____

_____

_____

_____

Contrasts   The final type of speaking task asks you to contrast ideas. Here are some helpful phrases to use when contrasting ideas.

- in **contrast to**...
- one **difference between**...
- **unlike**...
- one **distinction between**...
- **dissimilarly**...
- one **disagreement between**...
- one **inconsistency between**...
- one point at **issue** is...
- one point of **disagreement** is...

Let's look at a task that requires us to contrast two things.

Read the following passage:

For more than three hundred years, the world understood physics as a predictable system. Isaac Newton's three laws of motion allowed physicists to predict the motion of not just falling apples and thrown balls, but comets, planets, and stars as well. The amazing degree of accuracy of these predictions had convinced scientists that the universe obeyed precise laws, a belief that in many ways was reassuring because it was comforting to think of the universe as an orderly, predictable place.

Now read the following lecture on the same topic:

What would you guys think if I told you I could walk right through that wall over there? You probably wouldn't believe me. As you all know from, uh, basic physics, two solid objects cannot occupy the same space. But the truth is that...is that neither I nor the wall am really solid. That's right...I am mostly made up of empty space. I know it's weird, but think about it. I'm made of atoms, and atoms are mostly empty space. And it was in the early um, early twentieth century when the discovery was made that atoms can pass through other objects. If you shoot a number of atoms...I think it was Niels Bohr who did this experiment...at a sheet of metal, some of them will pass right through it. And although the probability is extremely unlikely...because I have so many atoms in my body...if I walked into that wall an infinite number of times, at some point I would pass right through it. So our world isn't as nice and predictable as we may believe.

Explain how the lecture casts doubt on or otherwise relates to the reading.

This asks us to contrast the information presented in both selections. (To "cast doubt" means "to cause something to be doubted.") Here's a sample response, with the contrasting terms shown in boldface.

One **difference between** the two is the predictable nature of physics. The reading states that the universe is predictable. In **contrast to** this idea, the professor says the world isn't always predictable. **Unlike** the reading, the lecture gives some information on how atoms can be unpredictable. This is **inconsistent with** the reading, which talks about larger objects, such as planets. However, the biggest point at **issue between** the two is whether or not we can predict events in the universe.

Can you find other contrasting ideas in the lecture? Use the contrasting phrases listed above in your response. You can also practice on your own. A good place to look for contrasting ideas is in the editorial pages of your local newspaper. Find two articles or opinions on the same topic and try to contrast them.

Basic Principle #3: What You Say

One key to scoring well on the Speaking section is to make sure the ideas about which you are talking are clearly connected to one another. You should use transitions to relate the parts of your speech together.

Here are some of the common transition words you will need to use on the TOEFL.

Words that indicate a *sequence* or progression

First	Second	Third	Next	After	Lastly
Then	Previously	Before	Following	Finally	

Words that indicate a *connection* between ideas

Because	Therefore	Thus	And
Also	Furthermore	Additionally	So

Words that indicate a *contradiction* between ideas

However	Despite	Yet	Although
But	In contrast to	On the other hand	

Now practice using these transitions in the exercise that follows.

PRACTICE: USING TRANSITIONS

Read the following sentences aloud, connecting them with the appropriate transition word or words.

1. Jane would like to go home during the holiday break, _____ she doesn't have enough money.
2. Sasha intends to major in mathematics _____ it is her favorite subject.
3. First, you must mix the two chemicals together. _____, wait for the reaction to occur.

4. One of the main reasons Jose took the job was the salary; _____, the location was a factor.

5. _____ Ming had never met Anna before, they acted like old friends.

6. The professor is known for his harsh grading scale; _____, students say that he is one of the best teachers at the school.

7. The class requires students to write a 20-page research paper. _____, the students have to complete a group project.

8. Marco had _____ believed that he wanted to go to business school, but now he plans to attend law school.

9. It is very difficult to do well in this class without doing the required reading. _____, I recommend keeping up with the assignments.

10. Neela was sure that she had failed the exam, _____ she received a passing grade.

ANSWERS AND EXPLANATIONS FOR PRACTICE: USING TRANSITIONS

Here are the appropriate transitions.

1. Jane would like to go home during the holiday break, **but** she doesn't have enough money.

This sentence *contrasts* two ideas. You also could have used *although*.

2. Sasha intends to major in mathematics **because** it is her favorite subject.

Here, we need to *connect* the two ideas. The first part is explained by the second part of the sentence.

3. First, you must mix the two chemicals together. **Then** wait for the reaction to occur.

There is a *progression* of ideas in this sentence. You also may have used *next* or *second*.

4. One of the main reasons Jose took the job was the salary; **additionally,** the location was a factor.

We need to *connect* both of the reasons together. Other possible responses include *furthermore* and *also*.

5. **Although** Ming had never met Anna before, they acted like old friends.

There is a *contrast* between the first idea and the second one.

6. The professor is known for his harsh grading scale; **however,** students say that he is one of the best teachers at the school.

Another *contrasting* set of ideas. The first part says something negative, whereas the second part expresses something positive.

7. The class requires students to write a 20-page research paper. **Furthermore,** the students have to complete a group project.

Both of the requirements need to be *connected*. You could have used *also* or *additionally* as well.

8. Marco had **previously** believed that he wanted to go to business school, but now he plans to attend law school.

This sentence shows a *progression* of ideas.

9. It is very difficult to do well in this class without doing the required reading. **Therefore,** I recommend keeping up with the assignments.

The first part and the second part are *connected* to each other. You could have also used *thus*.

10. Neela was sure that she had failed the exam, **yet** she received a passing grade.

These two ideas *contrast* with one another. You also could have used *but*.

You can practice this drill on your own. Try making statements that require using each of the transitions presented on the previous page.

CRACKING THE SPEAKING SECTION: BASIC APPROACH

Now that we've gone over the basic principles, we're ready to think about strategic ways to approach the Speaking section. To do so, complete the following:

> 1. **Learn the appropriate template for each task,** and use it for your response.
> 2. **Use the appropriate vocabulary for each task.** Remember to use words that describe, contrast, and summarize, as well as words that show preferences. Transitions are also important to help the grader follow your train of thought.
> 3. **Listen to and practice speaking English as often as possible.** There's no better way to improve your speaking ability than to actually practice speaking.

Let's spend some more time on the first step because it is one of the keys to doing well on this section.

Step 1: Learn the Appropriate Templates

Remember the three qualities that the graders are listening for? How you sound, your use of language, and what you say. The best way to attack all three aspects on a regular basis is to have a structured plan of attack for each task. The following templates provide exactly that—a strategic plan for each individual assignment. Memorize them! Then all you have to do on test day is adapt them a little bit to respond to the actual questions you are asked.

INDEPENDENT TASKS

Template #1: Personal Preference Question

The first speaking task on the TOEFL typically asks you to describe something that you would prefer to do, see, or experience. These tasks may also ask you to talk about something important to you. Regardless of the exact question, these tasks require you to pick the thing, person, or event you are going to discuss. You'll have 15 seconds to organize your thoughts and then 45 seconds to respond.

Here's the template:

> State your preference
> Reason #1
> Detail for Reason #1
> Reason #2
> Detail for Reason #2

And here's a typical example:

> Describe a place you would like to visit, and explain why you chose this location. Use details and examples to support your position.

One possible response might be as follows:

State personal preference	I would like to visit Italy.
Reason #1	I would choose to visit Italy because it has a lot of history.
Specific detail for reason #1	**For example,** Italy has many interesting Roman ruins. It would be interesting to see these historic sites.
Reason #2	**Another reason** I would like to visit Italy is for the culture.
Specific detail for reason #2	Italy has been home to many great artists and the museums there contain some of the most famous works of art.
Reason #3	**Finally,** I would like to visit Italy to sample the food.
Specific detail for reason #3	I love Italian food and would really like the chance to try some authentic Italian cooking.

The boldfaced words are examples of transitions and other phrases you can use in your speech.

Depending on how quickly you speak, you may be able to provide only two reasons in the time given. That's acceptable. And although this response may appear simple, it is much harder when you are under pressure.

Before you go on, go back and read the sample response out loud. There's no better way to improve your speaking than to actually speak!

Now, practice using the template for the following prompt. Remember to use the descriptive words you've learned. Time yourself: give yourself 15 seconds to prepare and 45 seconds to respond.

Describe your favorite hobby, and explain why you enjoy it. Use details and examples to support your point.

State personal preference	
Reason #1	
Specific detail for reason #1	
Reason #2	
Specific detail for reason #2	
Reason #3	
Specific detail for reason #3	

Practice using this template on your own. Think of your favorite food, color, article of clothing, activity, and so on, and try to provide reasons and details as to why they are your favorites. Don't forget to use transitions.

Template #2: Choose an Option Question

The second type of task on the TOEFL presents you with two options. You'll have to decide which one you believe is better and support your decision.

Here's the template:

> State better option
> Reason #1
> Detail for Reason #1
> Reason #2
> Detail for Reason #2

Look familiar? It should! It's almost exactly the same as Template #1! The only difference is that in the second task, you will need to choose between two options that are presented to you.

Here's a sample prompt:

Some universities give financial aid in the form of grants, which don't have to be paid back, whereas others provide financial assistance in the form of loans, which must be paid back. Which option do you think is better and why? Support your decision with reasons and examples.

The following would have been an acceptable response:

State better option	I think it is better to offer student loans.
Reason #1	**I prefer** loans because they make the student responsible.
Specific detail for reason #1	A student who has to pay back a loan becomes personally responsible for his or her education.
Reason #2	**Furthermore**, loans are safer for the school.
Specific detail for reason #2	Grants require the school to give away large amounts of money, and there is no guarantee that the school will get the money back.
Reason #3	**Lastly**, a student with a loan is probably more likely to stay in school.
Specific detail for reason #3	If the student doesn't complete the degree, it will be harder to pay back the money.

Did you remember to read the sample response aloud? If not, go for it!

Now, practice this template. Remember to use the descriptive words that you've learned. As before, keep track of your time: you'll have 15 seconds to prepare and 45 seconds to respond.

> Some people believe that universities should require students to take classes on ethics, whereas others believe a school should focus only on academic issues. Which do you think is better? Support your decision with reasons and examples.

State better option	
Reason #1	
Specific detail for reason #1	
Reason #2	
Specific detail for reason #2	
Reason #3	
Specific detail for reason #3	

INTEGRATED TASKS—READING, LISTENING, SPEAKING

Template #3: Summarize an Opinion Question

The third task requires you to read a brief passage and listen to a conversation about it. Then you'll have to summarize the opinion or position given in the conversation.

Reading: You'll have 45 seconds to read the passage, which will usually discuss some sort of campus life issue. Most likely, you won't need to take notes while you read the passage.

Listening: The conversation will start automatically, so be ready to listen! During the 60–90 seconds you're listening, pay attention to the speaker's opinion or attitude about the reading, and pay close attention to the *reasons* the speaker gives for his or her position. Write them down if you can.

Here's the template you should keep in mind as you read and listen:

State the requested opinion
Reason #1 for opinion
Detail for Reason #1
Reason #2 for opinion
Detail for Reason #2

Once again, the template looks similar, focusing not only on the answer to the question (in this case, the speaker's opinion), but also on the reasons behind the answer.

Here's an example.

Read the following announcement from the university president:

Due to recent budget constraints, the university has decided to close the computer labs during weekends and reduce their operating hours during the week from 8:00 A.M. to 10:00 P.M. to 9:00 A.M. to 8:00 P.M. These changes are necessary in order to compensate for an unexpected budget shortfall. Without these cutbacks, the school would be forced to reduce service in other important areas, such as the library and the cafeteria.

Headphones On!

Play Track 9 on the accompanying CD (or in your Student Tools). Transcripts of all the audio tracks in this chapter begin on page 393.

The woman offers her opinion of the announcement. State what her opinion is and what reasons she gives for having that view.

You'll have 30 seconds to prepare and 60 seconds to respond.

Here's the template for our response.

State opinion	The woman **believes** that the decision to reduce the hours of the computer lab is a **bad** idea.
Reason #1	Her first **reason for claiming this** is that she needs a computer for her class work.
Detail for reason #1	The woman **states that** she doesn't have a computer and that some of her classes require her to use one.
Reason #2	**Also,** the woman **claims** it will be harder to complete all of her work.
Detail for reason #2	**According** to the woman, the best time to do work is on the weekends. Now she fears that the labs will be too full during the week.

Did you practice reading the response aloud?

As you can see, all you have to do is basically repeat the reasons given by the speaker. You won't be required to do anything else. Now, it's your turn to try the template with the following example.

You'll have 45 seconds to read the passage.

Read the following announcement from the president of a university:

Effective immediately, the university is instituting a new policy on off-campus visitors. Any guests are now required to register with campus security and obtain a guest pass which must be worn at all times. This new policy is necessary in order to keep all the students safe and to increase campus safety's knowledge of who is on campus.

Play Track 10 on the accompanying CD (or in your Student Tools).

The man gives his opinion on the announcement. State the man's opinion and provide the reasons he gives for holding it.

Headphones On!

Give yourself 30 seconds to prepare and 60 seconds to respond.

State requested opinion	
Reason #1	
Detail for reason #1	
Reason #2	
Detail for reason #2	

Template #4: Summarize/Contrast Question

The fourth task will begin with a reading passage and then be followed by an academic lecture that will either agree or disagree with the reading. Your job is to show how the lecture relates to or contrasts with the reading. Both the lecture and the reading will present some characteristics of a given topic.

Reading: Once again, you'll have 45 seconds to read the passage. While you read, take brief notes about the characteristics mentioned—typically there will be three to five characteristics to track.

Listening: The lecture will start automatically, so be ready to listen! You will be able to tell within the first couple sentences whether the lecture agrees or disagrees with the reading passage. While you listen to the lecture, listen for the characteristics mentioned and jot them down if you can. Think about how the characteristics in the lecture agree or disagree with the information in the reading.

Here's the template you should keep in mind as you read and listen:

> Main Response
> Characteristic #1 from reading
> Detail #1 from lecture
> Characteristic #2 from reading
> Detail #2 from lecture
> Characteristic #3 from reading
> Detail #3 from lecture

Since this task asks you to compare or contrast the reading with the lecture, you should think about how you take your notes. Your most efficient approach will likely be to create two columns, one for your notes about the reading and one for your notes about the listening. Then, as you take notes on the characteristics, you can line them up to be better able to compare them. Try it out with the sample below, and compare your notes to our suggestions that appear below.

Here's a sample. You'll have 45 seconds to read a passage like this.

Read the following passage about captive breeding:

Both environmentalists and animal rights activists consider captive breeding a solution to the threat of extinction of certain endangered species. In captive breeding, endangered animals are caught and bred, and the offspring is then released back into the wild. Unfortunately, the results of this program have been mixed. In many cases, the animals that are released back into the wild are unable to survive. The time spent in human captivity makes it more difficult for them to acquire food and to fit in with other members of their species.

Play Track 11 on the accompanying CD (or in your Student Tools).

Headphones On!

The professor describes the results of a captive breeding experiment. Explain how the results of the experiment relate to the reading on the topic.

Here's what your notes might look like:

Reading
Captive breeding
    breed in captivity, set babies free
Mixed results
    Many released animals can't survive

Listening
Problems re: reintroduce
    animal into wild
"Working out"
1st time—Lynx died
    Taught them to hunt
    Kept together so they
    can get along

Notice that we can easily see that the reading says there are "mixed results," but just to the right of that we noted that there's been a situation in which reintroducing animals into the wild is "working out." This can be helpful in crafting your response to the prompt.

Once the lecture is finished, you'll have 30 seconds to prepare and then 60 seconds to speak.

Here's a possible response to the prompt:

Main response	The experiment with the lynx shows that captive breeding can be successful.
Characteristic #1 from reading	**One problem** with captive breeding, **according to** the reading, is that animals do not always survive when reintroduced into the wild.
Detail #1 from lecture	**But** the scientists seemed to be having good luck reintroducing the lynx into the wild.
Characteristic #2 from reading	The reading **states that** a major problem is that the animals don't know how to hunt.
Detail #2 from lecture	**However,** for the experiment, biologists first taught the animals how to hunt before releasing them.
Characteristic #3 from reading	**Another** problem in the reading is that the animals don't know how to interact with other members of the species.
Detail #3 from lecture	Scientists were able to get around this, **however,** by keeping the lynx together in a group.

Did you read this one aloud? If not, go back and do so—it's great practice!

For this type of question, it's acceptable if you run out of time before you list all of the characteristics. Your goal while speaking is to be as clear as possible, so don't rush through the details because it may make you harder to understand.

Try this template with the following example. You have 30 seconds to prepare and 60 seconds to respond.

Read the following passage about methane:

Methane is a colorless, odorless gas that occurs naturally as a result of the decomposition of plant and animal matters. Methane is a hydrocarbon like coal and oil, and it's all that remains of long-dead plants, dinosaurs, and other prehistoric animals. Although methane can be produced by volcanic activity, scientists usually connect the presence of methane with the presence of biological life. Many microorganisms excrete methane as a waste product, and scientists often infer the presence of these creatures by measuring the amount of methane in the air.

Play Track 12 on the accompanying CD (or in your Student Tools).

Headphones On!

The professor presents some facts about Mars. Explain how these facts may indicate life.

You have 30 seconds to prepare and 60 seconds to respond.

Main response	
Characteristic #1 from reading	
Detail #1 from lecture	
Characteristic #2 from reading	
Detail #2 from lecture	
Characteristic #3 from reading	
Detail #3 from lecture	

INTEGRATED TASKS—LISTENING AND SPEAKING

Template #5: Summarize/Preference Question

The fifth task asks you to listen to a 1- to 2-minute conversation, usually about a problem. Then you'll have 20 seconds to organize your thoughts and 60 seconds to summarize the problem and any solutions offered and state your preferred solution.

Listening: Pay attention to the problem and the solutions offered.

Keep this template in mind as you listen:

> State the problem.
> State the solutions offered.
> State your preferred solution.
> Reason #1
> Detail for reason #1
> Reason #2
> Detail for reason #2

Here's an example.

Play Track 13 on the accompanying CD (or in your Student Tools).

Headphones On!

> The students discuss two possible solutions to the problem.
> Describe the problem and state which of the two solutions you prefer and why.

The most important component of your response is the list of solutions to the problem—this shows that you were able to understand what was said. As far as your preferred solution, there is no right or wrong answer, so all you have to do is pick whichever solution is easier for you to talk about.

Here's a sample response, with the summarizing and preference terms shown in boldface.

State the problem	The man's problem is that he has two projects due at the same time.
State the solutions	His friend **offers** two possible solutions. He can ask for an extension, or he can drop the class.
State your preference	I think asking for an extension is a **better** solution.
Reason #1	An extension is better **because** dropping the class is too drastic.
Detail for reason #1	It seems silly to drop the entire class just because of one conflict.
Reason #2	I **also** think an extension is better because the professor will probably give the student one.
Detail for reason #2	The friend told of a similar situation, and she was able to get an extension.

Did you read the sample response out loud for practice?

Now practice using the template on the following example.

Play Track 14 on the accompanying CD (or in your Student Tools).

Headphones On!

The students discuss two possible solutions to the problem. Describe the problem and state which of the two solutions you prefer and why.

You have 20 seconds to prepare and 60 seconds to respond.

State the problem	
State the solutions	
State your preference	
Reason #1	
Detail for reason #1	
Reason #2	
Detail for reason #2	

Template #6: Summarize Question

The final task asks you to listen to a 1- to 2-minute lecture and show how the speaker's points support his or her main idea.

Listening: While listening to the lecture, focus on identifying the main idea. Don't worry about identifying every detail—you need only enough details so that you can talk for a minute.

Keep this template in mind as you listen:

> State the main idea
> State Reason #1
> Detail for reason #1
> Link between reason #1 and main idea
> State Reason #2
> Detail for reason #2
> Link between reason #2 and main idea

Notice that this template is a little bit different: you have to do more than just list the reasons and details. You also have to take the final step to explain how the reasons support the main idea. When you respond, make sure you state the main idea right away. If you focus too much on the details, you'll lose points.

Step 3: Consider Your Audience

TOEFL graders are trained to look for certain features in your writing. By ensuring that your essay contains these features, you'll improve your score. Make sure your essay contains the following:

1. **An introduction, body paragraphs, and a conclusion.** More details on these can be found in Core Concept: Writing.
2. **Specific examples.** Your essay must use specific examples. The more detail you use, the better your essay will be.
3. **Transitions.** One of the things TOEFL graders look for in an essay is "unity and coherence." That means that all the ideas must flow easily. They should be linked together with appropriate transitions.

Similarly, there are some elements to avoid in your writing. Make sure you avoid the following:

1. **Repeating phrases from the reading or prompt word for word.** Always put the examples and reasons into your own words. Although repeating a word or two is acceptable, you should *never* copy long phrases directly from the text on screen. TOEFL graders will penalize you for this.
2. **Writing your essay as one long paragraph.** Make sure you divide your essay into separate paragraphs. *Do not* just write a single block of text.
3. **Including material not relevant to the task.** Your essay must remain on topic. *Do not* include any reasons or examples that do not connect or relate to the task.

By keeping these points in mind, you'll ensure that your essay is well received by the TOEFL graders.

Step 4: Use Your Time Wisely

If you had unlimited time, you would surely be able to achieve a top score on the Writing section. Unfortunately, your time on the TOEFL is extremely limited. Thus, you must make sure to use your time wisely. The following tables provide a good guide for how to spend your time.

Task #1: 20 minutes

Time	Task
5 minutes	Organize your essay.
2 minutes	Write your introduction.
10 minutes	Write your body paragraphs.
2 minutes	Write your conclusion.
1 minute	Proofread your essay to correct any mistakes.

Task #2: 30 minutes

Time	Task
7 minutes	Organize your essay.
2 minutes	Write your introduction.
16 minutes	Write your body paragraphs.
2 minutes	Write your conclusion.
3 minutes	Proofread your essay to correct any mistakes.

To stick to these guidelines, you'll have to know exactly what your essay is going to look like. Use the templates from Step 1 to focus as you read.

Now you're ready to try some practice writing drills.

Writing Summary

Congratulations! You now know how to crack all parts of the TOEFL. But before you move on, keep the following points in mind for cracking the Writing section:

o **Answer the question!** Even if you write well, you won't receive a top score unless you address the task. Make sure you know what each task requires.

o **Focus on form.** The structure and organization of your essay is crucial. Make sure you know how to put your essay together.

o **Make the graders' jobs easy.** You know what the TOEFL graders are looking for, so make them happy by giving them a structured essay that uses detailed examples and good transitions.

Let's practice some writing with the drills in the next chapter. Then, if you feel ready, go on to Part IV and take the full-length practice TOEFL exam. If not, review the lessons in the previous chapters until you are confident you know how to crack the test.

Chapter 17
Writing Practice Drills

You're now ready to crack the Writing section. Try the following practice prompts. After you've finished, read through the sample essays in the next chapter to get an idea of what TOEFL graders are looking for in the essay responses.

Writing Practice Drill #1

The first type of writing question will provide you with the following directions:

> You will have 3 minutes to read the following passage. You may take notes during your reading. After the 3 minutes are up, you will hear a lecture on the topic. You may take notes during the lecture as well.
>
> After the lecture ends, you will have 20 minutes to write your response. An effective response is generally 150–225 words long. You may use your notes to help you answer, and you may refer to the reading passage. Your essay will be graded on the quality of your writing and on the completeness of the content.

Now let's look at a writing question. On the actual test, you will hear a prompt that will ask you to read a passage in 3 minutes. For our purposes here, you will need to stop the audio to read the passage and either time yourself or ask a friend to time you. After 3 minutes, resume the audio for the listening passage.

Begin playing Track 23 on the CD or in your Student Tools.

Narrator: Now read the passage about the first grain-based food. You have 3 minutes to read the passage. Begin reading now.

[Stop the audio for 3 minutes while you read the passage on the next page.]

Scant physical evidence remains of the first human domestication of grain. Still, there is enough to conclude that ancient peoples, motivated by the nutritional value of bread or cakes made of wild wheat, looked for controlled ways to grow it to provide a consistent food supply. Three related discoveries are likely to have led to the introduction of bread as the first grain-based food.

The first discovery was that wheat could be prepared for use by grinding. People probably began consuming wheat by chewing it raw. Because wheat is very hard, they gradually discovered that it was less trouble to eat if crushed to paste between two stones. The result would have been the ancestor of the drier, more powdery wheat flour we use today.

From there, it was a short step to the next breakthrough—baking the simplest bread, which requires no technology but fire. Loaves of wheat paste, when baked into bread, could be stored for long periods, certainly longer than raw seeds. This kept the food value of wheat available for an extended period after it had been harvested.

Finally, ancient peoples found that if the paste was allowed to sit in the open, yeast spores from the air settled on it and began fermenting the wheat. This natural process of fermentation caused bubbles to form in the wheat paste, suggesting that it would be lighter in texture and even easier to eat when baked.

Resume playing Track 23.

N: Now listen to part of a lecture on the topic you just read about.

N: Summarize the points made in the lecture you just heard, explaining how they cast doubt on the contents of the reading. You may refer to the passage as you write.

> *For the Writing Drills, make sure you have a word processing document open on your computer and practice typing your response, as you will on test day.*

Directions: You have 20 minutes to plan and write your response. Your response will be graded on the quality of your writing and on how well your response presents the points in the lecture and their relationship to the reading passage. Typically, an effective response will be 150–225 words.

Question: Summarize the points made in the lecture you just heard, explaining how they cast doubt on the contents of the reading. You may refer to the passage as you write.

| Copy | Cut | Paste | | Word Count: 0 |

Scant physical evidence remains of the first human domestication of grain. Still, there is enough to conclude that ancient peoples, motivated by the nutritional value of bread or cakes made of wild wheat, looked for controlled ways to grow it to provide a consistent food supply. Three related discoveries are likely to have led to the introduction of bread as the first grain-based food.

The first discovery was that wheat could be prepared for use by grinding. People probably began consuming wheat by chewing it raw. Because wheat is very hard, they gradually discovered that it was less trouble to eat if crushed to paste between two stones—the result would have been the ancestor of the drier, more powdery wheat flour we use today.

From there, it was a short step to the next breakthrough: baking the simplest bread, which requires no technology but fire. Loaves of wheat paste, when baked into bread, could be stored for long periods, certainly longer than raw seeds. This kept the food value of wheat available for an extended period after it had been harvested.

Finally, ancient peoples found that if the paste was allowed to sit in the open, yeast spores from the air settled on it and began fermenting the wheat. This natural process of fermentation caused bubbles to form in the wheat paste, suggesting that it would be lighter in texture and even easier to eat when baked.

Writing Practice Drill #2

The second type of writing question asks you to write a response to a question in 30 minutes. It will look something like the following:

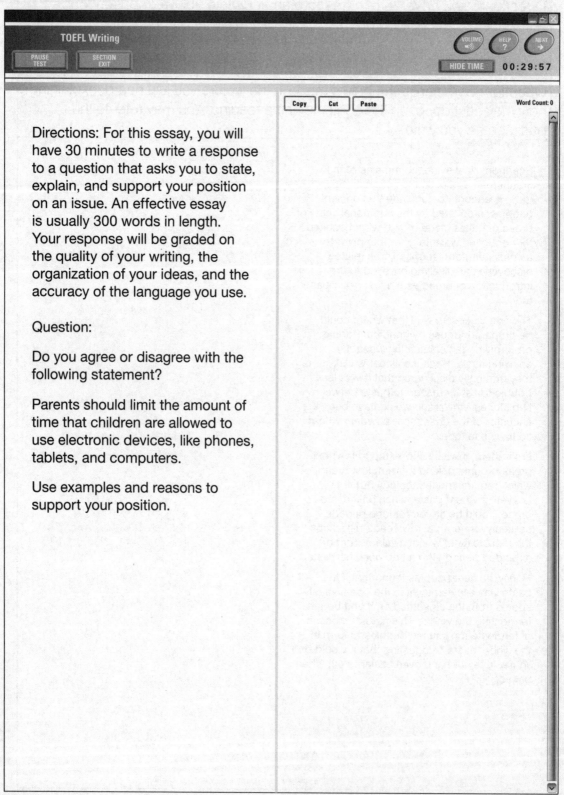

TOEFL Writing

PAUSE TEST   SECTION EXIT

VOLUME   HELP ?   NEXT →

HIDE TIME   00:29:57

Copy   Cut   Paste   Word Count: 0

Directions: For this essay, you will have 30 minutes to write a response to a question that asks you to state, explain, and support your position on an issue. An effective essay is usually 300 words in length. Your response will be graded on the quality of your writing, the organization of your ideas, and the accuracy of the language you use.

Question:

Do you agree or disagree with the following statement?

Parents should limit the amount of time that children are allowed to use electronic devices, like phones, tablets, and computers.

Use examples and reasons to support your position.

Writing Practice Drill #3

This drill again asks you to write a response to a question in 30 minutes.

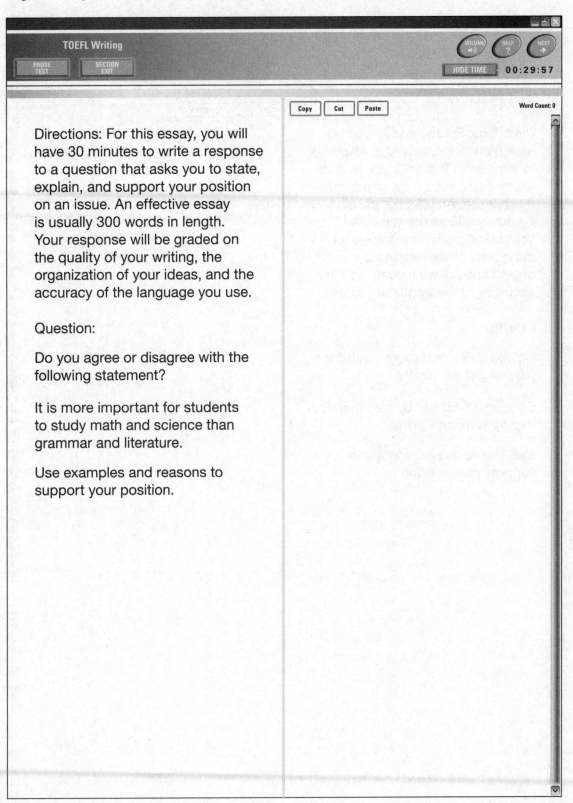

TOEFL Writing

PAUSE TEST   SECTION EXIT

VOLUME   HELP ?   NEXT →

HIDE TIME   00:29:57

Copy   Cut   Paste

Word Count: 0

Directions: For this essay, you will have 30 minutes to write a response to a question that asks you to state, explain, and support your position on an issue. An effective essay is usually 300 words in length. Your response will be graded on the quality of your writing, the organization of your ideas, and the accuracy of the language you use.

Question:

Do you agree or disagree with the following statement?

It is more important for students to study math and science than grammar and literature.

Use examples and reasons to support your position.

Writing Practice Drill #4

This is another opportunity for you to write a response to a question in 30 minutes.

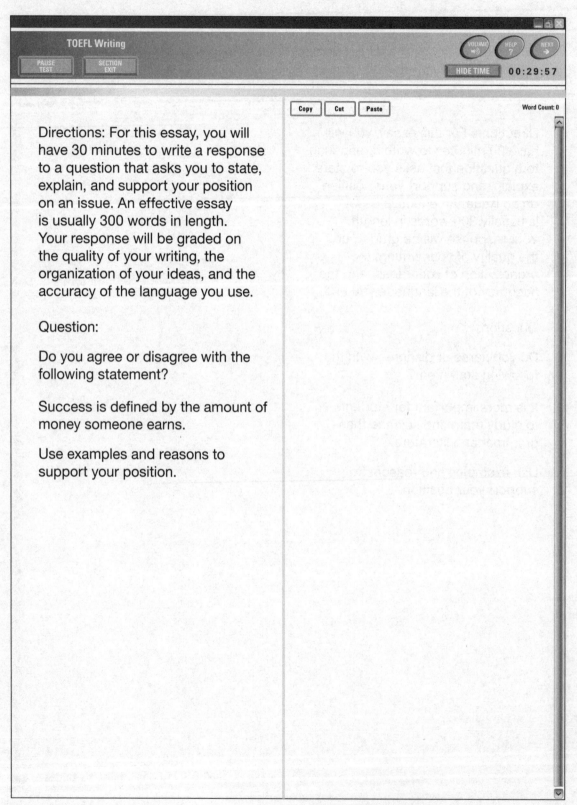

TOEFL Writing

PAUSE TEST   SECTION EXIT

VOLUME   HELP ?   NEXT →

HIDE TIME   00:29:57

Copy   Cut   Paste   Word Count: 0

Directions: For this essay, you will have 30 minutes to write a response to a question that asks you to state, explain, and support your position on an issue. An effective essay is usually 300 words in length. Your response will be graded on the quality of your writing, the organization of your ideas, and the accuracy of the language you use.

Question:

Do you agree or disagree with the following statement?

Success is defined by the amount of money someone earns.

Use examples and reasons to support your position.

Writing Practice Drill #5

Here's another chance to write a response to a question in 30 minutes.

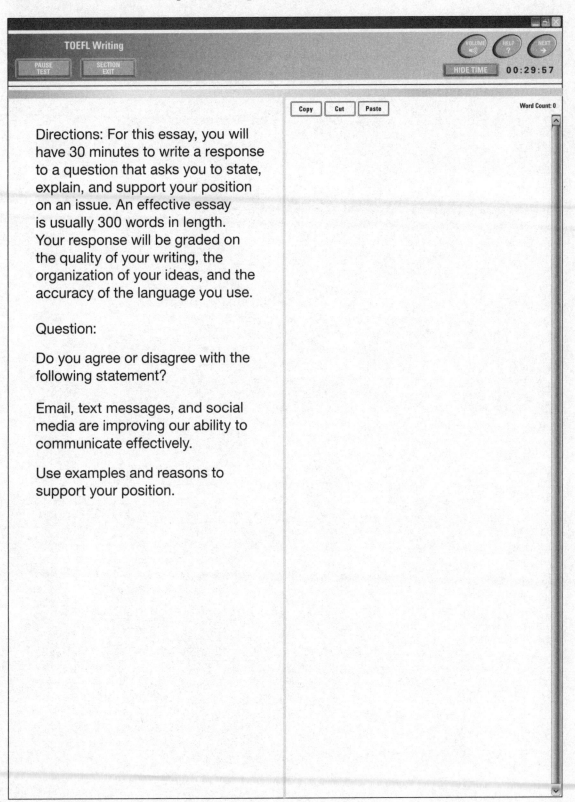

TOEFL Writing

PAUSE TEST   SECTION EXIT

VOLUME   HELP ?   NEXT →

HIDE TIME   00:29:57

Copy   Cut   Paste

Word Count: 0

Directions: For this essay, you will have 30 minutes to write a response to a question that asks you to state, explain, and support your position on an issue. An effective essay is usually 300 words in length. Your response will be graded on the quality of your writing, the organization of your ideas, and the accuracy of the language you use.

Question:

Do you agree or disagree with the following statement?

Email, text messages, and social media are improving our ability to communicate effectively.

Use examples and reasons to support your position.

Chapter 18
Writing Practice
Answers and
Explanations

Read through the following sample responses to the drills you completed in the previous chapter and compare your essays with them. If possible, have a friend who is a native speaker or highly proficient in English look over your essays.

As always, your writing does not have to match ours exactly. Just check to see if your essay accomplishes the important points highlighted in the high-scoring essays.

WRITING PRACTICE DRILL #1

Take a look at the first task.

> *Narrator:* Now read the passage about the first grain-based food. You have 3 minutes to read the passage. Begin reading now.

Scant physical evidence remains of the first human domestication of grain. Still, there is enough to conclude that ancient peoples, motivated by the nutritional value of bread or cakes made of wild wheat, looked for controlled ways to grow it to provide a consistent food supply. Three related discoveries are likely to have led to the introduction of bread as the first grain-based food.

The first discovery was that wheat could be prepared for use by grinding. People probably began consuming wheat by chewing it raw. Because wheat is very hard, they gradually discovered that it was less trouble to eat if crushed to paste between two stones—the result would have been the ancestor of the drier, more powdery wheat flour we use today.

From there, it was a short step to the next breakthrough: baking the simplest bread, which requires no technology but fire. Loaves of wheat paste, when baked into bread, could be stored for long periods, certainly longer than raw seeds. This kept the food value of wheat available for an extended period after it had been harvested.

Finally, ancient peoples found that if the paste was allowed to sit in the open, yeast spores from the air settled on it and began fermenting the wheat. This natural process of fermentation caused bubbles to form in the wheat paste that suggested it would be lighter in texture and even easier to eat when baked.

> *Narrator:* Now listen to part of a lecture on the topic you just read about.

> *Professor:* Conventional wisdom says that a very primitive kind of bread was the first grain food that human societies ate. But, you know, for the last few decades, there's been an alternative hypothesis that quite a few anthropologists are starting to give a closer look. That hypothesis says that it was, in fact, beer—not bread—that was the first grain food. Sound strange? Consider a couple of things.
>
> For one thing, you don't have to grind wheat to make it easier to eat. If you keep it in a moist environment, it naturally starts sprouting, with a new baby plant splitting the hard seed case in half. Sprouted wheat is sweeter, softer, and actually more nutritious than whole wheat seeds—and it would have developed without human

More Available

9. The author implies that the most complex phase of tree worship involves

   a. the belief that all trees are sacred
   b. distinguishing between male and female tree spirits
   c. different ceremonies for different seasons
   d. the use of trees as symbols

The Veneration of Trees

In *The Golden Bough,* his classic catalog of mythologies, Sir James George Frazer extensively documents the significance of trees in world religion. His chapters on tree spirits roam from Northern Europe to the Eastern Seaboard of what is now the United States
5 to the islands of the Pacific. Despite the lack of contact among these regions, the veneration of trees united them. The woods that covered large areas of Europe and North America, in particular, were difficult to penetrate and dangerous to cross. It was not a great mental leap for people to see the trees that populated them
10 as embodiments of the natural forces that governed their lives.

On the basis of Frazer's classification, one can derive three loose stages of tree worship. In the first, a society sees the tree as the physical body of the spirit that inhabits it, much as the human body
15 can be seen as housing the mind. It is known that both the Celtic and the Germanic tribes that inhabited ancient Northern Europe regarded certain trees as sacred, setting them apart by species (as the Druids worshipped oaks) or by location (the way certain natural groves were regarded as natural temples or sacred spaces in what
20 is now Germany). Early on, each of these trees was regarded as an animate being with both spirit and body. It had a distinct identity, like an individual person. This suggests that it was believed to have the same impulses and reactions as the people who venerated it.

25 Accordingly, ancient peoples had elaborate taboos designed to avoid causing offense to trees. These taboos were taken very seriously. In some places, one could be punished severely for injuring the bark of a tree or stealing its fruit. Before a tree was felled for human use, woodcutters in many world cultures would offer it
30 both apologies and thanks for the resources it was about to provide them. This was necessary to avoid insulting the tree and inviting bad fortune. It was also the case, however, that injuries were said to cause suffering to trees as they did to people. In some societies, it was claimed that trees cry out in pain when struck or cut into. A
35 tree's spirit and body are considered inseparable in this first stage.

A society makes a leap in sophistication and reaches Frazer's second stage when it begins to regard them as separate. That is, the spirit exists independently of the physical tree, even if it
40 chooses to dwell there most of the time. The same spirit may thus take up residence in any tree of a forest; it is not killed when an individual tree is cut down. It is not bound to a single tree but rather stands for a group. The distinction may seem small, but it is a significant first step toward symbolic thinking. A forest, after
45 all, is more than the sum of its parts. It encompasses not only its trees but also the animals and brush that flourish among them. The dangers of the forest are hidden; a traveler may or may not encounter them on a given journey. To think about a tree spirit identified with the forest as a whole, therefore, people had to
50 think about phenomena that were removed from them in time and space—ideas rather than things. Such a tree spirit represented the potential and abstract rather than the concrete and immediate.

That transition is completed in the third stage. Liberated from each
55 other, trees and their spirits can begin to be seen as symbols and embodiments of other natural processes of significance to primitive life: the power of weather and seasons to produce good or bad harvests, the mysteries of childbirth and disease. At that point, the veneration of trees reaches its stage of greatest complexity.
60 Societies in both Eastern Europe and the South Pacific presented ceremonial offerings to trees in the hopes that they would furnish rain and sunshine. Women who hoped to bear children might be instructed to embrace special trees thought to give fertility. The appearance of these beliefs, in which the fruitfulness of trees
65 suggests the fruitfulness of harvests and family-building, indicates that a society has made its first steps toward symbolic and abstract thinking.

More Available

10. The word furnish in the passage is closest in meaning to

a.   explain
b.   provide
c.   avoid
d.   refuse

The Veneration of Trees

In *The Golden Bough,* his classic catalog of mythologies, Sir James George Frazer extensively documents the significance of trees in world religion. His chapters on tree spirits roam from Northern Europe to the Eastern Seaboard of what is now the United States
5   to the islands of the Pacific. Despite the lack of contact among these regions, the veneration of trees united them. The woods that covered large areas of Europe and North America, in particular, were difficult to penetrate and dangerous to cross. It was not a great mental leap for people to see the trees that populated them as
10 embodiments of the natural forces that governed their lives.

On the basis of Frazer's classification, one can derive three loose stages of tree worship. In the first, a society sees the tree as the physical body of the spirit that inhabits it, much as the human body
15 can be seen as housing the mind. It is known that both the Celtic and the Germanic tribes that inhabited ancient Northern Europe regarded certain trees as sacred, setting them apart by species (as the Druids worshipped oaks) or by location (the way certain natural groves were regarded as natural temples or sacred spaces in what
20 is now Germany). Early on, each of these trees was regarded as an animate being with both spirit and body. It had a distinct identity, like an individual person. This suggests that it was believed to have the same impulses and reactions as the people who venerated it.

25 Accordingly, ancient peoples had elaborate taboos designed to avoid causing offense to trees. These taboos were taken very seriously. In some places, one could be punished severely for injuring the bark of a tree or stealing its fruit. Before a tree was felled for human use, woodcutters in many world cultures would offer it
30 both apologies and thanks for the resources it was about to provide them. This was necessary to avoid insulting the tree and inviting bad fortune. It was also the case, however, that injuries were said to cause suffering to trees as they did to people. In some societies, it was claimed that trees cry out in pain when struck or cut into. A
35 tree's spirit and body are considered inseparable in this first stage.

A society makes a leap in sophistication and reaches Frazer's second stage when it begins to regard them as separate. That is, the spirit exists independently of the physical tree, even if it
40 chooses to dwell there most of the time. The same spirit may thus take up residence in any tree of a forest; it is not killed when an individual tree is cut down. It is not bound to a single tree but rather stands for a group. The distinction may seem small, but it is a significant first step toward symbolic thinking. A forest, after all, is
45 more than the sum of its parts. It encompasses not only its trees but also the animals and brush that flourish among them. The dangers of the forest are hidden; a traveler may or may not encounter them on a given journey. To think about a tree spirit identified with the forest as a whole, therefore, people had to think about phenomena
50 that were removed from them in time and space—ideas rather than things. Such a tree spirit represented the potential and abstract rather than the concrete and immediate.

That transition is completed in the third stage. Liberated from each
55 other, trees and their spirits can begin to be seen as symbols and embodiments of other natural processes of significance to primitive life: the power of weather and seasons to produce good or bad harvests, the mysteries of childbirth and disease. At that point, the veneration of trees reaches its stage of greatest complexity.
60 Societies in both Eastern Europe and the South Pacific presented ceremonial offerings to trees in the hopes that they would furnish rain and sunshine. Women who hoped to bear children might be instructed to embrace special trees thought to give fertility. The appearance of these beliefs, in which the fruitfulness of trees
65 suggests the fruitfulness of harvests and family-building, indicates that a society has made its first steps toward symbolic and abstract thinking.

11. According to paragraph 5 of the passage, ancient peoples saw special meaning in

a.   the ability of trees to bear fruit

b.   the three stages in the life cycle of a tree

c.   trees that required little rain and sun

d.   the raising of trees by women

Paragraph 5 is marked with an arrow [→]

The Veneration of Trees

In *The Golden Bough,* his classic catalog of mythologies, Sir James George Frazer extensively documents the significance of trees in world religion. His chapters on tree spirits roam from Northern Europe to the Eastern Seaboard of what is now the United States
5   to the islands of the Pacific. Despite the lack of contact among these regions, the veneration of trees united them. The woods that covered large areas of Europe and North America, in particular, were difficult to penetrate and dangerous to cross. It was not a great mental leap for people to see the trees that populated them
10   as embodiments of the natural forces that governed their lives.

On the basis of Frazer's classification, one can derive three loose stages of tree worship. In the first, a society sees the tree as the physical body of the spirit that inhabits it, much as the human body
15   can be seen as housing the mind. It is known that both the Celtic and the Germanic tribes that inhabited ancient Northern Europe regarded certain trees as sacred, setting them apart by species (as the Druids worshipped oaks) or by location (the way certain natural groves were regarded as natural temples or sacred spaces in what
20   is now Germany). Early on, each of these trees was regarded as an animate being with both spirit and body. It had a distinct identity, like an individual person. This suggests that it was believed to have the same impulses and reactions as the people who venerated it.

25   Accordingly, ancient peoples had elaborate taboos designed to avoid causing offense to trees. These taboos were taken very seriously. In some places, one could be punished severely for injuring the bark of a tree or stealing its fruit. Before a tree was felled for human use, woodcutters in many world cultures would offer it
30   both apologies and thanks for the resources it was about to provide them. This was necessary to avoid insulting the tree and inviting bad fortune. It was also the case, however, that injuries were said to cause suffering to trees as they did to people. In some societies, it was claimed that trees cry out in pain when struck or cut into. A
35   tree's spirit and body are considered inseparable in this first stage.

A society makes a leap in sophistication and reaches Frazer's second stage when it begins to regard them as separate. That is, the spirit exists independently of the physical tree, even if it
40   chooses to dwell there most of the time. The same spirit may thus take up residence in any tree of a forest; it is not killed when an individual tree is cut down. It is not bound to a single tree but rather stands for a group. The distinction may seem small, but it is a significant first step toward symbolic thinking. A forest, after
45   all, is more than the sum of its parts. It encompasses not only its trees but also the animals and brush that flourish among them. The dangers of the forest are hidden; a traveler may or may not encounter them on a given journey. To think about a tree spirit identified with the forest as a whole, therefore, people had to
50   think about phenomena that were removed from them in time and space—ideas rather than things. Such a tree spirit represented the potential and abstract rather than the concrete and immediate.

→ That transition is completed in the third stage. Liberated from
55   each other, trees and their spirits can begin to be seen as symbols and embodiments of other natural processes of significance to primitive life: the power of weather and seasons to produce good or bad harvests, the mysteries of childbirth and disease. At that point, the veneration of trees reaches its stage of greatest complexity.
60   Societies in both Eastern Europe and the South Pacific presented ceremonial offerings to trees in the hopes that they would furnish rain and sunshine. Women who hoped to bear children might be instructed to embrace special trees thought to give fertility. The appearance of these beliefs, in which the fruitfulness of trees
65   suggests the fruitfulness of harvests and family-building, indicates that a society has made its first steps toward symbolic and abstract thinking.

12. Directions: An introductory sentence for a brief summary of the passage is provided below. Complete the summary by selecting the THREE answer choices that express the most important ideas in the passage. Some sentences do not belong in the summary because they express ideas that are not presented in the passage or are minor ideas in the passage. *This question is worth 2 points.*

Three basic levels of tree worship can be observed in *The Golden Bough*.

- •
- •
- •

Answer Choices	
It was forbidden to cut down certain trees because they would be seriously offended by an injury.	Ancient Germans believed certain groves were sacred and used them as temples, but Druids venerated the oak tree in particular.
Certain peoples came to believe that tree spirits were independent of individual trees and instead represented a whole forest.	Some societies believed each tree had an individual spirit, the way a human being has a distinct mind.
More is known about the ceremonies of Europe than about the ceremonies of North America and the South Pacific.	A basis for abstract thinking was achieved when tree spirits were believed to control natural forces such as crops and human fertility.

More Available

Mercury Pollution

When most people think or talk about dangers to our environment, they focus on general terms like "pollution," "smog," and "acid rain." Also, they often focus on the

5 impact of supposedly man-made chemicals and compounds. But to truly understand the risks to our environment, it's helpful to focus on the danger of specific chemicals, which are often otherwise naturally-

10 occurring elements that have been spread harmfully by man. One of the largest threats to our environment is mercury: Hg on the periodic table of elements.

15 At room temperature, mercury, a metal, exists as a silvery-white liquid. However, it vaporizes readily when heat is applied, and it can stay suspended in the air for more than a year. The largest sources of mercury

20 pollution in the United States are coal-fired power plants. Emissions from these plants account for 70 percent of the mercury that enters our oceans, lakes, and streams. Air currents carry these particles far from the

25 source and are capable of polluting bodies of water thousands of miles away.

Mercury particles released into the air fall into these waterways and quickly enter

30 aquatic food chains. First, mercury attaches to sediments (fragments of organic and inorganic material that settle to the bottom of the body of water). Second, bacteria change the mercury into methyl mercury, a

35 highly toxic substance. Third, phytoplankton feed on the organic matter in sediments and absorb the methyl mercury. Fourth, fish then eat the mercury-contaminated phytoplankton; the larger the fish and the

40 longer it lives, the more concentrated the methyl mercury in its system becomes.

More Available

The mercury can then move higher up the food chain when humans eat fish that have
45 absorbed high amounts of mercury.

Studies indicate that mercury levels in U.S. waterways have increased anywhere from 100 to 400 percent over the course of the
50 last century, and no river, lake, or ocean seems immune. It is important to note that, thanks to the U.S. Clean Air Act and efforts by industry to curb unnecessary discharges as well as better sewage treatment methods,
55 the levels have been in slow decline since the 1970s. However, this minor decline is relatively miniscule in comparison to the major increase in the years prior.

60 If you've ever experienced that "rotten egg" smell during low tide at a coastal area, you've seen (or smelled) methylation in action. Methylation is the conversion of mercury in sediments to methyl mercury
65 by sulfate-reducing bacteria. While this methylation is a natural process, the industrial discharge of mercury has greatly accelerated the process beyond what the ecosystem is able to absorb safely. This
70 methylation not only impacts aquatic species, but also harms humans and other land-based wildlife.

Most of the fish and shellfish that humans
75 eat live solely in coastal areas or frequent coastal areas and feed on the fish that live there. At the same time, most methylation takes place in coastal areas. Therefore, methyl mercury moves up the food chain
80 from plankton to lobster, bluefish, winter flounder, tuna, and many other species eaten extensively by man. The methyl mercury binds to the protein in fish, residing in the muscle of the fish. This muscle is
85 exactly what we eat: the fillet.

The short-term impact of digestion of toxic methyl mercury is obviously a concern. ■ More troubling, however, is its long-term
90 impact on species up and down the food chain. ■ In Wisconsin, scientists have studied the decline of chick production in loons (aquatic birds). ■ They have made a positive link to mercury concentration
95 in eggs which exceeds the concentration found to be toxic in laboratory studies. ■ Through that example, the lasting impact of methyl mercury far from the source of the pollution can be seen.
100

One of the great wonders of the Earth is the interconnectivity of all the world's ecosystems. This interconnectivity gives us the range and diversity of wildlife that we all
105 enjoy and it also allowed life on the planet to endure through cataclysmic events, such as asteroid impacts and the ice ages. However, it is this very interconnectivity that makes our ecosystems so vulnerable.
110 Mercury pollution is unfortunately one of many examples of an environmental impact far removed from the source of the pollution; understanding the process by which the pollution spreads up the food chain is one
115 of many steps to ameliorate the impact of such pollution.

More Available

13. The word applied in the passage is closest in meaning to

a. improved
b. created
c. used
d. reduced

Mercury Pollution

When most people think or talk about dangers to our environment, they focus on general terms like "pollution," "smog," and "acid-rain." Also, they often focus on the impact of supposedly man-made chemicals and compounds. But to truly understand the risks to our environment,
5 it's helpful to focus on the danger of specific chemicals, which are often otherwise naturally-occurring elements that have been spread harmfully by man. One of the largest threats to our environment is mercury: Hg on the periodic table of elements.

10 At room temperature, mercury, a metal, exists as a silvery-white liquid. However, it vaporizes readily when heat is applied, and can stay suspended in the air for more than a year. The largest sources of mercury pollution in the United States are coal-fired power plants. Emissions from these plants account for 70 percent of the mercury
15 that enters our oceans, lakes, and streams. Air currents carry these particles far from the source and are capable of polluting bodies of water thousands of miles away.

Mercury particles released into the air fall into these waterways and
20 quickly enter aquatic food chains. First, mercury attaches to sediments (fragments of organic and inorganic material that settle to the bottom of the body of water). Second, bacteria change the mercury into methyl mercury, a highly toxic substance. Third, phytoplankton feed on the organic matter in sediments and absorb the methyl mercury. Fourth, fish
25 then eat the mercury-contaminated phytoplankton; the larger the fish and the longer it lives, the more concentrated the methyl mercury in its system becomes. The mercury can then move higher up the food chain when humans eat fish that have absorbed high amounts of mercury.

30 Studies indicate that mercury levels in U.S. waterways have increased anywhere from 100 to 400 percent over the course of the last century, and no river, lake, or ocean seems immune. It is important to note that, thanks to the U.S. Clean Air Act and efforts by industry to curb unnecessary discharges as well as better sewage treatment methods,
35 the levels have been in slow decline since the 1970s. However, this minor decline is relatively miniscule in comparison to the major increase in the years prior.

If you've ever experienced that "rotten egg" smell during low tide
40 at a coastal area, you've seen (or smelled) methylation in action. Methylation is the conversion of mercury in sediments to methyl mercury by sulfate-reducing bacteria. While this methylation is a natural process, the industrial discharge of mercury has greatly accelerated the process beyond what the ecosystem is able to absorb safely. This
45 methylation not only impacts aquatic species, but also harms humans and other land-based wildlife.

Most of the fish and shellfish that humans eat live solely in coastal areas or frequent coastal areas and feed on the fish that live there.
50 At the same time, most methylation takes place in coastal areas. Therefore, methyl mercury moves up the food chain from plankton to lobster, bluefish, winter flounder, tuna, and many other species eaten extensively by man. The methyl mercury binds to the protein in fish, residing in the muscle of the fish. This muscle is exactly what we eat:
55 the fillet.

The short-term impact of digestion of toxic methyl mercury is obviously a concern. ■ More troubling, however, is its long-term impact on species up and down the food chain. ■ In Wisconsin, scientists have
60 studied the decline of chick production in loons (aquatic birds). ■ They have made a positive link to mercury concentration in eggs which exceeds the concentration found to be toxic in laboratory studies. ■ Through that example, the lasting impact of methyl mercury far from the source of the pollution can be seen.
65
One of the great wonders of the Earth is the interconnectivity of all the world's ecosystems. This interconnectivity gives us the range and diversity of wildlife that we all enjoy and it also allowed life on the planet to endure through cataclysmic events, such as asteroid impacts
70 and the ice ages. However, it is this very interconnectivity that makes our ecosystems so vulnerable. Mercury pollution is unfortunately one of many examples of an environmental impact far removed from the source of the pollution; understanding the process by which the pollution spreads up the food chain is one of many steps to ameliorate
75 the impact of such pollution.

TOEFL Reading

14 of 38

REVIEW   HELP   BACK   NEXT
?

PAUSE TEST   SECTION EXIT

HIDE TIME   00:08:45

More Available

14. According to paragraph 2, what accounts for 70% of toxic mercury pollution?

a.   Air currents
b.   Vaporization
c.   Coal-fired power plants
d.   A silvery-white liquid

Paragraph 2 is marked with an arrow [→]

Mercury Pollution

When most people think or talk about dangers to our environment, they focus on general terms like "pollution," "smog," and "acid-rain." Also, they often focus on the impact of supposedly man-made chemicals and compounds. But to truly understand the risks to our environment,
5   it's helpful to focus on the danger of specific chemicals, which are often otherwise naturally-occurring elements that have been spread harmfully by man. One of the largest threats to our environment is mercury: Hg on the periodic table of elements.

10 → At room temperature, mercury, a metal, exists as a silvery-white liquid. However, it vaporizes readily when heat is applied, and can stay suspended in the air for more than a year. The largest sources of mercury pollution in the United States are coal-fired power plants. Emissions from these plants account for 70 percent of the mercury
15   that enters our oceans, lakes, and streams. Air currents carry these particles far from the source and are capable of polluting bodies of water thousands of miles away.

Mercury particles released into the air fall into these waterways and
20   quickly enter aquatic food chains. First, mercury attaches to sediments (fragments of organic and inorganic material that settle to the bottom of the body of water). Second, bacteria change the mercury into methyl mercury, a highly toxic substance. Third, phytoplankton feed on the organic matter in sediments and absorb the methyl mercury. Fourth, fish
25   eat the mercury-contaminated phytoplankton; the larger the fish and the longer it lives, the more concentrated the methyl mercury in its system becomes. The mercury can then move higher up the food chain when humans eat fish that have absorbed high amounts of mercury.

30   Studies indicate that mercury levels in U.S. waterways have increased anywhere from 100 to 400 percent over the course of the last century, and no river, lake, or ocean seems immune. It is important to note that, thanks to the U.S. Clean Air Act and efforts by industry to curb unnecessary discharges as well as better sewage treatment methods,
35   the levels have been in slow decline since the 1970s. However, this minor decline is relatively miniscule in comparison to the major increase in the years prior.

If you've ever experienced that "rotten egg" smell during low tide
40   at a coastal area, you've seen (or smelled) methylation in action. Methylation is the conversion of mercury in sediments to methyl mercury by sulfate-reducing bacteria. While this methylation is a natural process, the industrial discharge of mercury has greatly accelerated the process beyond what the ecosystem is able to absorb
45   safely. This methylation not only impacts aquatic species, but also harms humans and other land-based wildlife.

Most of the fish and shellfish that humans eat live solely in coastal areas or frequent coastal areas and feed on the fish that live there.
50   At the same time, most methylation takes place in coastal areas. Therefore, methyl mercury moves up the food chain from plankton to lobster, bluefish, winter flounder, tuna, and many other species eaten extensively by man. The methyl mercury binds to the protein in fish, residing in the muscle of the fish. This muscle is exactly what we eat:
55   the fillet.

The short-term impact of digestion of toxic methyl mercury is obviously a concern. ■ More troubling, however, is its long-term impact on species up and down the food chain. ■ In Wisconsin, scientists have
60   studied the decline of chick production in loons (aquatic birds). ■ They have made a positive link to mercury concentration in eggs which exceeds the concentration found to be toxic in laboratory studies. ■ Through that example, the lasting impact of methyl mercury far from the source of the pollution can be seen.

65   One of the great wonders of the Earth is the interconnectivity of all the world's ecosystems. This interconnectivity gives us the range and diversity of wildlife that we all enjoy and it also allowed life on the planet to endure through cataclysmic events, such as asteroid impacts
70   and the ice ages. However, it is this very interconnectivity that makes our ecosystems so vulnerable. Mercury pollution is unfortunately one of many examples of an environmental impact far removed from the source of the pollution; understanding the process by which the pollution spreads up the food chain is one of many steps to ameliorate
75   the impact of such pollution.

More Available

15. In paragraph 3, what does the author say about the role of phytoplankton in the spread of mercury throughout the food chain?

a. It transforms mercury to methyl mercury.

b. It provides the link between the methyl mercury in sediments and fish.

c. It reduces the impact of methyl mercury on the coastal ecosystem.

d. It concentrates the mercury making it less toxic.

Paragraph 3 is marked with an arrow [→]

Mercury Pollution

When most people think or talk about dangers to our environment, they focus on general terms like "pollution," "smog," and "acid-rain." Also, they often focus on the impact of supposedly man-made chemicals and compounds. But to truly understand the risks to our environment,
5   it's helpful to focus on the danger of specific chemicals, which are often otherwise naturally-occurring elements that have been spread harmfully by man. One of the largest threats to our environment is mercury: Hg on the periodic table of elements.

At room temperature, mercury, a metal, exists as a silvery-white
10 liquid. However, it vaporizes readily when heat is applied, and can stay suspended in the air for more than a year. The largest sources of mercury pollution in the United States are coal-fired power plants. Emissions from these plants account for 70 percent of the mercury
15 that enters our oceans, lakes, and streams. Air currents carry these particles far from the source and are capable of polluting bodies of water thousands of miles away.

→ Mercury particles released into the air fall into these waterways and
20 quickly enter aquatic food chains. First, mercury attaches to sediments (fragments of organic and inorganic material that settle to the bottom of the body of water). Second, bacteria change the mercury into methyl mercury, a highly toxic substance. Third, phytoplankton feed on the organic matter in sediments and absorb the methyl mercury. Fourth, fish
25 then eat the mercury-contaminated phytoplankton; the larger the fish and the longer it lives, the more concentrated the methyl mercury in its system becomes. The mercury can then move higher up the food chain when humans eat fish that have absorbed high amounts of mercury.

Studies indicate that mercury levels in U.S. waterways have increased
30 anywhere from 100 to 400 percent over the course of the last century, and no river, lake, or ocean seems immune. It is important to note that, thanks to the U.S. Clean Air Act and efforts by industry to curb unnecessary discharges as well as better sewage treatment methods,
35 the levels have been in slow decline since the 1970s. However, this minor decline is relatively miniscule in comparison to the major increase in the years prior.

If you've ever experienced that "rotten egg" smell during low tide
40 at a coastal area, you've seen (or smelled) methylation in action. Methylation is the conversion of mercury in sediments to methyl mercury by sulfate-reducing bacteria. While this methylation is a natural process, the industrial discharge of mercury has greatly accelerated the process beyond what the ecosystem is able to absorb safely. This
45 methylation not only impacts aquatic species, but also harms humans and other land-based wildlife.

Most of the fish and shellfish that humans eat live solely in coastal areas or frequent coastal areas and feed on the fish that live there.
50 At the same time, most methylation takes place in coastal areas. Therefore, methyl mercury moves up the food chain from plankton to lobster, bluefish, winter flounder, tuna, and many other species eaten extensively by man. The methyl mercury binds to the protein in fish, residing in the muscle of the fish. This muscle is exactly what we eat:
55 the fillet.

The short-term impact of digestion of toxic methyl mercury is obviously a concern. ■ More troubling, however, is its long-term impact on species up and down the food chain. ■ In Wisconsin, scientists have
60 studied the decline of chick production in loons (aquatic birds). ■ They have made a positive link to mercury concentration in eggs which exceeds the concentration found to be toxic in laboratory studies. ■ Through that example, the lasting impact of methyl mercury far from the source of the pollution can be seen.
65

One of the great wonders of the Earth is the interconnectivity of all the world's ecosystems. This interconnectivity gives us the range and diversity of wildlife that we all enjoy and it also allowed life on the planet to endure through cataclysmic events, such as asteroid impacts
70 and the ice ages. However, it is this very interconnectivity that makes our ecosystems so vulnerable. Mercury pollution is unfortunately one of many examples of an environmental impact far removed from the source of the pollution; understanding the process by which the pollution spreads up the food chain is one of many steps to ameliorate
75 the impact of such pollution.

More Available

16. The word concentrated in the passage is closest in meaning to

a. clustered
b. thought
c. separated
d. reduced

Mercury Pollution

When most people think or talk about dangers to our environment, they focus on general terms like "pollution," "smog," and "acid-rain." Also, they often focus on the impact of supposedly man-made chemicals and compounds. But to truly understand the risks to our environment,
5 it's helpful to focus on the danger of specific chemicals, which are often otherwise naturally-occurring elements that have been spread harmfully by man. One of the largest threats to our environment is mercury: Hg on the periodic table of elements.

10 At room temperature, mercury, a metal, exists as a silvery-white liquid. However, it vaporizes readily when heat is applied, and can stay suspended in the air for more than a year. The largest sources of mercury pollution in the United States are coal-fired power plants. Emissions from these plants account for 70 percent of the mercury
15 that enters our oceans, lakes, and streams. Air currents carry these particles far from the source and are capable of polluting bodies of water thousands of miles away.

Mercury particles released into the air fall into these waterways and
20 quickly enter aquatic food chains. First, mercury attaches to sediments (fragments of organic and inorganic material that settle to the bottom of the body of water). Second, bacteria change the mercury into methyl mercury, a highly toxic substance. Third, phytoplankton feed on the organic matter in sediments and absorb the methyl mercury. Fourth, fish
25 then eat the mercury-contaminated phytoplankton; the larger the fish and the longer it lives, the more concentrated the methyl mercury in its system becomes. The mercury can then move higher up the food chain when humans eat fish that have absorbed high amounts of mercury.

30 Studies indicate that mercury levels in U.S. waterways have increased anywhere from 100 to 400 percent over the course of the last century, and no river, lake, or ocean seems immune. It is important to note that, thanks to the U.S. Clean Air Act and efforts by industry to curb unnecessary discharges as well as better sewage treatment methods,
35 the levels have been in slow decline since the 1970s. However, this minor decline is relatively miniscule in comparison to the major increase in the years prior.

If you've ever experienced that "rotten egg" smell during low tide
40 at a coastal area, you've seen (or smelled) methylation in action. Methylation is the conversion of mercury in sediments to methyl mercury by sulfate-reducing bacteria. While this methylation is a natural process, the industrial discharge of mercury has greatly accelerated the process beyond what the ecosystem is able to absorb
45 safely. This methylation not only impacts aquatic species, but also harms humans and other land-based wildlife.

Most of the fish and shellfish that humans eat live solely in coastal areas or frequent coastal areas and feed on the fish that live there.
50 At the same time, most methylation takes place in coastal areas. Therefore, methyl mercury moves up the food chain from plankton to lobster, bluefish, winter flounder, tuna, and many other species eaten extensively by man. The methyl mercury binds to the protein in fish, residing in the muscle of the fish. This muscle is exactly what we eat:
55 the fillet.

The short-term impact of digestion of toxic methyl mercury is obviously a concern. ■ More troubling, however, is its long-term impact on species up and down the food chain. ■ In Wisconsin, scientists have
60 studied the decline of chick production in loons (aquatic birds). ■ They have made a positive link to mercury concentration in eggs which exceeds the concentration found to be toxic in laboratory studies. ■ Through that example, the lasting impact of methyl mercury far from the source of the pollution can be seen.
65
One of the great wonders of the Earth is the interconnectivity of all the world's ecosystems. This interconnectivity gives us the range and diversity of wildlife that we all enjoy and it also allowed life on the planet to endure through cataclysmic events, such as asteroid impacts
70 and the ice ages. However, it is this very interconnectivity that makes our ecosystems so vulnerable. Mercury pollution is unfortunately one of many examples of an environmental impact far removed from the source of the pollution; understanding the process by which the pollution spreads up the food chain is one of many steps to ameliorate
75 the impact of such pollution.

More Available

17. Which of the following can be inferred from paragraph 4 about the U.S. Clean Air Act?

a.   It was aimed to increase air pollution.

b.   It existed prior to the effects of pollution on the environment were known.

c.   It was part of the reason industries reduced harmful emissions into the air.

d.   It has been unsuccessful in slowing air pollution.

Paragraph 4 is marked with an arrow [→]

Mercury Pollution

When most people think or talk about dangers to our environment, they focus on general terms like "pollution," "smog," and "acid-rain." Also, they often focus on the impact of supposedly man-made chemicals and compounds. But to truly understand the risks to our environment,
5   it's helpful to focus on the danger of specific chemicals, which are often otherwise naturally-occurring elements that have been spread harmfully by man. One of the largest threats to our environment is mercury: Hg on the periodic table of elements.

At room temperature, mercury, a metal, exists as a silvery-white
10   liquid. However, it vaporizes readily when heat is applied, and can stay suspended in the air for more than a year. The largest sources of mercury pollution in the United States are coal-fired power plants. Emissions from these plants account for 70 percent of the mercury
15   that enters our oceans, lakes, and streams. Air currents carry these particles far from the source and are capable of polluting bodies of water thousands of miles away.

Mercury particles released into the air fall into these waterways and
20   quickly enter aquatic food chains. First, mercury attaches to sediments (fragments of organic and inorganic material that settle to the bottom of the body of water). Second, bacteria change the mercury into methyl mercury, a highly toxic substance. Third, phytoplankton feed on the organic matter in sediments and absorb the methyl mercury. Fourth, fish
25   then eat the mercury-contaminated phytoplankton; the larger the fish and the longer it lives, the more concentrated the methyl mercury in its system becomes. The mercury can then move higher up the food chain when humans eat fish that have absorbed high amounts of mercury.

30   → Studies indicate that mercury levels in U.S. waterways have increased anywhere from 100 to 400 percent over the course of the last century, and no river, lake, or ocean seems immune. It is important to note that, thanks to the U.S. Clean Air Act and efforts by industry to curb unnecessary discharges as well as better sewage treatment
35   methods, the levels have been in slow decline since the 1970s. However, this minor decline is relatively miniscule in comparison to the major increase in the years prior.

If you've ever experienced that "rotten egg" smell during low tide
40   at a coastal area, you've seen (or smelled) methylation in action. Methylation is the conversion of mercury in sediments to methyl mercury by sulfate-reducing bacteria. While this methylation is a natural process, the industrial discharge of mercury has greatly accelerated the process beyond what the ecosystem is able to absorb safely. This
45   methylation not only impacts aquatic species, but also harms humans and other land-based wildlife.

Most of the fish and shellfish that humans eat live solely in coastal areas or frequent coastal areas and feed on the fish that live there.
50   At the same time, most methylation takes place in coastal areas. Therefore, methyl mercury moves up the food chain from plankton to lobster, bluefish, winter flounder, tuna, and many other species eaten extensively by man. The methyl mercury binds to the protein in fish, residing in the muscle of the fish. This muscle is exactly what we eat:
55   the fillet.

The short-term impact of digestion of toxic methyl mercury is obviously a concern. ■ More troubling, however, is its long-term impact on species up and down the food chain. ■ In Wisconsin, scientists have
60   studied the decline of chick production in loons (aquatic birds). ■ They have made a positive link to mercury concentration in eggs which exceeds the concentration found to be toxic in laboratory studies. ■ Through that example, the lasting impact of methyl mercury far from the source of the pollution can be seen.
65
One of the great wonders of the Earth is the interconnectivity of all the world's ecosystems. This interconnectivity gives us the range and diversity of wildlife that we all enjoy and it also allowed life on the planet to endure through cataclysmic events, such as asteroid impacts
70   and the ice ages. However, it is this very interconnectivity that makes our ecosystems so vulnerable. Mercury pollution is unfortunately one of many examples of an environmental impact far removed from the source of the pollution; understanding the process by which the pollution spreads up the food chain is one of many steps to ameliorate
75   the impact of such pollution.

More Available

18. All of the following are mentioned in the passage as reasons why mercury levels in the environment have been in slow decline since the 1970s EXCEPT

a. the Clean Air Act
b. reduction in sulfate-producing bacteria
c. better sewage treatment
d. changes in industrial practice

Mercury Pollution

When most people think or talk about dangers to our environment, they focus on general terms like "pollution," "smog," and "acid-rain." Also, they often focus on the impact of supposedly man-made chemicals and compounds. But to truly understand the risks to our environment,
5   it's helpful to focus on the danger of specific chemicals, which are often otherwise naturally-occurring elements that have been spread harmfully by man. One of the largest threats to our environment is mercury: Hg on the periodic table of elements.

10 At room temperature, mercury, a metal, exists as a silvery-white liquid. However, it vaporizes readily when heat is applied, and can stay suspended in the air for more than a year. The largest sources of mercury pollution in the United States are coal-fired power plants. Emissions from these plants account for 70 percent of the mercury
15 that enters our oceans, lakes, and streams. Air currents carry these particles far from the source and are capable of polluting bodies of water thousands of miles away.

Mercury particles released into the air fall into these waterways and
20 quickly enter aquatic food chains. First, mercury attaches to sediments (fragments of organic and inorganic material that settle to the bottom of the body of water). Second, bacteria change the mercury into methyl mercury, a highly toxic substance. Third, phytoplankton feed on the organic matter in sediments and absorb the methyl mercury. Fourth, fish
25 then eat the mercury-contaminated phytoplankton; the larger the fish and the longer it lives, the more concentrated the methyl mercury in its system becomes. The mercury can then move higher up the food chain when humans eat fish that have absorbed high amounts of mercury.

30 Studies indicate that mercury levels in U.S. waterways have increased anywhere from 100 to 400 percent over the course of the last century, and no river, lake, or ocean seems immune. It is important to note that, thanks to the U.S. Clean Air Act and efforts by industry to curb unnecessary discharges as well as better sewage treatment methods,
35 the levels have been in slow decline since the 1970s. However, this minor decline is relatively miniscule in comparison to the major increase in the years prior.

If you've ever experienced that "rotten egg" smell during low tide
40 at a coastal area, you've seen (or smelled) methylation in action. Methylation is the conversion of mercury in sediments to methyl mercury by sulfate-reducing bacteria. While this methylation is a natural process, the industrial discharge of mercury has greatly accelerated the process beyond what the ecosystem is able to absorb
45 safely. This methylation not only impacts aquatic species, but also harms humans and other land-based wildlife.

Most of the fish and shellfish that humans eat live solely in coastal areas or frequent coastal areas and feed on the fish that live there.
50 At the same time, most methylation takes place in coastal areas. Therefore, methyl mercury moves up the food chain from plankton to lobster, bluefish, winter flounder, tuna, and many other species eaten extensively by man. The methyl mercury binds to the protein in fish, residing in the muscle of the fish. This muscle is exactly what we eat:
55 the fillet.

The short-term impact of digestion of toxic methyl mercury is obviously a concern. ■ More troubling, however, is its long-term impact on species up and down the food chain. ■ In Wisconsin, scientists have
60 studied the decline of chick production in loons (aquatic birds). ■ They have made a positive link to mercury concentration in eggs which exceeds the concentration found to be toxic in laboratory studies. ■ Through that example, the lasting impact of methyl mercury far from the source of the pollution can be seen.

65
One of the great wonders of the Earth is the interconnectivity of all the world's ecosystems. This interconnectivity gives us the range and diversity of wildlife that we all enjoy and it also allowed life on the planet to endure through cataclysmic events, such as asteroid impacts
70 and the ice ages. However, it is this very interconnectivity that makes our ecosystems so vulnerable. Mercury pollution is unfortunately one of many examples of an environmental impact far removed from the source of the pollution; understanding the process by which the pollution spreads up the food chain is one of many steps to ameliorate
75 the impact of such pollution.

More Available

19. According to paragraph 6, coastal areas are the locations for most

a.   tuna
b.   methylation
c.   mercury pollution sources
d.   ecosystems

Paragraph 6 is marked with an arrow [→]

Mercury Pollution

When most people think or talk about dangers to our environment, they focus on general terms like "pollution," "smog," and "acid-rain." Also, they often focus on the impact of supposedly man-made chemicals and compounds. But to truly understand the risks to our environment, 5 it's helpful to focus on the danger of specific chemicals, which are often otherwise naturally-occurring elements that have been spread harmfully by man. One of the largest threats to our environment is mercury: Hg on the periodic table of elements.

10 At room temperature, mercury, a metal, exists as a silvery-white liquid. However, it vaporizes readily when heat is applied, and can stay suspended in the air for more than a year. The largest sources of mercury pollution in the United States are coal-fired power plants. Emissions from these plants account for 70 percent of the mercury 15 that enters our oceans, lakes, and streams. Air currents carry these particles far from the source and are capable of polluting bodies of water thousands of miles away.

Mercury particles released into the air fall into these waterways and 20 quickly enter aquatic food chains. First, mercury attaches to sediments (fragments of organic and inorganic material that settle to the bottom of the body of water). Second, bacteria change the mercury into methyl mercury, a highly toxic substance. Third, phytoplankton feed on the organic matter in sediments and absorb the methyl mercury. Fourth, fish 25 then eat the mercury-contaminated phytoplankton; the larger the fish and the longer it lives, the more concentrated the methyl mercury in its system becomes. The mercury can then move higher up the food chain when humans eat fish that have absorbed high amounts of mercury.

30 Studies indicate that mercury levels in U.S. waterways have increased anywhere from 100 to 400 percent over the course of the last century, and no river, lake, or ocean seems immune. It is important to note that, thanks to the U.S. Clean Air Act and efforts by industry to curb unnecessary discharges as well as better sewage treatment methods, 35 the levels have been in slow decline since the 1970s. However, this minor decline is relatively miniscule in comparison to the major increase in the years prior.

If you've ever experienced that "rotten egg" smell during low tide 40 at a coastal area, you've seen (or smelled) methylation in action. Methylation is the conversion of mercury in sediments to methyl mercury by sulfate-reducing bacteria. While this methylation is a natural process, the industrial discharge of mercury has greatly accelerated the process beyond what the ecosystem is able to absorb safely. This 45 methylation not only impacts aquatic species, but also harms humans and other land-based wildlife.

→ Most of the fish and shellfish that humans eat live solely in coastal areas or frequent coastal areas and feed on the fish that live there. 50 At the same time, most methylation takes place in coastal areas. Therefore, methyl mercury moves up the food chain from plankton to lobster, bluefish, winter flounder, tuna, and many other species eaten extensively by man. The methyl mercury binds to the protein in fish, residing in the muscle of the fish. This muscle is exactly what we eat: 55 the fillet.

The short-term impact of digestion of toxic methyl mercury is obviously a concern. ■ More troubling, however, is its long-term impact on species up and down the food chain. ■ In Wisconsin, scientists have 60 studied the decline of chick production in loons (aquatic birds). ■ They have made a positive link to mercury concentration in eggs which exceeds the concentration found to be toxic in laboratory studies. ■ Through that example, the lasting impact of methyl mercury far from the source of the pollution can be seen.

65
One of the great wonders of the Earth is the interconnectivity of all the world's ecosystems. This interconnectivity gives us the range and diversity of wildlife that we all enjoy and it also allowed life on the planet to endure through cataclysmic events, such as asteroid impacts 70 and the ice ages. However, it is this very interconnectivity that makes our ecosystems so vulnerable. Mercury pollution is unfortunately one of many examples of an environmental impact far removed from the source of the pollution; understanding the process by which the pollution spreads up the food chain is one of many steps to ameliorate 75 the impact of such pollution.

More Available

20. The word its in the passage refers to

a.   long-term impact
b.   methyl mercury
c.   food chain
d.   digestion

Mercury Pollution

When most people think or talk about dangers to our environment, they focus on general terms like "pollution," "smog," and "acid-rain." Also, they often focus on the impact of supposedly man-made chemicals and compounds. But to truly understand the risks to our environment,
5 it's helpful to focus on the danger of specific chemicals, which are often otherwise naturally-occurring elements that have been spread harmfully by man. One of the largest threats to our environment is mercury: Hg on the periodic table of elements.

10 At room temperature, mercury, a metal, exists as a silvery-white liquid. However, it vaporizes readily when heat is applied, and can stay suspended in the air for more than a year. The largest sources of mercury pollution in the United States are coal-fired power plants. Emissions from these plants account for 70 percent of the mercury
15 that enters our oceans, lakes, and streams. Air currents carry these particles far from the source and are capable of polluting bodies of water thousands of miles away.

Mercury particles released into the air fall into these waterways and
20 quickly enter aquatic food chains. First, mercury attaches to sediments (fragments of organic and inorganic material that settle to the bottom of the body of water). Second, bacteria change the mercury into methyl mercury, a highly toxic substance. Third, phytoplankton feed on the organic matter in sediments and absorb the methyl mercury. Fourth, fish
25 then eat the mercury-contaminated phytoplankton; the larger the fish and the longer it lives, the more concentrated the methyl mercury in its system becomes. The mercury can then move higher up the food chain when humans eat fish that have absorbed high amounts of mercury.

30 Studies indicate that mercury levels in U.S. waterways have increased anywhere from 100 to 400 percent over the course of the last century, and no river, lake, or ocean seems immune. It is important to note that, thanks to the U.S. Clean Air Act and efforts by industry to curb unnecessary discharges as well as better sewage treatment methods,
35 the levels have been in slow decline since the 1970s. However, this minor decline is relatively miniscule in comparison to the major increase in the years prior.

If you've ever experienced that "rotten egg" smell during low tide
40 at a coastal area, you've seen (or smelled) methylation in action. Methylation is the conversion of mercury in sediments to methyl mercury by sulfate-reducing bacteria. While this methylation is a natural process, the industrial discharge of mercury has greatly accelerated the process beyond what the ecosystem is able to absorb
45 safely. This methylation not only impacts aquatic species, but also harms humans and other land-based wildlife.

Most of the fish and shellfish that humans eat live solely in coastal areas or frequent coastal areas and feed on the fish that live there.
50 At the same time, most methylation takes place in coastal areas. Therefore, methyl mercury moves up the food chain from plankton to lobster, bluefish, winter flounder, tuna, and many other species eaten extensively by man. The methyl mercury binds to the protein in fish, residing in the muscle of the fish. This muscle is exactly what we eat:
55 the fillet.

The short-term impact of digestion of toxic methyl mercury is obviously a concern. ■ More troubling, however, is its long-term impact on species up and down the food chain. ■ In Wisconsin, scientists have
60 studied the decline of chick production in loons (aquatic birds). ■ They have made a positive link to mercury concentration in eggs which exceeds the concentration found to be toxic in laboratory studies. ■ Through that example, the lasting impact of methyl mercury far from the source of the pollution can be seen.

65

One of the great wonders of the Earth is the interconnectivity of all the world's ecosystems. This interconnectivity gives us the range and diversity of wildlife that we all enjoy and it also allowed life on the planet to endure through cataclysmic events, such as asteroid impacts
70 and the ice ages. However, it is this very interconnectivity that makes our ecosystems so vulnerable. Mercury pollution is unfortunately one of many examples of an environmental impact far removed from the source of the pollution; understanding the process by which the pollution spreads up the food chain is one of many steps to ameliorate
75 the impact of such pollution.

More Available

21. Which of the following is mentioned in paragraph 7 as one of the long-term impacts of methyl mercury pollution?

a. Increase in sulfate-reducing bacteria in sediment
b. Reduction in the number of fish in coastal areas
c. Danger to the reproductive cycle of birds
d. Concentrated mercury in lobsters

Paragraph 7 is marked with an arrow [➔]

Mercury Pollution

When most people think or talk about dangers to our environment, they focus on general terms like "pollution," "smog," and "acid-rain." Also, they often focus on the impact of supposedly man-made chemicals and compounds. But to truly understand the risks to our environment,
5 it's helpful to focus on the danger of specific chemicals, which are often otherwise naturally-occurring elements that have been spread harmfully by man. One of the largest threats to our environment is mercury: Hg on the periodic table of elements.

10 At room temperature, mercury, a metal, exists as a silvery-white liquid. However, it vaporizes readily when heat is applied, and can stay suspended in the air for more than a year. The largest sources of mercury pollution in the United States are coal-fired power plants. Emissions from these plants account for 70 percent of the mercury
15 that enters our oceans, lakes, and streams. Air currents carry these particles far from the source and are capable of polluting bodies of water thousands of miles away.

Mercury particles released into the air fall into these waterways and
20 quickly enter aquatic food chains. First, mercury attaches to sediments (fragments of organic and inorganic material that settle to the bottom of the body of water). Second, bacteria change the mercury into methyl mercury, a highly toxic substance. Third, phytoplankton feed on the organic matter in sediments and absorb the methyl mercury. Fourth, fish
25 then eat the mercury-contaminated phytoplankton; the larger the fish and the longer it lives, the more concentrated the methyl mercury in its system becomes. The mercury can then move higher up the food chain when humans eat fish that have absorbed high amounts of mercury.

30 Studies indicate that mercury levels in U.S. waterways have increased anywhere from 100 to 400 percent over the course of the last century, and no river, lake, or ocean seems immune. It is important to note that, thanks to the U.S. Clean Air Act and efforts by industry to curb unnecessary discharges as well as better sewage treatment methods,
35 the levels have been in slow decline since the 1970s. However, this minor decline is relatively miniscule in comparison to the major increase in the years prior.

If you've ever experienced that "rotten egg" smell during low tide
40 at a coastal area, you've seen (or smelled) methylation in action. Methylation is the conversion of mercury in sediments to methyl mercury by sulfate-reducing bacteria. While this methylation is a natural process, the industrial discharge of mercury has greatly accelerated the process beyond what the ecosystem is able to absorb safely. This
45 methylation not only impacts aquatic species, but also harms humans and other land-based wildlife.

Most of the fish and shellfish that humans eat live solely in coastal areas or frequent coastal areas and feed on the fish that live there.
50 At the same time, most methylation takes place in coastal areas. Therefore, methyl mercury moves up the food chain from plankton to lobster, bluefish, winter flounder, tuna, and many other species eaten extensively by man. The methyl mercury binds to the protein in fish, residing in the muscle of the fish. This muscle is exactly what we eat:
55 the fillet.

➔ The short-term impact of digestion of toxic methyl mercury is obviously a concern. ■ More troubling, however, is its long-term impact on species up and down the food chain. ■ In Wisconsin, scientists
60 have studied the decline of chick production in loons (aquatic birds). ■ They have made a positive link to mercury concentration in eggs which exceeds the concentration found to be toxic in laboratory studies. ■ Through that example, the lasting impact of methyl mercury far from the source of the pollution can be seen.
65
One of the great wonders of the Earth is the interconnectivity of all the world's ecosystems. This interconnectivity gives us the range and diversity of wildlife that we all enjoy and it also allowed life on the planet to endure through cataclysmic events, such as asteroid impacts
70 and the ice ages. However, it is this very interconnectivity that makes our ecosystems so vulnerable. Mercury pollution is unfortunately one of many examples of an environmental impact far removed from the source of the pollution; understanding the process by which the pollution spreads up the food chain is one of many steps to ameliorate
75 the impact of such pollution.

More Available

22. According to paragraph 8, the interconnectivity of the Earth's ecosystems is also

  a.   the reason the ecosystems are so susceptible to pollution

  b.   the cause of mercury pollution

  c.   the reason methyl mercury is such a harmful substance

  d.   the cure for pollution from coal-fired power plants

Paragraph 8 is marked with an arrow [→]

Mercury Pollution

When most people think or talk about dangers to our environment, they focus on general terms like "pollution," "smog," and "acid-rain." Also, they often focus on the impact of supposedly man-made chemicals and compounds. But to truly understand the risks to our environment,
5 it's helpful to focus on the danger of specific chemicals, which are often otherwise naturally-occurring elements that have been spread harmfully by man. One of the largest threats to our environment is mercury: Hg on the periodic table of elements.

10 At room temperature, mercury, a metal, exists as a silvery-white liquid. However, it vaporizes readily when heat is applied, and can stay suspended in the air for more than a year. The largest sources of mercury pollution in the United States are coal-fired power plants. Emissions from these plants account for 70 percent of the mercury
15 that enters our oceans, lakes, and streams. Air currents carry these particles far from the source and are capable of polluting bodies of water thousands of miles away.

Mercury particles released into the air fall into these waterways and
20 quickly enter aquatic food chains. First, mercury attaches to sediments (fragments of organic and inorganic material that settle to the bottom of the body of water). Second, bacteria change the mercury into methyl mercury, a highly toxic substance. Third, phytoplankton feed on the organic matter in sediments and absorb the methyl mercury. Fourth, fish
25 then eat the mercury-contaminated phytoplankton; the larger the fish and the longer it lives, the more concentrated the methyl mercury in its system becomes. The mercury can then move higher up the food chain when humans eat fish that have absorbed high amounts of mercury.

30 Studies indicate that mercury levels in U.S. waterways have increased anywhere from 100 to 400 percent over the course of the last century, and no river, lake, or ocean seems immune. It is important to note that, thanks to the U.S. Clean Air Act and efforts by industry to curb unnecessary discharges as well as better sewage treatment methods,
35 the levels have been in slow decline since the 1970s. However, this minor decline is relatively miniscule in comparison to the major increase in the years prior.

If you've ever experienced that "rotten egg" smell during low tide
40 at a coastal area, you've seen (or smelled) methylation in action. Methylation is the conversion of mercury in sediments to methyl mercury by sulfate-reducing bacteria. While this methylation is a natural process, the industrial discharge of mercury has greatly accelerated the process beyond what the ecosystem is able to absorb
45 safely. This methylation not only impacts aquatic species, but also harms humans and other land-based wildlife.

Most of the fish and shellfish that humans eat live solely in coastal areas or frequent coastal areas and feed on the fish that live there.
50 At the same time, most methylation takes place in coastal areas. Therefore, methyl mercury moves up the food chain from plankton to lobster, bluefish, winter flounder, tuna, and many other species eaten extensively by man. The methyl mercury binds to the protein in fish, residing in the muscle of the fish. This muscle is exactly what we eat:
55 the fillet.

The short-term impact of digestion of toxic methyl mercury is obviously a concern. ■ More troubling, however, is its long-term impact on species up and down the food chain. ■ In Wisconsin, scientists have
60 studied the decline of chick production in loons (aquatic birds). ■ They have made a positive link to mercury concentration in eggs which exceeds the concentration found to be toxic in laboratory studies. ■ Through that example, the lasting impact of methyl mercury far from the source of the pollution can be seen.

65
→ One of the great wonders of the Earth is the interconnectivity of all the world's ecosystems. This interconnectivity gives us the range and diversity of wildlife that we all enjoy and it also allowed life on the planet to endure through cataclysmic events, such as asteroid impacts
70 and the ice ages. However, it is this very interconnectivity that makes our ecosystems so vulnerable. Mercury pollution is unfortunately one of many examples of an environmental impact far removed from the source of the pollution; understanding the process by which the pollution spreads up the food chain is one of many steps to ameliorate
75 the impact of such pollution.

TOEFL Reading

23 of 38

PAUSE
TEST   SECTION
EXIT

REVIEW   HELP   BACK   NEXT

HIDE TIME   00:08:45

More Available

23. The word ameliorate in the passage is closest in meaning to

a. enlarge
b. impact
c. summarize
d. lessen

Mercury Pollution

When most people think or talk about dangers to our environment, they focus on general terms like "pollution," "smog," and "acid-rain." Also, they often focus on the impact of supposedly man-made chemicals and compounds. But to truly understand the risks to our environment,
5 it's helpful to focus on the danger of specific chemicals, which are often otherwise naturally-occurring elements that have been spread harmfully by man. One of the largest threats to our environment is mercury: Hg on the periodic table of elements.

10 At room temperature, mercury, a metal, exists as a silvery-white liquid. However, it vaporizes readily when heat is applied, and can stay suspended in the air for more than a year. The largest sources of mercury pollution in the United States are coal-fired power plants. Emissions from these plants account for 70 percent of the mercury
15 that enters our oceans, lakes, and streams. Air currents carry these particles far from the source and are capable of polluting bodies of water thousands of miles away.

Mercury particles released into the air fall into these waterways and
20 quickly enter aquatic food chains. First, mercury attaches to sediments (fragments of organic and inorganic material that settle to the bottom of the body of water). Second, bacteria change the mercury into methyl mercury, a highly toxic substance. Third, phytoplankton feed on the organic matter in sediments and absorb the methyl mercury. Fourth, fish
25 then eat the mercury-contaminated phytoplankton; the larger the fish and the longer it lives, the more concentrated the methyl mercury in its system becomes. The mercury can then move higher up the food chain when humans eat fish that have absorbed high amounts of mercury.

30 Studies indicate that mercury levels in U.S. waterways have increased anywhere from 100 to 400 percent over the course of the last century, and no river, lake, or ocean seems immune. It is important to note that, thanks to the U.S. Clean Air Act and efforts by industry to curb unnecessary discharges as well as better sewage treatment methods,
35 the levels have been in slow decline since the 1970s. However, this minor decline is relatively miniscule in comparison to the major increase in the years prior.

If you've ever experienced that "rotten egg" smell during low tide
40 at a coastal area, you've seen (or smelled) methylation in action. Methylation is the conversion of mercury in sediments to methyl mercury by sulfate-reducing bacteria. While this methylation is a natural process, the industrial discharge of mercury has greatly accelerated the process beyond what the ecosystem is able to absorb safely. This
45 methylation not only impacts aquatic species, but also harms humans and other land-based wildlife.

Most of the fish and shellfish that humans eat live solely in coastal areas or frequent coastal areas and feed on the fish that live there.
50 At the same time, most methylation takes place in coastal areas. Therefore, methyl mercury moves up the food chain from plankton to lobster, bluefish, winter flounder, tuna, and many other species eaten extensively by man. The methyl mercury binds to the protein in fish, residing in the muscle of the fish. This muscle is exactly what we eat:
55 the fillet.

The short-term impact of digestion of toxic methyl mercury is obviously a concern. ■ More troubling, however, is its long-term impact on species up and down the food chain. ■ In Wisconsin, scientists have
60 studied the decline of chick production in loons (aquatic birds). ■ They have made a positive link to mercury concentration in eggs which exceeds the concentration found to be toxic in laboratory studies. ■ Through that example, the lasting impact of methyl mercury far from the source of the pollution can be seen.
65
One of the great wonders of the Earth is the interconnectivity of all the world's ecosystems. This interconnectivity gives us the range and diversity of wildlife that we all enjoy and it also allowed life on the planet to endure through cataclysmic events, such as asteroid impacts
70 and the ice ages. However, it is this very interconnectivity that makes our ecosystems so vulnerable. Mercury pollution is unfortunately one of many examples of an environmental impact far removed from the source of the pollution; understanding the process by which the pollution spreads up the food chain is one of many steps to ameliorate
75 the impact of such pollution.

TOEFL Reading

24 of 38

REVIEW   HELP   BACK   NEXT
?

PAUSE TEST   SECTION EXIT

HIDE TIME   00:08:45

More Available

24. Look at the four squares ■ that indicate where the following sentence can be added to the passage.

Thus, the harmful effects of methyl mercury are passed from adult to young and will impact the health of the species for years to come.

Where would the sentence best fit?

Click on a square ■ to add the sentence to the passage.

[Here, on this practice test, circle your answer below.]

a.   Square 1
b.   Square 2
c.   Square 3
d.   Square 4

Mercury Pollution

When most people think or talk about dangers to our environment, they focus on general terms like "pollution," "smog," and "acid-rain." Also, they often focus on the impact of supposedly man-made chemicals and compounds. But to truly understand the risks to our environment,
5   it's helpful to focus on the danger of specific chemicals, which are often otherwise naturally-occurring elements that have been spread harmfully by man. One of the largest threats to our environment is mercury: Hg on the periodic table of elements.

10 At room temperature, mercury, a metal, exists as a silvery-white liquid. However, it vaporizes readily when heat is applied, and can stay suspended in the air for more than a year. The largest sources of mercury pollution in the United States are coal-fired power plants. Emissions from these plants account for 70 percent of the mercury
15 that enters our oceans, lakes, and streams. Air currents carry these particles far from the source and are capable of polluting bodies of water thousands of miles away.

Mercury particles released into the air fall into these waterways and
20 quickly enter aquatic food chains. First, mercury attaches to sediments (fragments of organic and inorganic material that settle to the bottom of the body of water). Second, bacteria change the mercury into methyl mercury, a highly toxic substance. Third, phytoplankton feed on the organic matter in sediments and absorb the methyl mercury. Fourth, fish
25 then eat the mercury-contaminated phytoplankton; the larger the fish and the longer it lives, the more concentrated the methyl mercury in its system becomes. The mercury can then move higher up the food chain when humans eat fish that have absorbed high amounts of mercury.

30 Studies indicate that mercury levels in U.S. waterways have increased anywhere from 100 to 400 percent over the course of the last century, and no river, lake, or ocean seems immune. It is important to note that, thanks to the U.S. Clean Air Act and efforts by industry to curb unnecessary discharges as well as better sewage treatment methods,
35 the levels have been in slow decline since the 1970s. However, this minor decline is relatively miniscule in comparison to the major increase in the years prior.

If you've ever experienced that "rotten egg" smell during low tide
40 at a coastal area, you've seen (or smelled) methylation in action. Methylation is the conversion of mercury in sediments to methyl mercury by sulfate-reducing bacteria. While this methylation is a natural process, the industrial discharge of mercury has greatly accelerated the process beyond what the ecosystem is able to absorb
45 safely. This methylation not only impacts aquatic species, but also harms humans and other land-based wildlife.

Most of the fish and shellfish that humans eat live solely in coastal areas or frequent coastal areas and feed on the fish that live there.
50 At the same time, most methylation takes place in coastal areas. Therefore, methyl mercury moves up the food chain from plankton to lobster, bluefish, winter flounder, tuna, and many other species eaten extensively by man. The methyl mercury binds to the protein in fish, residing in the muscle of the fish. This muscle is exactly what we eat:
55 the fillet.

The short-term impact of digestion of toxic methyl mercury is obviously a concern. ■ More troubling, however, is its long-term impact on species up and down the food chain. ■ In Wisconsin, scientists have
60 studied the decline of chick production in loons (aquatic birds). ■ They have made a positive link to mercury concentration in eggs which exceeds the concentration found to be toxic in laboratory studies. ■ Through that example, the lasting impact of methyl mercury far from the source of the pollution can be seen.

65
One of the great wonders of the Earth is the interconnectivity of all the world's ecosystems. This interconnectivity gives us the range and diversity of wildlife that we all enjoy and it also allowed life on the planet to endure through cataclysmic events, such as asteroid impacts
70 and the ice ages. However, it is this very interconnectivity that makes our ecosystems so vulnerable. Mercury pollution is unfortunately one of many examples of an environmental impact far removed from the source of the pollution; understanding the process by which the pollution spreads up the food chain is one of many steps to ameliorate
75 the impact of such pollution.

25. Directions: An introductory sentence for a brief summary of the passage is provided below. Complete the summary by selecting the THREE answer choices that express the most important ideas in the passage. Some sentences do not belong in the summary because they express ideas that are not presented in the passage or are minor ideas in the passage. *This question is worth 2 points.*

Mercury pollution is one example of a type of pollution that has short-term and long-term effects far from the source of the pollution.

-
-
-

Answer Choices	
Air currents carry Mercury particles far from the source and are capable of polluting bodies of water thousands of miles away.	Mercury pollution is increasing in the United States despite the U.S. Clean Air Act and efforts of industry.
Mercury is transformed into the toxic methyl mercury and moves up the food chain to cause harm for organisms at every level all the way up to humans.	The methyl mercury binds to the protein in fish, residing in the muscle.
Sulfate-reducing bacteria cause the "rotten egg" smell that exists at coastal areas during low tide.	The harmful effects of methyl mercury are passed from adult to young and will impact the health of many species for years to come.

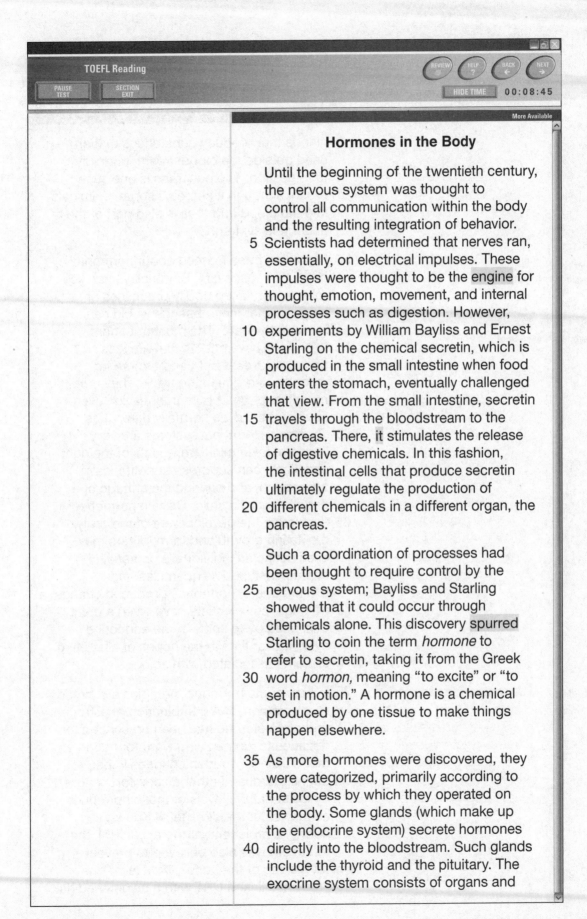

Hormones in the Body

Until the beginning of the twentieth century, the nervous system was thought to control all communication within the body and the resulting integration of behavior.

5 Scientists had determined that nerves ran, essentially, on electrical impulses. These impulses were thought to be the engine for thought, emotion, movement, and internal processes such as digestion. However,

10 experiments by William Bayliss and Ernest Starling on the chemical secretin, which is produced in the small intestine when food enters the stomach, eventually challenged that view. From the small intestine, secretin

15 travels through the bloodstream to the pancreas. There, it stimulates the release of digestive chemicals. In this fashion, the intestinal cells that produce secretin ultimately regulate the production of

20 different chemicals in a different organ, the pancreas.

Such a coordination of processes had been thought to require control by the

25 nervous system; Bayliss and Starling showed that it could occur through chemicals alone. This discovery spurred Starling to coin the term *hormone* to refer to secretin, taking it from the Greek

30 word *hormon,* meaning "to excite" or "to set in motion." A hormone is a chemical produced by one tissue to make things happen elsewhere.

35 As more hormones were discovered, they were categorized, primarily according to the process by which they operated on the body. Some glands (which make up the endocrine system) secrete hormones

40 directly into the bloodstream. Such glands include the thyroid and the pituitary. The exocrine system consists of organs and

TOEFL Reading

PAUSE
TEST
SECTION
EXIT

REVIEW
HELP
?
BACK
←
NEXT
→

HIDE TIME   00:08:45

More Available

glands that produce substances that are used outside the bloodstream, primarily
45 for digestion. The pancreas is one such organ, although it secretes some chemicals into the blood and thus is also part of the endocrine system.

50 Much has been learned about hormones since their discovery. Some play such key roles in regulating bodily processes or behavior that their absence would cause immediate death. The most abundant
55 hormones have effects that are less obviously urgent but can be more far-reaching and difficult to track: They modify moods and affect human behavior, even some behavior we normally think of as
60 voluntary. Hormonal systems are very intricate. Even minute amounts of the right chemicals can suppress appetite, calm aggression, and change the attitude of a parent toward a child. Certain hormones
65 accelerate the development of the body, regulating growth and form; others may even define an individual's personality characteristics. The quantities and proportions of hormones produced change
70 with age, so scientists have given a great deal of study to shifts in the endocrine system over time in the hopes of alleviating ailments associated with aging.

75 In fact, some hormone therapies are already very common. ■ A combination of estrogen and progesterone has been prescribed for decades to women who want to reduce mood swings, sudden changes in body
80 temperature, and other discomforts caused by lower natural levels of those hormones as they enter middle age. ■ Known as hormone replacement therapy (HRT), the treatment was also believed to prevent
85 weakening of the bones. ■ At least one study has linked HRT with a heightened risk

of heart disease and certain types of cancer. HRT may also increase the likelihood that blood clots—dangerous because they

90 could travel through the bloodstream and block major blood vessels—will form. Some proponents of HRT have tempered their enthusiasm in the face of this new evidence, recommending it only to patients whose

95 symptoms interfere with their abilities to live normal lives. ■

Human growth hormone may also be given to patients who are secreting abnormally

100 low amounts on their own. Because of the complicated effects the growth hormone has on the body, such treatments are generally restricted to children who would be pathologically small in stature without it.

105 Growth hormone affects not just physical size but also the digestion of food and the aging process. Researchers and family physicians tend to agree that it is foolhardy to dispense it in cases in which the risks are

110 not clearly outweighed by the benefits.

More Available

26. The word engine in the passage is closest in meaning to

a. desire
b. origin
c. science
d. chemical

Hormones in the Body

Until the beginning of the twentieth century, the nervous system was thought to control all communication within the body and the resulting integration of behavior. Scientists had determined that nerves ran, essentially, on electrical impulses. These impulses were
5   thought to be the engine for thought, emotion, movement, and internal processes such as digestion. However, experiments by William Bayliss and Ernest Starling on the chemical secretin, which is produced in the small intestine when food enters the stomach, eventually challenged that view. From the small intestine, secretin
10 travels through the bloodstream to the pancreas. There, it stimulates the release of digestive chemicals. In this fashion, the intestinal cells that produce secretin ultimately regulate the production of different chemicals in a different organ, the pancreas.

15 Such a coordination of processes had been thought to require control by the nervous system; Bayliss and Starling showed that it could occur through chemicals alone. This discovery spurred Starling to coin the term hormone to refer to secretin, taking it from the Greek word hormon, meaning "to excite" or "to set in motion." A hormone is
20 a chemical produced by one tissue to make things happen elsewhere.

As more hormones were discovered, they were categorized, primarily according to the process by which they operated on the body. Some glands (which make up the endocrine system) secrete hormones
25 directly into the bloodstream. Such glands include the thyroid and the pituitary. The exocrine system consists of organs and glands that produce substances that are used outside the bloodstream, primarily for digestion. The pancreas is one such organ, although it secretes some chemicals into the blood and thus is also part of the endocrine
30 system.

Much has been learned about hormones since their discovery. Some play such key roles in regulating bodily processes or behavior that their absence would cause immediate death. The most abundant
35 hormones have effects that are less obviously urgent but can be more far-reaching and difficult to track: They modify moods and affect human behavior, even some behavior we normally think of as voluntary. Hormonal systems are very intricate. Even minute amounts of the right chemicals can suppress appetite, calm aggression, and
40 change the attitude of a parent toward a child. Certain hormones accelerate the development of the body, regulating growth and form; others may even define an individual's personality characteristics. **The quantities and proportions of hormones produced change with age, so scientists have given a great deal of study to shifts
45 in the endocrine system over time in the hopes of alleviating ailments associated with aging.**

In fact, some hormone therapies are already very common. ■ **A combination of estrogen and progesterone has been prescribed
50 for decades to women who want to reduce mood swings, sudden changes in body temperature, and other discomforts caused by lower natural levels of those hormones as they enter middle age.** ■ Known as hormone replacement therapy (HRT), the treatment was also believed to prevent weakening of the bones. ■
55 At least one study has linked HRT with a heightened risk of heart disease and certain types of cancer. **HRT may also increase the likelihood that blood clots—dangerous because they could travel through the bloodstream and block major blood vessels— will form.** Some proponents of HRT have tempered their enthusiasm
60 in the face of this new evidence, recommending it only to patients whose symptoms interfere with their abilities to live normal lives. ■

Human growth hormone may also be given to patients who are secreting abnormally low amounts on their own. **Because of the
65 complicated effects the growth hormone has on the body, such treatments are generally restricted to children who would be pathologically small in stature without it.** Growth hormone affects not just physical size but also the digestion of food and the aging process. Researchers and family physicians tend to agree that it is
70 foolhardy to dispense it in cases in which the risks are not clearly outweighed by the benefits.

More Available

27. The word **it** in the passage refers to

a. secretin
b. small intestine
c. bloodstream
d. pancreas

Hormones in the Body

Until the beginning of the twentieth century, the nervous system was thought to control all communication within the body and the resulting integration of behavior. Scientists had determined that nerves ran, essentially, on electrical impulses. These impulses were
5 thought to be the engine for thought, emotion, movement, and internal processes such as digestion. However, experiments by William Bayliss and Ernest Starling on the chemical secretin, which is produced in the small intestine when food enters the stomach, eventually challenged that view. From the small intestine, secretin
10 travels through the bloodstream to the pancreas. There, it stimulates the release of digestive chemicals. In this fashion, the intestinal cells that produce secretin ultimately regulate the production of different chemicals in a different organ, the pancreas.

15 Such a coordination of processes had been thought to require control by the nervous system; Bayliss and Starling showed that it could occur through chemicals alone. This discovery spurred Starling to coin the term *hormone* to refer to secretin, taking it from the Greek word *hormon,* meaning "to excite" or "to set in motion." A hormone is
20 a chemical produced by one tissue to make things happen elsewhere.

As more hormones were discovered, they were categorized, primarily according to the process by which they operated on the body. Some glands (which make up the endocrine system) secrete hormones
25 directly into the bloodstream. Such glands include the thyroid and the pituitary. The exocrine system consists of organs and glands that produce substances that are used outside the bloodstream, primarily for digestion. The pancreas is one such organ, although it secretes some chemicals into the blood and thus is also part of the
30 endocrine system.

Much has been learned about hormones since their discovery. Some play such key roles in regulating bodily processes or behavior that their absence would cause immediate death. The most abundant
35 hormones have effects that are less obviously urgent but can be more far-reaching and difficult to track: They modify moods and affect human behavior, even some behavior we normally think of as voluntary. Hormonal systems are very intricate. Even minute amounts of the right chemicals can suppress appetite, calm aggression, and
40 change the attitude of a parent toward a child. Certain hormones accelerate the development of the body, regulating growth and form; others may even define an individual's personality characteristics. **The quantities and proportions of hormones produced change with age, so scientists have given a great deal of study to shifts**
45 **in the endocrine system over time in the hopes of alleviating ailments associated with aging.**

In fact, some hormone therapies are already very common. ■ **A combination of estrogen and progesterone has been prescribed**
50 **for decades to women who want to reduce mood swings, sudden changes in body temperature, and other discomforts caused by lower natural levels of those hormones as they enter middle age.** ■ Known as hormone replacement therapy (HRT), the treatment was also believed to prevent weakening of the bones. ■
55 At least one study has linked HRT with a heightened risk of heart disease and certain types of cancer. **HRT may also increase the likelihood that blood clots—dangerous because they could travel through the bloodstream and block major blood vessels— will form.** Some proponents of HRT have tempered their enthusiasm
60 in the face of this new evidence, recommending it only to patients whose symptoms interfere with their abilities to live normal lives. ■

Human growth hormone may also be given to patients who are secreting abnormally low amounts on their own. **Because of the**
65 **complicated effects the growth hormone has on the body, such treatments are generally restricted to children who would be pathologically small in stature without it.** Growth hormone affects not just physical size but also the digestion of food and the aging process. Researchers and family physicians tend to agree that it is
70 foolhardy to dispense it in cases in which the risks are not clearly outweighed by the benefits.

More Available

28. The word spurred in the passage is closest in meaning to

a. remembered
b. surprised
c. invented
d. motivated

Hormones in the Body

Until the beginning of the twentieth century, the nervous system was thought to control all communication within the body and the resulting integration of behavior. Scientists had determined that nerves ran, essentially, on electrical impulses. These impulses were
5   thought to be the engine for thought, emotion, movement, and internal processes such as digestion. However, experiments by William Bayliss and Ernest Starling on the chemical secretin, which is produced in the small intestine when food enters the stomach, eventually challenged that view. From the small intestine, secretin
10 travels through the bloodstream to the pancreas. There, it stimulates the release of digestive chemicals. In this fashion, the intestinal cells that produce secretin ultimately regulate the production of different chemicals in a different organ, the pancreas.

15 Such a coordination of processes had been thought to require control by the nervous system; Bayliss and Starling showed that it could occur through chemicals alone. This discovery spurred Starling to coin the term *hormone* to refer to secretin, taking it from the Greek word *hormon,* meaning "to excite" or "to set in motion." A hormone is
20 a chemical produced by one tissue to make things happen elsewhere.

As more hormones were discovered, they were categorized, primarily according to the process by which they operated on the body. Some glands (which make up the endocrine system) secrete hormones
25 directly into the bloodstream. Such glands include the thyroid and the pituitary. The exocrine system consists of organs and glands that produce substances that are used outside the bloodstream, primarily for digestion. The pancreas is one such organ, although it secretes some chemicals into the blood and thus is also part of the endocrine
30 system.

Much has been learned about hormones since their discovery. Some play such key roles in regulating bodily processes or behavior that their absence would cause immediate death. The most abundant
35 hormones have effects that are less obviously urgent but can be more far-reaching and difficult to track: They modify moods and affect human behavior, even some behavior we normally think of as voluntary. Hormonal systems are very intricate. Even minute amounts of the right chemicals can suppress appetite, calm aggression, and
40 change the attitude of a parent toward a child. Certain hormones accelerate the development of the body, regulating growth and form; others may even define an individual's personality characteristics. **The quantities and proportions of hormones produced change with age, so scientists have given a great deal of study to shifts
45 in the endocrine system over time in the hopes of alleviating ailments associated with aging.**

In fact, some hormone therapies are already very common. ■ **A combination of estrogen and progesterone has been prescribed
50 for decades to women who want to reduce mood swings, sudden changes in body temperature, and other discomforts caused by lower natural levels of those hormones as they enter middle age.** ■ Known as hormone replacement therapy (HRT), the treatment was also believed to prevent weakening of the bones. ■
55 At least one study has linked HRT with a heightened risk of heart disease and certain types of cancer. **HRT may also increase the likelihood that blood clots—dangerous because they could travel through the bloodstream and block major blood vessels— will form.** Some proponents of HRT have tempered their enthusiasm
60 in the face of this new evidence, recommending it only to patients whose symptoms interfere with their abilities to live normal lives. ■

Human growth hormone may also be given to patients who are secreting abnormally low amounts on their own. **Because of the
65 complicated effects the growth hormone has on the body, such treatments are generally restricted to children who would be pathologically small in stature without it.** Growth hormone affects not just physical size but also the digestion of food and the aging process. Researchers and family physicians tend to agree that it is
70 foolhardy to dispense it in cases in which the risks are not clearly outweighed by the benefits.

More Available

29. To be considered a hormone, a chemical produced in the body must

a. be part of the digestive process
b. influence the operations of the nervous system
c. affect processes in a different part of the body
d. regulate attitudes and behavior

Hormones in the Body

Until the beginning of the twentieth century, the nervous system was thought to control all communication within the body and the resulting integration of behavior. Scientists had determined that nerves ran, essentially, on electrical impulses. These impulses were
5 thought to be the engine for thought, emotion, movement, and internal processes such as digestion. However, experiments by William Bayliss and Ernest Starling on the chemical secretin, which is produced in the small intestine when food enters the stomach, eventually challenged that view. From the small intestine, secretin
10 travels through the bloodstream to the pancreas. There, it stimulates the release of digestive chemicals. In this fashion, the intestinal cells that produce secretin ultimately regulate the production of different chemicals in a different organ, the pancreas.

15 Such a coordination of processes had been thought to require control by the nervous system; Bayliss and Starling showed that it could occur through chemicals alone. This discovery spurred Starling to coin the term *hormone* to refer to secretin, taking it from the Greek word *hormon*, meaning "to excite" or "to set in motion." A hormone is
20 a chemical produced by one tissue to make things happen elsewhere.

As more hormones were discovered, they were categorized, primarily according to the process by which they operated on the body. Some glands (which make up the endocrine system) secrete hormones
25 directly into the bloodstream. Such glands include the thyroid and the pituitary. The exocrine system consists of organs and glands that produce substances that are used outside the bloodstream, primarily for digestion. The pancreas is one such organ, although it secretes some chemicals into the blood and thus is also part of the
30 endocrine system.

Much has been learned about hormones since their discovery. Some play such key roles in regulating bodily processes or behavior that their absence would cause immediate death. The most abundant
35 hormones have effects that are less obviously urgent but can be more far-reaching and difficult to track: They modify moods and affect human behavior, even some behavior we normally think of as voluntary. Hormonal systems are very intricate. Even minute amounts of the right chemicals can suppress appetite, calm aggression, and
40 change the attitude of a parent toward a child. Certain hormones accelerate the development of the body, regulating growth and form; others may even define an individual's personality characteristics. **The quantities and proportions of hormones produced change with age, so scientists have given a great deal of study to shifts**
45 **in the endocrine system over time in the hopes of alleviating ailments associated with aging.**

In fact, some hormone therapies are already very common. ■ **A combination of estrogen and progesterone has been prescribed**
50 **for decades to women who want to reduce mood swings, sudden changes in body temperature, and other discomforts caused by lower natural levels of those hormones as they enter middle age.** ■ Known as hormone replacement therapy (HRT), the treatment was also believed to prevent weakening of the bones. ■
55 At least one study has linked HRT with a heightened risk of heart disease and certain types of cancer. **HRT may also increase the likelihood that blood clots—dangerous because they could travel through the bloodstream and block major blood vessels— will form.** Some proponents of HRT have tempered their enthusiasm
60 in the face of this new evidence, recommending it only to patients whose symptoms interfere with their abilities to live normal lives. ■

Human growth hormone may also be given to patients who are secreting abnormally low amounts on their own. **Because of the**
65 **complicated effects the growth hormone has on the body, such treatments are generally restricted to children who would be pathologically small in stature without it.** Growth hormone affects not just physical size but also the digestion of food and the aging process. Researchers and family physicians tend to agree that it is
70 foolhardy to dispense it in cases in which the risks are not clearly outweighed by the benefits.

More Available

30. The glands and organs mentioned in paragraph 3 are categorized according to

a. whether scientists understand their function

b. how frequently they release hormones into the body

c. whether the hormones they secrete influence the aging process

d. whether they secrete chemicals into the blood

Paragraph 3 is marked with an arrow [→]

Hormones in the Body

Until the beginning of the twentieth century, the nervous system was thought to control all communication within the body and the resulting integration of behavior. Scientists had determined that nerves ran, essentially, on electrical impulses. These impulses were
5   thought to be the engine for thought, emotion, movement, and internal processes such as digestion. However, experiments by William Bayliss and Ernest Starling on the chemical secretin, which is produced in the small intestine when food enters the stomach, eventually challenged that view. From the small intestine, secretin
10   travels through the bloodstream to the pancreas. There, it stimulates the release of digestive chemicals. In this fashion, the intestinal cells that produce secretin ultimately regulate the production of different chemicals in a different organ, the pancreas.

15   Such a coordination of processes had been thought to require control by the nervous system; Bayliss and Starling showed that it could occur through chemicals alone. This discovery spurred Starling to coin the term *hormone* to refer to secretin, taking it from the Greek word *hormon,* meaning "to excite" or "to set in motion." A hormone is
20   a chemical produced by one tissue to make things happen elsewhere.

→ As more hormones were discovered, they were categorized, primarily according to the process by which they operated on the body. Some glands (which make up the endocrine system) secrete
25   hormones directly into the bloodstream. Such glands include the thyroid and the pituitary. The exocrine system consists of organs and glands that produce substances that are used outside the bloodstream, primarily for digestion. The pancreas is one such organ, although it secretes some chemicals into the blood and thus is also
30   part of the endocrine system.

Much has been learned about hormones since their discovery. Some play such key roles in regulating bodily processes or behavior that their absence would cause immediate death. The most abundant
35   hormones have effects that are less obviously urgent but can be more far-reaching and difficult to track: They modify moods and affect human behavior, even some behavior we normally think of as voluntary. Hormonal systems are very intricate. Even minute amounts of the right chemicals can suppress appetite, calm aggression, and
40   change the attitude of a parent toward a child. Certain hormones accelerate the development of the body, regulating growth and form; others may even define an individual's personality characteristics. **The quantities and proportions of hormones produced change with age, so scientists have given a great deal of study to shifts
45   in the endocrine system over time in the hopes of alleviating ailments associated with aging.**

In fact, some hormone therapies are already very common. ■ **A combination of estrogen and progesterone has been prescribed
50   for decades to women who want to reduce mood swings, sudden changes in body temperature, and other discomforts caused by lower natural levels of those hormones as they enter middle age.** ■ Known as hormone replacement therapy (HRT), the treatment was also believed to prevent weakening of the bones. ■
55   At least one study has linked HRT with a heightened risk of heart disease and certain types of cancer. **HRT may also increase the likelihood that blood clots—dangerous because they could travel through the bloodstream and block major blood vessels— will form.** Some proponents of HRT have tempered their enthusiasm
60   in the face of this new evidence, recommending it only to patients whose symptoms interfere with their abilities to live normal lives. ■

Human growth hormone may also be given to patients who are secreting abnormally low amounts on their own. **Because of the
65   complicated effects the growth hormone has on the body, such treatments are generally restricted to children who would be pathologically small in stature without it.** Growth hormone affects not just physical size but also the digestion of food and the aging process. Researchers and family physicians tend to agree that it is
70   foolhardy to dispense it in cases in which the risks are not clearly outweighed by the benefits.

More Available

31. The word key in the passage is closest in meaning to

a. misunderstood
b. precise
c. significant
d. simple

Hormones in the Body

Until the beginning of the twentieth century, the nervous system was thought to control all communication within the body and the resulting integration of behavior. Scientists had determined that nerves ran, essentially, on electrical impulses. These impulses were
5 thought to be the engine for thought, emotion, movement, and internal processes such as digestion. However, experiments by William Bayliss and Ernest Starling on the chemical secretin, which is produced in the small intestine when food enters the stomach, eventually challenged that view. From the small intestine, secretin
10 travels through the bloodstream to the pancreas. There, it stimulates the release of digestive chemicals. In this fashion, the intestinal cells that produce secretin ultimately regulate the production of different chemicals in a different organ, the pancreas.

Such a coordination of processes had been thought to require control
15 by the nervous system; Bayliss and Starling showed that it could occur through chemicals alone. This discovery spurred Starling to coin the term *hormone* to refer to secretin, taking it from the Greek word *hormon,* meaning "to excite" or "to set in motion." A hormone is
20 a chemical produced by one tissue to make things happen elsewhere.

As more hormones were discovered, they were categorized, primarily according to the process by which they operated on the body. Some glands (which make up the endocrine system) secrete hormones
25 directly into the bloodstream. Such glands include the thyroid and the pituitary. The exocrine system consists of organs and glands that produce substances that are used outside the bloodstream, primarily for digestion. The pancreas is one such organ, although it secretes some chemicals into the blood and thus is also part of the
30 endocrine system.

Much has been learned about hormones since their discovery. Some play such key roles in regulating bodily processes or behavior that their absence would cause immediate death. The most abundant
35 hormones have effects that are less obviously urgent but can be more far-reaching and difficult to track: They modify moods and affect human behavior, even some behavior we normally think of as voluntary. Hormonal systems are very intricate. Even minute amounts of the right chemicals can suppress appetite, calm aggression, and
40 change the attitude of a parent toward a child. Certain hormones accelerate the development of the body, regulating growth and form; others may even define an individual's personality characteristics. **The quantities and proportions of hormones produced change with age, so scientists have given a great deal of study to shifts**
45 **in the endocrine system over time in the hopes of alleviating ailments associated with aging.**

In fact, some hormone therapies are already very common. ■ **A combination of estrogen and progesterone has been prescribed**
50 **for decades to women who want to reduce mood swings, sudden changes in body temperature, and other discomforts caused by lower natural levels of those hormones as they enter middle age.** ■ Known as hormone replacement therapy (HRT), the treatment was also believed to prevent weakening of the bones. ■
55 At least one study has linked HRT with a heightened risk of heart disease and certain types of cancer. **HRT may also increase the likelihood that blood clots—dangerous because they could travel through the bloodstream and block major blood vessels— will form.** Some proponents of HRT have tempered their enthusiasm
60 in the face of this new evidence, recommending it only to patients whose symptoms interfere with their abilities to live normal lives. ■

Human growth hormone may also be given to patients who are secreting abnormally low amounts on their own. **Because of the**
65 **complicated effects the growth hormone has on the body, such treatments are generally restricted to children who would be pathologically small in stature without it.** Growth hormone affects not just physical size but also the digestion of food and the aging process. Researchers and family physicians tend to agree that it is
70 foolhardy to dispense it in cases in which the risks are not clearly outweighed by the benefits.

More Available

32. The word minute in the passage is closest in meaning to

   a.   sudden
   b.   small
   c.   seconds
   d.   noticeable

Hormones in the Body

Until the beginning of the twentieth century, the nervous system was thought to control all communication within the body and the resulting integration of behavior. Scientists had determined that nerves ran, essentially, on electrical impulses. These impulses were
5 thought to be the engine for thought, emotion, movement, and internal processes such as digestion. However, experiments by William Bayliss and Ernest Starling on the chemical secretin, which is produced in the small intestine when food enters the stomach, eventually challenged that view. From the small intestine, secretin
10 travels through the bloodstream to the pancreas. There, it stimulates the release of digestive chemicals. In this fashion, the intestinal cells that produce secretin ultimately regulate the production of different chemicals in a different organ, the pancreas.

15 Such a coordination of processes had been thought to require control by the nervous system; Bayliss and Starling showed that it could occur through chemicals alone. This discovery spurred Starling to coin the term *hormone* to refer to secretin, taking it from the Greek word *hormon,* meaning "to excite" or "to set in motion." A hormone is
20 a chemical produced by one tissue to make things happen elsewhere.

As more hormones were discovered, they were categorized, primarily according to the process by which they operated on the body. Some glands (which make up the endocrine system) secrete hormones
25 directly into the bloodstream. Such glands include the thyroid and the pituitary. The exocrine system consists of organs and glands that produce substances that are used outside the bloodstream, primarily for digestion. The pancreas is one such organ, although it secretes some chemicals into the blood and thus is also part of the endocrine
30 system.

Much has been learned about hormones since their discovery. Some play such key roles in regulating bodily processes or behavior that their absence would cause immediate death. The most abundant
35 hormones have effects that are less obviously urgent but can be more far-reaching and difficult to track: They modify moods and affect human behavior, even some behavior we normally think of as voluntary. Hormonal systems are very intricate. Even minute amounts of the right chemicals can suppress appetite, calm aggression, and
40 change the attitude of a parent toward a child. Certain hormones accelerate the development of the body, regulating growth and form; others may even define an individual's personality characteristics. **The quantities and proportions of hormones produced change with age, so scientists have given a great deal of study to shifts**
45 **in the endocrine system over time in the hopes of alleviating ailments associated with aging.**

In fact, some hormone therapies are already very common. ■ **A combination of estrogen and progesterone has been prescribed**
50 **for decades to women who want to reduce mood swings, sudden changes in body temperature, and other discomforts caused by lower natural levels of those hormones as they enter middle age.** ■ Known as hormone replacement therapy (HRT), the treatment was also believed to prevent weakening of the bones. ■
55 At least one study has linked HRT with a heightened risk of heart disease and certain types of cancer. **HRT may also increase the likelihood that blood clots—dangerous because they could travel through the bloodstream and block major blood vessels— will form.** Some proponents of HRT have tempered their enthusiasm
60 in the face of this new evidence, recommending it only to patients whose symptoms interfere with their abilities to live normal lives. ■

Human growth hormone may also be given to patients who are secreting abnormally low amounts on their own. **Because of the**
65 **complicated effects the growth hormone has on the body, such treatments are generally restricted to children who would be pathologically small in stature without it.** Growth hormone affects not just physical size but also the digestion of food and the aging process. Researchers and family physicians tend to agree that it is
70 foolhardy to dispense it in cases in which the risks are not clearly outweighed by the benefits.

More Available

33. Which of the sentences below best expresses the essential information in the highlighted sentence in the passage? *Incorrect* answer choices change the meaning in important ways or leave out essential information.

a. Most moods and actions are not voluntary because they are actually produced by the production of hormones in the body.

b. Because the effects of hormones are difficult to measure, scientists remain unsure how far-reaching their effects on moods and actions are.

c. When the body is not producing enough hormones, urgent treatment may be necessary to avoid psychological damage.

d. The influence of many hormones is not easy to measure, but they can affect both people's psychology and actions extensively.

Hormones in the Body

Until the beginning of the twentieth century, the nervous system was thought to control all communication within the body and the resulting integration of behavior. Scientists had determined that nerves ran, essentially, on electrical impulses. These impulses were
5 thought to be the engine for thought, emotion, movement, and internal processes such as digestion. However, experiments by William Bayliss and Ernest Starling on the chemical secretin, which is produced in the small intestine when food enters the stomach, eventually challenged that view. From the small intestine, secretin
10 travels through the bloodstream to the pancreas. There, it stimulates the release of digestive chemicals. In this fashion, the intestinal cells that produce secretin ultimately regulate the production of different chemicals in a different organ, the pancreas.

15 Such a coordination of processes had been thought to require control by the nervous system; Bayliss and Starling showed that it could occur through chemicals alone. This discovery spurred Starling to coin the term *hormone* to refer to secretin, taking it from the Greek word *hormon*, meaning "to excite" or "to set in motion." A hormone is
20 a chemical produced by one tissue to make things happen elsewhere.

As more hormones were discovered, they were categorized, primarily according to the process by which they operated on the body. Some glands (which make up the endocrine system) secrete hormones
25 directly into the bloodstream. Such glands include the thyroid and the pituitary. The exocrine system consists of organs and glands that produce substances that are used outside the bloodstream, primarily for digestion. The pancreas is one such organ, although it secretes some chemicals into the blood and thus is also part of the
30 endocrine system.

Much has been learned about hormones since their discovery. Some play such key roles in regulating bodily processes or behavior that their absence would cause immediate death. The most abundant
35 hormones have effects that are less obviously urgent but can be more far-reaching and difficult to track: They modify moods and affect human behavior, even some behavior we normally think of as voluntary. Hormonal systems are very intricate. Even minute amounts of the right chemicals can suppress appetite, calm aggression, and
40 change the attitude of a parent toward a child. Certain hormones accelerate the development of the body, regulating growth and form; others may even define an individual's personality characteristics. **The quantities and proportions of hormones produced change with age, so scientists have given a great deal of study to shifts**
45 **in the endocrine system over time in the hopes of alleviating ailments associated with aging.**

In fact, some hormone therapies are already very common. ■ **A combination of estrogen and progesterone has been prescribed**
50 **for decades to women who want to reduce mood swings, sudden changes in body temperature, and other discomforts caused by lower natural levels of those hormones as they enter middle age.** ■ Known as hormone replacement therapy (HRT), the treatment was also believed to prevent weakening of the bones. ■
55 At least one study has linked HRT with a heightened risk of heart disease and certain types of cancer. **HRT may also increase the likelihood that blood clots—dangerous because they could travel through the bloodstream and block major blood vessels— will form.** Some proponents of HRT have tempered their enthusiasm
60 in the face of this new evidence, recommending it only to patients whose symptoms interfere with their abilities to live normal lives. ■

Human growth hormone may also be given to patients who are secreting abnormally low amounts on their own. **Because of the**
65 **complicated effects the growth hormone has on the body, such treatments are generally restricted to children who would be pathologically small in stature without it.** Growth hormone affects not just physical size but also the digestion of food and the aging process. Researchers and family physicians tend to agree that it is
70 foolhardy to dispense it in cases in which the risks are not clearly outweighed by the benefits.

More Available

34. The word tempered in the passage is closest in meaning to

a. decreased
b. advertised
c. prescribed
d. researched

Hormones in the Body

Until the beginning of the twentieth century, the nervous system was thought to control all communication within the body and the resulting integration of behavior. Scientists had determined that nerves ran, essentially, on electrical impulses. These impulses were
5 thought to be the engine for thought, emotion, movement, and internal processes such as digestion. However, experiments by William Bayliss and Ernest Starling on the chemical secretin, which is produced in the small intestine when food enters the stomach, eventually challenged that view. From the small intestine, secretin
10 travels through the bloodstream to the pancreas. There, it stimulates the release of digestive chemicals. In this fashion, the intestinal cells that produce secretin ultimately regulate the production of different chemicals in a different organ, the pancreas.

15 Such a coordination of processes had been thought to require control by the nervous system; Bayliss and Starling showed that it could occur through chemicals alone. This discovery spurred Starling to coin the term *hormone* to refer to secretin, taking it from the Greek word *hormon*, meaning "to excite" or "to set in motion." A hormone is
20 a chemical produced by one tissue to make things happen elsewhere.

As more hormones were discovered, they were categorized, primarily according to the process by which they operated on the body. Some glands (which make up the endocrine system) secrete hormones
25 directly into the bloodstream. Such glands include the thyroid and the pituitary. The exocrine system consists of organs and glands that produce substances that are used outside the bloodstream, primarily for digestion. The pancreas is one such organ, although it secretes some chemicals into the blood and thus is also part of the endocrine
30 system.

Much has been learned about hormones since their discovery. Some play such key roles in regulating bodily processes or behavior that their absence would cause immediate death. The most abundant
35 hormones have effects that are less obviously urgent but can be more far-reaching and difficult to track: They modify moods and affect human behavior, even some behavior we normally think of as voluntary. Hormonal systems are very intricate. Even minute amounts of the right chemicals can suppress appetite, calm aggression, and
40 change the attitude of a parent toward a child. Certain hormones accelerate the development of the body, regulating growth and form; others may even define an individual's personality characteristics. **The quantities and proportions of hormones produced change with age, so scientists have given a great deal of study to shifts
45 in the endocrine system over time in the hopes of alleviating ailments associated with aging.**

In fact, some hormone therapies are already very common. ■ **A combination of estrogen and progesterone has been prescribed
50 for decades to women who want to reduce mood swings, sudden changes in body temperature, and other discomforts caused by lower natural levels of those hormones as they enter middle age.** ■ Known as hormone replacement therapy (HRT), the treatment was also believed to prevent weakening of the bones. ■
55 At least one study has linked HRT with a heightened risk of heart disease and certain types of cancer. **HRT may also increase the likelihood that blood clots—dangerous because they could travel through the bloodstream and block major blood vessels— will form.** Some proponents of HRT have tempered their enthusiasm
60 in the face of this new evidence, recommending it only to patients whose symptoms interfere with their abilities to live normal lives. ■

Human growth hormone may also be given to patients who are secreting abnormally low amounts on their own. **Because of the
65 complicated effects the growth hormone has on the body, such treatments are generally restricted to children who would be pathologically small in stature without it.** Growth hormone affects not just physical size but also the digestion of food and the aging process. Researchers and family physicians tend to agree that it is
70 foolhardy to dispense it in cases in which the risks are not clearly outweighed by the benefits.

More Available

35. Which patients are usually treated with growth hormone?

a. Adults of smaller stature than normal

b. Adults with strong digestive systems

c. Children who are not at risk from the treatment

d. Children who may remain abnormally small

Hormones in the Body

Until the beginning of the twentieth century, the nervous system was thought to control all communication within the body and the resulting integration of behavior. Scientists had determined that nerves ran, essentially, on electrical impulses. These impulses were
5 thought to be the engine for thought, emotion, movement, and internal processes such as digestion. However, experiments by William Bayliss and Ernest Starling on the chemical secretin, which is produced in the small intestine when food enters the stomach, eventually challenged that view. From the small intestine, secretin
10 travels through the bloodstream to the pancreas. There, it stimulates the release of digestive chemicals. In this fashion, the intestinal cells that produce secretin ultimately regulate the production of different chemicals in a different organ, the pancreas.

15 Such a coordination of processes had been thought to require control by the nervous system; Bayliss and Starling showed that it could occur through chemicals alone. This discovery spurred Starling to coin the term *hormone* to refer to secretin, taking it from the Greek word *hormon,* meaning "to excite" or "to set in motion." A hormone is
20 a chemical produced by one tissue to make things happen elsewhere.

As more hormones were discovered, they were categorized, primarily according to the process by which they operated on the body. Some glands (which make up the endocrine system) secrete hormones
25 directly into the bloodstream. Such glands include the thyroid and the pituitary. The exocrine system consists of organs and glands that produce substances that are used outside the bloodstream, primarily for digestion. The pancreas is one such organ, although it secretes some chemicals into the blood and thus is also part of the
30 endocrine system.

Much has been learned about hormones since their discovery. Some play such key roles in regulating bodily processes or behavior that their absence would cause immediate death. The most abundant
35 hormones have effects that are less obviously urgent but can be more far-reaching and difficult to track: They modify moods and affect human behavior, even some behavior we normally think of as voluntary. Hormonal systems are very intricate. Even minute amounts of the right chemicals can suppress appetite, calm aggression, and
40 change the attitude of a parent toward a child. Certain hormones accelerate the development of the body, regulating growth and form; others may even define an individual's personality characteristics. **The quantities and proportions of hormones produced change with age, so scientists have given a great deal of study to shifts
45 in the endocrine system over time in the hopes of alleviating ailments associated with aging.**

In fact, some hormone therapies are already very common. ■ **A combination of estrogen and progesterone has been prescribed
50 for decades to women who want to reduce mood swings, sudden changes in body temperature, and other discomforts caused by lower natural levels of those hormones as they enter middle age.** ■ Known as hormone replacement therapy (HRT), the treatment was also believed to prevent weakening of the bones. ■
55 At least one study has linked HRT with a heightened risk of heart disease and certain types of cancer. **HRT may also increase the likelihood that blood clots—dangerous because they could travel through the bloodstream and block major blood vessels— will form.** Some proponents of HRT have tempered their enthusiasm
60 in the face of this new evidence, recommending it only to patients whose symptoms interfere with their abilities to live normal lives. ■

Human growth hormone may also be given to patients who are secreting abnormally low amounts on their own. **Because of the
65 complicated effects the growth hormone has on the body, such treatments are generally restricted to children who would be pathologically small in stature without it.** Growth hormone affects not just physical size but also the digestion of food and the aging process. Researchers and family physicians tend to agree that it is
70 foolhardy to dispense it in cases in which the risks are not clearly outweighed by the benefits.

More Available

Hormones in the Body

36. Click on the sentence (in bold text in the passage and repeated below) in the passage where the author explains the primary goal of hormone replacement therapy.

a. The quantities and proportions of hormones produced change with age, so scientists have given a great deal of study to shifts in the endocrine system over time in the hopes of alleviating ailments associated with aging.

b. A combination of estrogen and progesterone has been prescribed for decades to women who want to reduce mood swings, sudden changes in body temperature, and other discomforts caused by lower natural levels of those hormones as they enter middle age.

c. HRT may also increase the likelihood that blood clots—dangerous because they could travel through the bloodstream and block major blood vessels—will form.

d. Because of the complicated effects growth hormone has on the body, such treatments are generally restricted to children who would be pathologically small in stature without it.

Until the beginning of the twentieth century, the nervous system was thought to control all communication within the body and the resulting integration of behavior. Scientists had determined that nerves ran, essentially, on electrical impulses. These impulses were thought to be the engine for thought, emotion, movement, and internal processes such as digestion. However, experiments by William Bayliss and Ernest Starling on the chemical secretin, which is produced in the small intestine when food enters the stomach, eventually challenged that view. From the small intestine, secretin travels through the bloodstream to the pancreas. There, it stimulates the release of digestive chemicals. In this fashion, the intestinal cells that produce secretin ultimately regulate the production of different chemicals in a different organ, the pancreas.

Such a coordination of processes had been thought to require control by the nervous system; Bayliss and Starling showed that it could occur through chemicals alone. This discovery spurred Starling to coin the term *hormone* to refer to secretin, taking it from the Greek word *hormon,* meaning "to excite" or "to set in motion." A hormone is a chemical produced by one tissue to make things happen elsewhere.

As more hormones were discovered, they were categorized, primarily according to the process by which they operated on the body. Some glands (which make up the endocrine system) secrete hormones directly into the bloodstream. Such glands include the thyroid and the pituitary. The exocrine system consists of organs and glands that produce substances that are used outside the bloodstream, primarily for digestion. The pancreas is one such organ, although it secretes some chemicals into the blood and thus is also part of the endocrine system.

Much has been learned about hormones since their discovery. Some play such key roles in regulating bodily processes or behavior that their absence would cause immediate death. The most abundant hormones have effects that are less obviously urgent but can be more far-reaching and difficult to track: They modify moods and affect human behavior, even some behavior we normally think of as voluntary. Hormonal systems are very intricate. Even minute amounts of the right chemicals can suppress appetite, calm aggression, and change the attitude of a parent toward a child. Certain hormones accelerate the development of the body, regulating growth and form; others may even define an individual's personality characteristics. **The quantities and proportions of hormones produced change with age, so scientists have given a great deal of study to shifts in the endocrine system over time in the hopes of alleviating ailments associated with aging.**

In fact, some hormone therapies are already very common. ■ **A combination of estrogen and progesterone has been prescribed for decades to women who want to reduce mood swings, sudden changes in body temperature, and other discomforts caused by lower natural levels of those hormones as they enter middle age.** ■ Known as hormone replacement therapy (HRT), the treatment was also believed to prevent weakening of the bones. ■ At least one study has linked HRT with a heightened risk of heart disease and certain types of cancer. **HRT may also increase the likelihood that blood clots—dangerous because they could travel through the bloodstream and block major blood vessels—will form.** Some proponents of HRT have tempered their enthusiasm in the face of this new evidence, recommending it only to patients whose symptoms interfere with their abilities to live normal lives. ■

Human growth hormone may also be given to patients who are secreting abnormally low amounts on their own. **Because of the complicated effects the growth hormone has on the body, such treatments are generally restricted to children who would be pathologically small in stature without it.** Growth hormone affects not just physical size but also the digestion of food and the aging process. Researchers and family physicians tend to agree that it is foolhardy to dispense it in cases in which the risks are not clearly outweighed by the benefits.

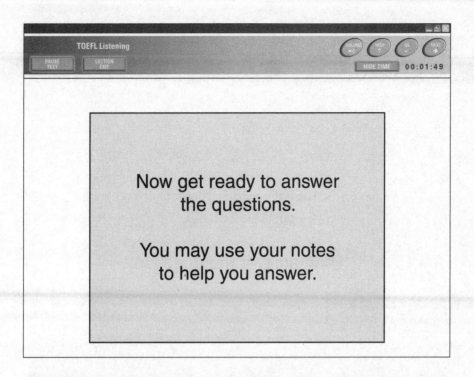

29. What did the professor mainly discuss?

    a.   Types of goods traded in the colonies
    b.   Major wars of the colonial period
    c.   How the colonists defeated new tax laws
    d.   How the British increased the flow of money from the colonies

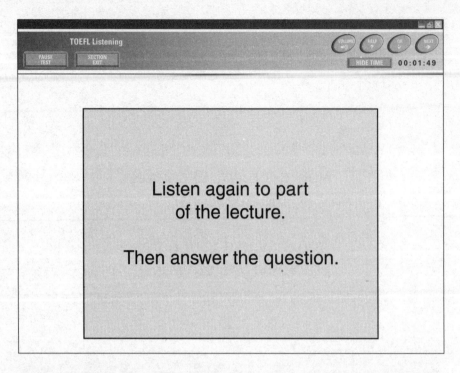

Listen again to part
of the lecture.

Then answer the question.

30. Why does the professor mention the documentary film?

    a.   He will have to show the class a different film.
    b.   He thinks one of the students borrowed the library copy.
    c.   He assumes some of the students have seen it.
    d.   There will be a change in the class schedule.

31. Why did Britain want to receive more money from the American colonies?

    a.   It had just finished a costly war.
    b.   Colonial paper currency had increased in value.
    c.   The colonies were producing more sugar.
    d.   Taxes in Britain had been lowered.

32. Which of the following did the professor mention as changes that accompanied the Sugar Act?

Click on 2 answers.

    a.   A greater number of commodities were taxed.
    b.   The taxes were collected more carefully.
    c.   The tax on sugar replaced the tax on coffee and wines.
    d.   The Stamp Act was no longer necessary.

33. Why does the professor say the colonists developed their own paper currency?

   a.   They needed more money to pay the sugar tax.
   b.   Their British currency was used to pay for British goods.
   c.   Property could be bought only with paper currency.
   d.   Paper currency was easier for laborers to transport.

34. According to the professor, why did the Stamp Act affect both merchants and laborers in the colonies?

   a.   It outlawed newspapers read by both groups.
   b.   Many colonists had fought in the French and Indian War.
   c.   Many everyday activities were taxed.
   d.   Both groups consumed large amounts of sugar.

THE SPEAKING SECTION

In this section, you will demonstrate your ability to speak about various topics. You will answer eight questions. Answer each question as completely as possible.

Questions 1 and 2 will ask you about familiar topics. For questions 3 and 4, you will first read a short text. Next, you will listen to a lecture on the same topic. You will then be asked a question about what you have read and heard. Questions 5 and 6 require you to listen to a short piece and a conversation between two students giving their reactions. Questions 7 and 8 require you to listen to a lecture first. You will then be asked two questions about what you just heard. You may take notes while you read and listen. You may use your notes to help you prepare.

For each task, you will be given a short period of time to prepare your response; to most closely simulate actual test conditions, you will need to pause and restart the audio CD as instructed in the following pages.

Note to students: If possible, record your responses or have someone proficient in English listen to your response. Compare your responses with the samples at the end of the test.

Speaking 1

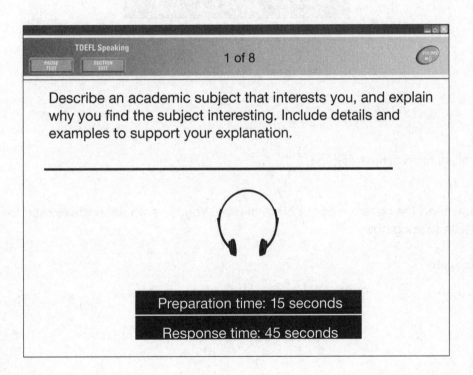

TOEFL Speaking

PAUSE TEST   SECTION EXIT

1 of 8

VOLUME

Describe an academic subject that interests you, and explain why you find the subject interesting. Include details and examples to support your explanation.

Preparation time: 15 seconds
Response time: 45 seconds

Speaking 2

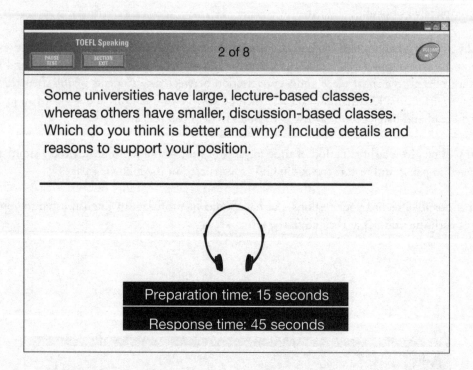

Some universities have large, lecture-based classes, whereas others have smaller, discussion-based classes. Which do you think is better and why? Include details and reasons to support your position.

Preparation time: 15 seconds

Response time: 45 seconds

Speaking 3

Please play Track 30 on the accompanying CD.

Narrator: Now read the passage about birds of prey. You have 45 seconds to read the passage. Begin reading now.

[Stop CD for 45 seconds]

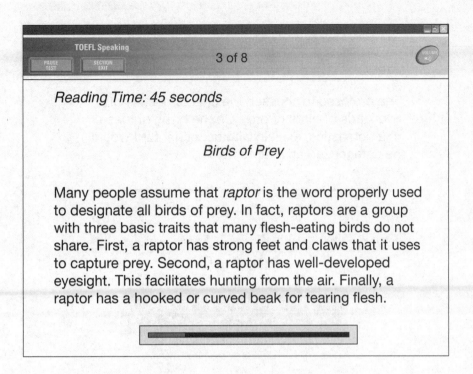

TOEFL Speaking

PAUSE TEST   SECTION EXIT

Reading Time: 45 seconds

Birds of Prey

Many people assume that *raptor* is the word properly used to designate all birds of prey. In fact, raptors are a group with three basic traits that many flesh-eating birds do not share. First, a raptor has strong feet and claws that it uses to capture prey. Second, a raptor has well-developed eyesight. This facilitates hunting from the air. Finally, a raptor has a hooked or curved beak for tearing flesh.

[Restart audio CD.]

Narrator: Now listen to part of a lecture on this topic given in a biology class.

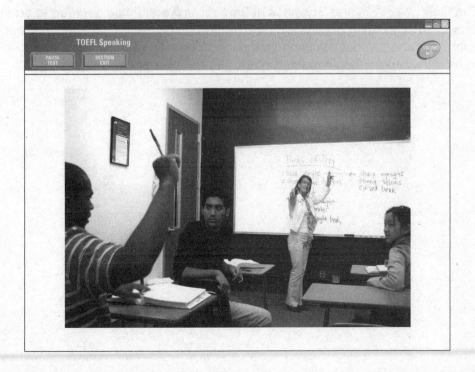

TOEFL Speaking

PAUSE TEST   SECTION EXIT

The professor discussed the characteristics of two kinds of birds of prey. On the basis of these characteristics, explain whether either bird would be categorized as a raptor.

Preparation time: 30 seconds

Response time: 60 seconds

Speaking 4

Please play Track 31 on the accompanying CD.

Narrator: The College of Arts and Sciences at Eastern University has decided to add a senior project to its existing graduation requirements. The campus newspaper printed the following report about the announcement of the new requirement. You have 45 seconds to read the report. Begin reading now.

[Stop CD for 45 seconds.]

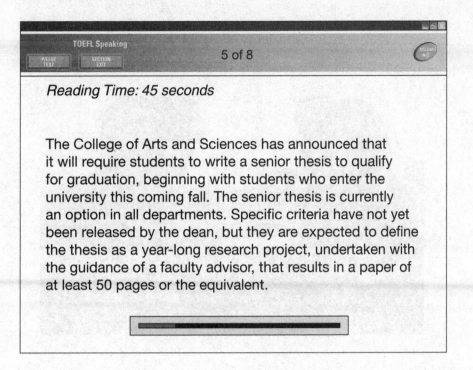

Reading Time: 45 seconds

The College of Arts and Sciences has announced that it will require students to write a senior thesis to qualify for graduation, beginning with students who enter the university this coming fall. The senior thesis is currently an option in all departments. Specific criteria have not yet been released by the dean, but they are expected to define the thesis as a year-long research project, undertaken with the guidance of a faculty advisor, that results in a paper of at least 50 pages or the equivalent.

[Restart audio CD.]

Narrator: Now listen to two students as they discuss the report.

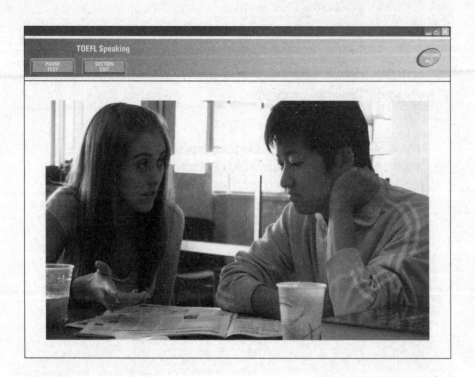

The woman explains her opinion of the announcement made by the College of Arts and Sciences. State her opinion, and explain the reasons she gives for holding that opinion.

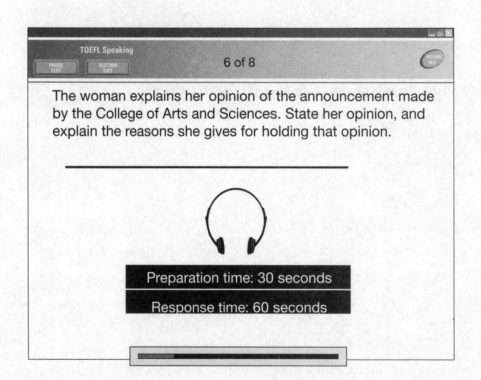

Preparation time: 30 seconds

Response time: 60 seconds

Speaking 5

Please play Track 32 on the accompanying CD.

Narrator: Now listen to a conversation between two students.

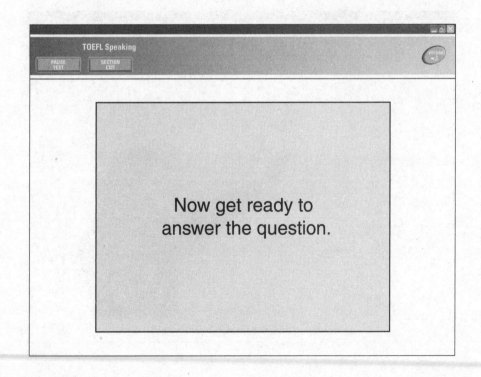

Now get ready to
answer the question.

The speakers discuss two possible solutions for the woman's problem. Describe the problem. Then state which of the two solutions you prefer, and explain why.

Preparation time: 20 seconds

Response time: 60 seconds

Speaking 6

Please play Track 33 on the accompanying CD.

Narrator: Now listen to part of a lecture in a history class.

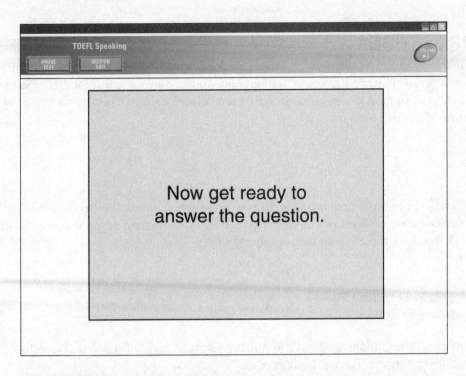

Now get ready to
answer the question.

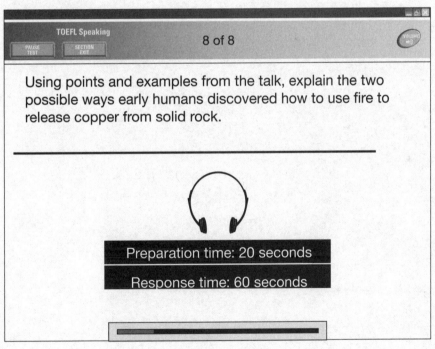

Using points and examples from the talk, explain the two possible ways early humans discovered how to use fire to release copper from solid rock.

Preparation time: 20 seconds

Response time: 60 seconds

THE WRITING SECTION

This section measures your ability to communicate in an academic environment. There are two writing tasks. The first task asks you to read a passage, listen to a lecture, and respond. You will answer the second question based on your own knowledge and experience. To most closely simulate actual test conditions, you will need to pause and restart the audio CD as instructed throughout this section.

Writing 1

Directions: You will have 20 minutes to plan and write your response. The break between the reading and lecture is not timed on the CD, because some students may need to practice untimed. Therefore, you will need to stop the CD for the duration of the break. You have three minutes to read the selection.

Please play Track 34 on the accompanying CD.

> *Narrator:* Now read the passage about the suppression of forest fires. You have three minutes to read the passage. Begin reading now.

[Stop CD for 3 minutes.]

TOEFL Writing

PAUSE
TEST

SECTION
EXIT

VOLUME

HELP
?

NEXT

HIDE TIME   00:29:57

Wilderness management has advanced greatly over the last century, due in part to such practices as the suppression of forest fires and limitations on the clear-cutting of trees. Monitoring forests for small brushfires is easier with aircraft, as is the use of large amounts of water and sophisticated chemical fire extinguishers to prevent fires from spreading.

The goals of decreasing the amount of destruction by fires and cutting are wide-ranging. One is simply the longer lives and improved health of trees. In some areas of hickory and oak forest on the Eastern Seaboard, fire suppression has allowed the maturation of so many trees that the treetops form a continuous canopy.

There is evidence of the healthful effects of fire suppression closer to the ground as well. Vines and low bushes that would be burned out in a forest fire can flourish when fires are suppressed, of course, but there is a more indirect way fires harm plant life. Chemical tests on areas that have recently experienced forest fires demonstrate that burning decreases the overall amount of nutrients in the soil. Suppressing fires prevents such a decrease. Ferns, wildflowers, and herbs grow without disturbance.

Finally, wildlife can benefit. In the eastern hickory and oak forests, the suppression of fires has meant that forest animals—ranging from small insects and birds to large deer and bears—are not burned to death. Deer populations, in particular, have increased notably.

[Restart audio CD.]

Narrator: Now listen to part of a lecture on the topic you just read about.

Directions: You have 20 minutes to plan and write your response. Your response will be graded on the quality of your writing and on how well your response presents the points in the lecture and their relationship to the reading passage. Typically, an effective response will be 150–225 words.

Question: Summarize the points made in the lecture you just heard, explaining how they cast doubt on the contents of the reading. You may refer to the passage as you write.

Copy   Cut   Paste

Word Count: 0

Wilderness management has advanced greatly over the last century, due in part to such practices as the suppression of forest fires and limitations on the clear-cutting of trees. Monitoring forests for small brushfires is easier with aircraft, as is the use of large amounts of water and sophisticated chemical fire extinguishers to prevent fires from spreading.

The goals of decreasing the amount of destruction by fires and cutting are wide-ranging. One is simply the longer lives and improved health of trees. In some areas of hickory and oak forest on the Eastern Seaboard, fire suppression has allowed the maturation of so many trees that the treetops form a continuous canopy.

There is evidence of the healthful effects of fire suppression closer to the ground as well. Vines and low bushes that would be burned out in a forest fire can flourish when fires are suppressed, of course, but there is a more indirect way fires harm plant life. Chemical tests on areas that have recently experienced forest fires demonstrate that burning decreases the overall amount of nutrients in the soil. Suppressing fires prevents such a decrease. Ferns, wildflowers, and herbs grow without disturbance.

Finally, wildlife can benefit. In the eastern hickory and oak forests, the suppression of fires has meant that forest animals—ranging from small insects and birds to large deer and bears—are not burned to death. Deer populations, in particular, have increased notably.

Writing 2

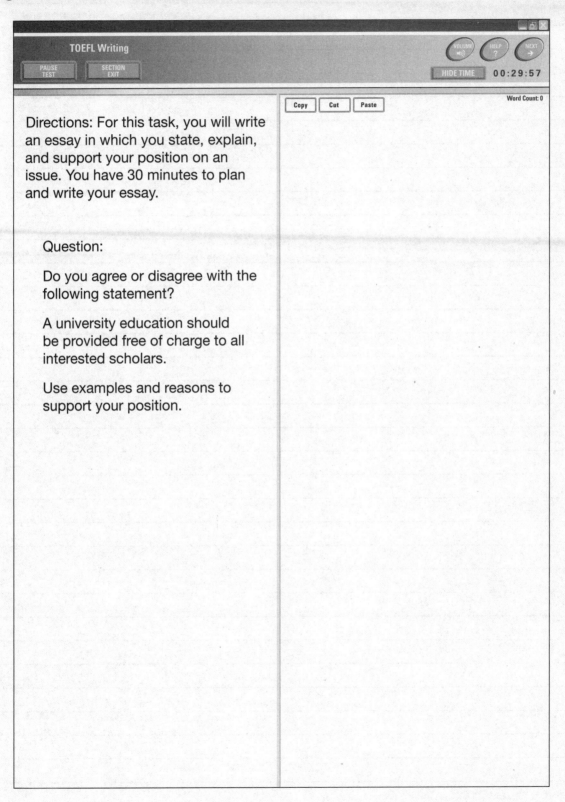

Directions: For this task, you will write an essay in which you state, explain, and support your position on an issue. You have 30 minutes to plan and write your essay.

Question:

Do you agree or disagree with the following statement?

A university education should be provided free of charge to all interested scholars.

Use examples and reasons to support your position.

TOEFL Writing

PAUSE TEST

SECTION EXIT

VOLUME

HELP ?

NEXT →

HIDE TIME   00:29:57

Copy   Cut   Paste

Word Count: 0

When the people took their pottery out of the oven, they found pieces of copper at the bottom.

N: Using points and examples from the talk, explain the two possible ways early humans discovered how to use fire to release copper from solid rock.

Here's how you may have answered this question.

State main idea	The professor states that it was an accident that humans discovered copper.
Reason #1	Humans may have discovered copper by using campfires.
Detail for reason #1	Copper is stuck inside rocks, and people used rocks to contain their fires.
Link between reason #1 and main idea	If the fire was hot enough, the people would have noticed pieces of copper in their fires.
Reason #2	Another way people could have discovered copper was through pottery.
Detail for reason #2	Sometimes the people decorated their pottery with stones.
Link between reason #2 and main idea	The heat caused the copper to melt and come out of the stones, and the people could have discovered it that way.

THE WRITING SECTION: SAMPLE RESPONSES

Look over your written responses. Make sure they answer the question effectively, are of the appropriate length, and are well organized. Use the following responses as guides.

Writing 1

Narrator: Now read the passage about the suppression of forest fires. You have three minutes to read the passage. Begin reading now.

Wilderness management has advanced greatly over the last century, due in part to such practices as the suppression of forest fires and limitations on the clear-cutting of trees. Monitoring forests for small brushfires is easier with aircraft, as is the use of large amounts of water and sophisticated chemical fire extinguishers to prevent fires from spreading.

The goals of decreasing the amount of destruction by fires and cutting are wide-ranging. One is simply the longer lives and improved health of trees. In some areas of hickory and oak forest on the Eastern Seaboard, fire suppression has allowed the maturation of so many trees that the treetops form a continuous canopy.

There is evidence of the healthful effects of fire suppression closer to the ground as well. Vines and low bushes that would be burned out in a forest fire can flourish when fires are suppressed, of course, but there is a more indirect way fires harm plant life. Chemical tests on areas that have recently experienced forest fires demonstrate that burning decreases the overall amount of nutrients in the soil. Suppressing fires prevents such a decrease. Ferns, wildflowers, and herbs grow without disturbance.

Finally, wildlife can benefit. In the eastern hickory and oak forests, the suppression of fires has meant that forest animals—ranging from small insects and birds to large deer and bears—are not burned to death. Deer populations, in particular, have increased notably.

Here is a transcript of the lecture (Track 34 on the accompanying CD and in your Student Tools).

N: Now listen to part of a lecture on the topic you just read about.

P: For years, forest fires were regarded as uniformly destructive, and forest managers put a lot of effort into preventing them. But it turns out that fire suppression may have destructive long-term effects on the forests it's supposed to protect.

For instance, mature oaks have grown so thickly in some places that little light reaches the forest floor. But young oak trees need light in order to grow properly. The lack of light has meant that new oaks aren't maturing rapidly enough to replace the older oaks. It also means that other tree species that don't need so much light, such as maples, are invading oak and hickory forests and competing for resources.

There are competition problems at ground level too. What forest fires, both natural and artificial, used to do is burn off some of the plants on the forest floor before they could grow into huge thickets. Now they run wild over the ground—and again, that means it's hard for young trees and other native plants to grow.

Then there's the increase in the deer population—this partially results from the lack of forest fires and partially from limitations on hunting—but the thing is, deer like to eat the leaves off oak saplings. So if one of those oak seedlings somehow does manage to get a good start, despite the shade and all the other plants competing for nutrients, it's likely to be killed by having its leaves eaten.

Oh, and one other thing: scientists are now finding that forest fires release nutrients from the plants and animals that are burned. That means that, even though the total amount of nutrients is decreased, there can actually be more nutrients available on the soil surface for plants that are trying to grow back afterward.

N: Summarize the points made in the lecture you just heard, explaining how they challenge specific claims made in the reading passage. You may refer to the passage as you write.

Sample High-Scoring Response

In the lecture, the professor made several points about the effects of forest fires. The professor argues that forest fires can actually be good for the forests, not bad. The talk by the professor however, is different from the reading. According to the reading, forest fires are harmful to the land and should be stopped. But the professor casts doubt on that view with several points.

The first point the teacher makes is that if there are too many trees, it is hard for some trees to get light and nutrition. This means that the trees are not healthy. The professor's point is different from the reading. The reading states that it is good to have a lot of trees in the forest. But the lecture shows that too many trees is actually bad for the forest.

Another point made by the professor is that burning a forest actually puts more nutrients into the land. This is not what the reading says. The reading says that fires take nutrients out of the soil. However, the professor says there are more nutrients at the top for plants to use.

In conclusion, the professor challenges the claims made in the reading by showing that forest fires are sometimes needed for a healthy forest.

Writing 2

Directions: For this task, you will write an essay in which you state, explain, and support your position on an issue. You have 30 minutes to plan and write your essay.

Question:

Do you agree or disagree with the following statement?

A university education should be provided free of charge to all interested scholars.

Use examples and reasons to support your position.

Sample High-Scoring Response

The issue stated by the topic is whether or not a university education should be provided free to all that are interested. This is a very important issue because the cost of education is rising and because education is very important. However, I believe that universities should not give an education for free.

I do not think that university education should be free because who is going to pay for it if the students do not? If the government has to pay for it then that means taxes are raised. This is not fair to the people because if they have to pay higher taxes they might not want to go to the university. That means they are paying for something they won't even use, which is not fair.

Furthermore, I don't think university education should be free because universities that have more money can give better education. The only way for the universities to get more money is to charge the students. If the education is free, how will the universities get money to buy computers, books, and hire good professors to teach? For this reason, we should not have a free university.

Finally, I think the university should not be free because there are many schools available and they have different prices. Poor students can go to a school that doesn't cost as much and still learn a lot. Also, many universities give aid or scholarships so a student can attend even if they don't have money. So there is no need to make a university education free.

In conclusion, university education should not be made free. I believe this because the colleges need the money to make them better. If the universities are free, taxes will be raised and people will have to pay for things they might not use. Since there are many schools available with scholarships and aid, university should not be made free.

IN CLOSING

OK, got all that? It's a lot, but if you have made it all the way back here, then you have pushed through it and done some serious studying and preparation. Bravo! Walk into the TOEFL feeling confident and prepared because you are. Best of luck!